The Gaiety Years

Also by Alan Hyman:

THE RISE AND FALL OF
HORATIO BOTTOMLEY

The Gaiety Years

Alan Hyman

CASSELL · LONDON

CASSELL & COMPANY LTD
an imprint of
Cassell & Collier Macmillan Publishers Ltd
35 Red Lion Square, London WC1R 4SG
and at Sydney, Auckland, Toronto, Johannesburg
and an affiliate of The Macmillan Company Inc, New York

First published 1975

ISBN 0 304 29372 5

Printed in Great Britain by
The Camelot Press Ltd. Southampton
F.1174

Contents

Illustrations

TO THE MEMORY OF
THE TALENTED MEN AND WOMEN
WHO MADE
THE GAIETY THEATRE
A BRITISH INSTITUTION

Foreword

I decided to tackle a biography of George Edwardes for several reasons. In the first place only one book had ever been written exclusively about him. Another factor was that he managed the Gaiety Theatre and Daly's during a very fascinating period and, since this was not so very long ago, one had a chance of recapturing its atmosphere, particularly by talking to men and women who were alive in the late Victorian and Edwardian eras. But the chief reason for embarking on this book is that I have loved the theatre ever since I was a small boy and was taken to the old theatre at Guildford every week to see all kinds of plays from *The Shop Girl* to Fred Terry in *The Scarlet Pimpernel*. I planned to write a theatrical biography about a man of action and George Edwardes, the 'Guv'nor', seemed an ideal choice.

The late Walter Macqueen Pope worked at the Gaiety for the Guv'nor and knew him extremely well; several of his books about the theatre give one a great insight into the character of George Edwardes. D. Forbes Winslow worked for Edwardes and used his experience to write a stimulating book about Daly's. But neither Macqueen Pope nor Winslow ever attempted a biography of Edwardes: the only one in existence was written by the indefatigable Miss Ursula Bloom and entitled *Curtain Call for the Guv'nor*. Now, Miss Bloom is a remarkable woman whom I admire immensely—she has something like four hundred and fifty books to her credit—but I am bound to say that she failed to do justice to George Edwardes.

Her book was charming, nostalgic and thoroughly romantic: my main objection was that Miss Bloom hardly ever showed the warts in her portrait of the great impresario. There was no hint, for instance, that he sometimes had affairs with actresses, or that he had such wonderful powers of persuasion that an actor would storm into his office to demand a rise and come out smiling, after agreeing to take a cut in salary. Miss Bloom also played down the fact that horse-racing was Edwardes's second love: winning the Ascot Gold Cup gave him almost as much pleasure as taking his bow on the triumphant first night of *The Merry Widow*.

However, Ursula Bloom is such a generous woman that I am sure she will take these comments in the right spirit. It was typical of her kindness that at my request she put me in touch with the descendants of George Edwardes. His grandson, David Sherbrooke, and his daughter, Mrs Norah Laye, have generously put at my disposal a trunk full of Edwardes's letters and scrap books and the Victorian diaries of his wife, Julia. David Sherbrooke helped me with my account of his grandfather's activities in the racing world, and Julius Edwardes, a great-nephew of George Edwardes, has made some excellent suggestions, which I have incorporated in my treatment. I am most grateful to him for them and for his splendid co-operation in checking some of my proofs.

It was essential to get a line on the legendary Gaiety Girls, whose charms brought the mashers flocking to the theatre. I had the privilege of meeting a few of these glamorous ladies and I thank them for all they have told me. Miss Ruby Miller first appeared at the Gaiety in *The Orchid* in 1903, when she was only a schoolgirl, but she will go down to posterity as the actress who had champagne drunk out of her slipper at Romano's. Two other Gaiety girls were Miss Trixie Hillier and her sister Miss Hope Hillier, who retired from the stage and as Mrs Mirabel Topham became the presiding genius of Aintree. Miss May Trevelyan once graced the Gaiety chorus and told me what it was like in Edwardian days. Miss Zena Dare, though she never appeared at the Gaiety, played for the Guv'nor in musical comedies at the Prince of Wales's and is the sister of Miss Phyllis Dare, who starred at the Gaiety in *The Sunshine Girl*. Miss Margaret Fraser, who danced so well at the Gaiety, died last year aged ninety; I heard about her from her daughter Mrs Margaret Barker.

Since the name of George Edwardes is hardly known to the present generation, I have aimed at presenting a picture of Edwardes and his world, which should broaden the appeal of this book and also help readers to appreciate the Guv'nor as a man of his time. Before he went into partnership with John Hollingshead at the Old Gaiety in 1885, Edwardes had been D'Oyly Carte's right-hand man at the Savoy Theatre. The influence of D'Oyly Carte and W. S. Gilbert played a vital part in his success. It was the golden age of the actor-managers: at their head was Sir Henry Irving, who formed a great partnership with Ellen Terry at the Lyceum. Other outstanding figures were George Alexander, who produced *The Importance of Being Earnest* and made a corner in high comedies at the St James's; Charles Wyndham, a fine actor whose company flourished at the Criterion and then played at Wyndham's and the New Theatres; and Herbert Beerbohm Tree, an inspired character actor whose magnificent productions drew the town to Her Majesty's.

I acknowledge my debt to the people who have assisted me with their knowledge of this period, and begin by thanking Peter Cotes, the distinguished stage director and producer. Peter Cotes has helped me in many ways and I am also grateful to him for reading my proofs. I am most grateful to those inimitable theatre historians, Raymond Mander and Joe Mitchenson—Raymond Mander has regaled me with a fund of stories about the Guv'nor and his shows and I have consulted them both about the illustrations in this book, many of which are from the Mander & Mitchenson Theatre Collection.

I also thank Clifford Mollison, Hubert Woodward and Sir Philip Brocklehurst for giving me their personal recollections of the period. Clifford Mollison, the comedian, is the son of William Mollison, who was in Irving's company at the Lyceum. Hubert Woodward, the veteran actor-manager, remembers this period as if it was yesterday. Sir Philip Brocklehurst, who went on Shackleton's first Polar expedition, was a young man about town in the Edwardian era.

I have dedicated this biography to the men and women who made the Gaiety a British institution. It is worth remembering that the Gaiety owed its phenomenal success to a team of men and women and not only to stars like Nellie Farren, Fred Leslie, Seymour Hicks, Ellaline Terriss, Gertie Millar, Teddy Payne and George Grossmith; chorus girls, stage staff, composers, authors and lyric writers all played their part in it. And some artists were so devoted to the Gaiety that they carried on almost literally until they dropped.

ALAN HYMAN

Steyning, September 1974

OLD GAIETY (1868–1886)

1 Laugh with Me, London

She was a peal of laughter, ringing its way
through life:
She was Gaiety's censure of London's serious
strife.
'Laugh with me, romp with me, London,' this
was her dinning song:
'Dance with me, frail and feeble: my music shall
make you strong.'

HENRY J. BYRON, *Tribute to Nellie Farren*

The Gaiety Theatre had been entertaining the public for a quarter of a century before George Edwardes brought the first musical comedy to its boards and soon made it world famous. The original playhouse stood at the eastern end of the Strand, near the beautiful church of St Mary-le-Strand, in the block bounded by Wellington Street, Catherine Street and Exeter Street. Its architect, C. J. Phipps, had designed it on similar lines to the Théâtre-Lyrique in Paris; it was considered an elegant building in 1868 and a great improvement on the heavy, dingy playhouses then existing. The gay colour scheme inside helped to produce an atmosphere of lightness and cheerfulness.

John Hollingshead had announced with some pride that he would open the new theatre on 21 December 1868, with an outstanding bill consisting of a French operetta, a new comic drama and a burlesque extravaganza by W. S. Gilbert; but as the day drew near people in the theatre world, who knew this was Hollingshead's first venture into management, believed he was being wildly optimistic. The pundits of the Green Room and Garrick Clubs were quite convinced that the theatre would never be ready before Christmas.

Hollingshead had met with a series of setbacks at the Gaiety. First, his builders had been held up owing to a dispute about 'Ancient Lights' with the *Morning Post,* the prominent Tory newspaper which occupied the premises next door in the Strand. The playhouse was already half-way up when the *Morning Post* decided that if it went any higher it would deprive their staff of essential light and air, so they applied for an injunction to stop the building. But John Hollingshead, who happened to be an experienced journalist, knew that all the staff would leave the *Morning Post* on Friday night and not return till Sunday afternoon. Before they had time to serve an injunction on him he went to see his landlord—Lionel Lawson of the *Daily Telegraph*—and they agreed on a course of action.

Hollingshead instructed his builders to pay their men overtime to work day and night over that weekend in order to complete the Gaiety structure. The brick walls went up as if by a miracle, the floors were laid down and in went the doors and windows. When the staff of the *Morning Post* returned on Sunday afternoon they had the shock of their lives: the whole of the theatre stood there, looking as permanent as the Strand itself.* The *Morning Post,* reasonably enough, decided to take no further action.

However, that had been only the start of Hollingshead's troubles. In late November he had a much greater setback: all the Gaiety scenery was burnt to a cinder at William Grieve's paintroom in Macklin Street, off Drury Lane. The fire at Grieve's would have been enough to make many managers lose heart; but Hollingshead, living up to his nickname of 'Practical John', persuaded old Grieve to have every item of scenery repainted. The only way to get it ready in time for the first night was by paying Grieve's men overtime to work all round the clock; Hollingshead also arranged for the new scenery to be stored in a dilapidated oilcloth factory at Camberwell.

During the following weeks he spent half his time jumping in and out of hansom cabs. He called on William Grieve and his men, painting the new scenery in the draughty factory at

* W. Macqueen Pope, *Gaiety, Theatre of Enchantment* (W. H. Allen, 1949).

Camberwell; he called at Covent Garden to hear Kettenus rehearsing the orchestra; he called at three different rehearsal rooms in the West End to watch the principals and the chorus of his three pieces and the corps de ballet. Then he took a cab back to the Gaiety to see how they were progressing with the auditorium. The theatre was packed with builders, decorators and upholsterers, all working flat out to get it ready in time. Hollingshead drove his people hard, though never harshly.

By these methods 'Practical John' got the costumes and scenery for the three pieces ready by December, but it was a very close thing. The workmen were so busy putting the finishing touches to the Gaiety stage that there was not time for a dress rehearsal. In fact, there was not even time for Hollingshead to call a lighting rehearsal to give the gas men their lighting cues. The carpenters and stage hands had no chance of handling the scenery or of rehearsing the strikings and settings, while the property men were completely at sea. But the most worrying thing of all was that he had to gamble on the ability of his three separate companies to make a success of an operetta, a drama and a burlesque, playing on a stage upon which they had never set foot.

Robert Soutar, his stage manager, was in a dreadful state at the prospect of coping with three different pieces, but John Hollingshead kept remarkably cool. At four o'clock he shooed the workmen off the stage, where they had been lingering in the hope of seeing a dress rehearsal, and shepherded his three companies on to the boards. Then Hollingshead, Soutar and the various other people connected with the performance held a sort of costume parade.

At twenty minutes past six—only ten minutes before the public was due to be admitted—the last of the workmen picked up their tools and filed off the stage. But instead of leaving the building they went through the 'pass door' from the stage to the auditorium, leaving behind them a trail of brickdust, lime and dirt. Eighty workmen climbed up to the upper balcony, sat down in the first two rows and made themselves comfortable. Hollingshead and Soutar were much too busy on the stage to realize what was happening.

The acting manager spotted the workmen; he yelled up and ordered them to leave the theatre immediately. The workmen refused to budge, so he appealed to them to give up their seats because people had already reserved them. When they ignored him he lost his temper and threatened to call in the police. One of the workmen shouted down to him, 'We've built the bloody theatre and we're going to see the bloody theatre open!'*

When Hollingshead was informed that the workmen had commandeered the first two rows of the upper balcony he decided to let them stay there. He felt there was a certain justice in their claim, and the last thing he wanted was a riot on his first night. The audience had already started to arrive.

The Gaiety had accommodation for 2,000 people. There were only five rows of stalls, the rest of the ground floor being taken up with the pit, where the public had to sit on backless benches. The domed roof was supported by pillars which came right through the balconies down to the floor; this was unfortunate as it meant that some of the people in the pit had an impeded view of the stage. The balcony had only three rows of seats, and behind them there were upper boxes facing the stage. Above this level came the upper balcony, and at the top a gallery with benches seating five hundred at a pinch. The decor was in neutral shades, but the alcoves on both sides of the proscenium had brightly coloured groups of statuary representing lyric and epic poetry. Over the proscenium there was a thirty-foot frieze of a medieval king and queen.

The curtain depicted a girl in a white dress with her long skirt held above her knees and caught over her left arm. She had a crimson rose in the middle of her low-cut bodice, and wore a pierrot ruffle with a white tricorne hat which set off her golden hair. She was parting the curtains of the Gaiety against a crimson background.

Punctually at seven o'clock the curtain rose on *The Two Harlequins*, a short operetta by Emile Jones, which all took place in a wood. It was followed by *On the Cards*, a comedy-drama in three acts adapted from the French. Alfred Wigan played a French character in his own inimitable style. The heroine was Madge Robertson, who 'acted with her usual grace, earnestness and intelligence', said the *Era*. She was to become one of the most notable actresses of the period under her married name of Mrs Madge Kendal. Nellie Farren, in the

* John Hollingshead, *Good Old Gaiety* (London, 1903).

role of a conjuror's assistant, was commended for 'her delightful archness and vivacity'.

The third piece, *Robert the Devil*, or *The Nun, the Dun and the Son of a Gun*, was a burlesque extravaganza by W. S. Gilbert, who had already made his name as the author and illustrator of the *Bab Ballads*. The music was a pot-pourri of the works of Offenbach and other Continental composers. Gilbert made fun of the Duke's brutal penance with a running fire of puns and changed the fiendish Bertram into a droll character. There was a scene in the waxworks of the Chamber of Horrors in which a body of nuns were 'resuscitated', and another one in Pandemonium.*

Burlesques, like pantomime, had a woman playing the leading male role, and Nellie Farren as Robert, Duke of Normandy, was the success of the evening. She had been born in Lancashire but brought up in London and had a Cockney accent. The fourth generation of an acting family, she had been on the stage since childhood and had appeared in straight parts in all types of plays; she had once played Ariel in *The Tempest*. The Press notices were full of praise for her. The *Examiner* said:

How pleasant it is to watch the face of Miss Farren. If a throng of people are on the stage, and she enters, what a smile, what a gleam in the eye! It is like turning on the gas! . . . We conclude by recording our sincere and cordial appreciation of the management of the Gaiety Theatre. Mr Hollingshead has performed an unparalleled feat. In a new theatre, with a new company where the members were strangers to each other, and under great difficulties . . . he performed an operetta, a drama and a burlesque without a single hitch, mistake or delay. . . . We are happy to welcome to the managerial chair a gentleman of so much intellect, taste and energy.

The remarkable feature of the Gaiety first night was that all Hollingshead's pieces had gone without a hitch—a great tribute to the work behind the scenes of Robert Soutar, the stage manager. He was married to Nellie Farren, so this was by way of being a family triumph.

* Raymond Mander and Joe Mitchenson, *The Lost Theatres of London* (Hart-Davis 1961).

The Gaiety Girls had been one of the main attractions in Hollingshead's opening production; most of them were in the chorus, and a few disported themselves in various fascinating poses in the corps de ballet. 'Practical John' fully appreciated that men formed the majority of the audiences who came to see his shows, so he always looked for pretty girls for them to feast their eyes on. 'A manager should never forget that there are in London many gentlemen, old and young, who will go to the theatre to admire the beauty of the female actresses,' he said.* If a girl had a good singing voice he would engage her although she might not be an oil painting, but in the ordinary way he chose his girls for their pretty faces and well-endowed figures. Hollingshead declared his stage was not a platform for the display of grandmothers and maiden aunts. The result was that every girl in the Gaiety chorus had the full breasts and well rounded thighs which were then the fashion.

John Hollingshead had been born in Hoxton in 1827 of parents who could not afford to give him a formal education. As a boy he formed the habit of walking for miles all over London, exploring different districts of the City and finding out all he could about any trade that was being carried on: thus he came to know London like the back of his hand by the time he grew up. His local knowledge and a natural bent for writing enabled him to become an admirable journalist. Charles Dickens engaged him to write for *Household Words* and he had been a regular contributor to the *Cornhill Magazine* under Thackeray's editorship. He wrote a play, *The Birthplace of Podgers*, specially for J. L. Toole, the comedian, and thanks to its success gained a footing in the theatre. Dickens gave him passes to London theatres and introduced him to the leading actors of the day. Since 1863 he had been drama critic of the *Daily News*.

Hollingshead had leased the Gaiety Theatre on reasonable terms from Lionel Lawson, the proprietor of the *Daily Telegraph*. They knew each other quite well as Hollingshead often contributed articles to that paper.

'I hear you are going to build a theatre in the Strand. I want to take it.' Hollingshead had said bluntly.

'Well, have you got any money?' asked Lawson.

* John Hollingshead, *Gaiety Chronicles* (Constable, 1898).

'Two hundred pounds and no debts,' replied Hollingshead.
'That's not much, is it?'

'Not a great deal, but I suppose I can get more if I want it.'

'You shall have the theatre,' said Lawson and they shook
hands on the deal.*

Though this may sound an extraordinary way to do business,
everything turned out satisfactorily. 'Practical John' met some
wealthy friends of his at the St James's Restaurant, Piccadilly.
Within a few hours they had agreed to put up capital of £5,000
for the running expenses of the theatre, and Hollingshead
calculated that so long as he took £6,000 a year at the Gaiety
he could make a profit. He soon earned a reputation for being
scrupulously honest in his dealings. Actors and actresses
learnt that his word was his bond, and once he had engaged an
artist there was no need of a formal contract, 'but we'll have
a piece of paper if you like', he would say.

Tall, well dressed and distinguished looking, John Hollingshead had turned forty when he became manager of the Gaiety.
He spoke in a high-pitched voice that was almost a falsetto.
He never employed an assistant, and left the day-to-day
running of the theatre to Robert Soutar, his stage manager
and right-hand man. He used to sit in his office at the Gaiety
with a watch in front of him as he often had to leave to keep
appointments all over London in connection with his interests
in music halls and other ventures. He had catholic tastes and
presented all kinds of pieces on his stage, but he specialized
in burlesque, whose plots were usually taken from plays, books,
stories, operas or legends. The burlesques were accompanied
by a musical hotchpotch made up from the work of Continental
composers.

In 1869 Hollingshead placed an 'electric light' on the roof
of the Gaiety, which was actually a searchlight run by a
primitive battery. Its rays lit up the streets from St Mary-le-
Strand to Charing Cross, making the Strand seem like daylight
every night. People visited the theatre just to see the 'electric
light'; this early publicity stunt helped to put the Gaiety on
the map.†

That same year Hollingshead produced a spectacular burlesque entitled *Columbus, or The Original Pitch in a Merry*

* J. B. Booth, *London Town* (Werner Laurie, 1929).
† Pope, *Gaiety*.

Key. (There was always a pun in the second titles of burlesques and the shows themselves were loaded with them: comedians would rattle off the most excruciating puns and be certain of getting a round of applause.) Nellie Farren played Little Christopher Columbus and had another triumph. The music was taken from various Continental composers and arranged by Meyer Lutz, the Gaiety's new conductor. Lutz, a serious, bespectacled German musician, also became the resident composer and chorus master, and even deputized as stage manager in an emergency.

In June Edward, Prince of Wales, arranged to bring Princess Alexandra to see *Columbus*—the first time royalty had visited the Gaiety. A Mr Chapman, a pompous individual employed by a theatre ticket agency, came to inspect the Royal Box and Retiring-Room a few days in advance. Chapman informed Hollingshead that there was not enough gold in the Royal Box for a royal personage and brought along to the theatre a large and cumbersome Louis Seize chair for the exclusive use of the Prince of Wales. As soon as Chapman left, Hollingshead had the Louis Seize chair removed and put back the original one.

His Royal Highness saw *Columbus* on 21 June and told Hollingshead he had spent a most enjoyable evening. Queen Victoria had cancelled all Command Performances and taken no interest in plays at all after Prince Albert's death in 1861, so the Prince of Wales had become the theatre's most important asset. The day after his visit to the Gaiety the takings almost doubled.

The original Gaiety chorus girls were tall, beautiful creatures who sauntered on to the stage in tights and had a diamond or two stuck on their shapely legs and 'sometimes in other ridiculous places'. All they really had to do was to appear on the stage looking lovely. They spent their time either staring at the gentlemen in the stalls with a charming, detached expression, or watching the artists on the stage with either disdain or total indifference.* Hollingshead's chorus girls were at first recruited from the lower social classes and not expected to be over-burdened with brains. A journalist interviewed one of them at home; she received him with her hair in curling-pins

* Ellaline Terriss, *Ellaline Terriss* (Cassell, 1928).

and 'There was nothing in the world she would not surrender to me in return for a newspaper notice a line long', he said. A few days later the same chorus girl, dressed in the height of fashion, drove up to the Gaiety in her own victoria. 'Hello, old chappie,' she called out to the journalist in an amusing affectation of well-bred condescension.* So many Gaiety girls had acquired their own carriages that John Hollingshead had a notice displayed prominently:

LADIES DRAWING LESS THAN 25 SHILLINGS A
WEEK ARE POLITELY
REQUESTED NOT TO ARRIVE AT THE THEATRE
IN BROUGHAMS

The chorus girls were often taken out to supper; some of them would boast of their illustrious ancestry when they were in their cups. One married a man of good family and made such a song and dance about her pedigree that he decided to call in a genealogist. All the latter could discover was that her grand-father had played the hind-legs of an elephant in a pantomime at Margate.

On 18 October 1869, 'Practical John' opened the Gaiety Restaurant with communicating entrances to the theatre. A great amenity for patrons, it had been built at a cost of £60,000 and in spite of fierce opposition from a score of public houses in the Strand. It had needed all the tenacity of a Hollingshead to persuade the London magistrates to give it a licence.

The Gaiety Restaurant soon became established as a favourite rendezvous for theatre people and for people coming to the West End to see plays or operas. It lived up to the wording in Hollingshead's advertisement:

Spacious Dining Saloons, Private Dining Rooms,
English, French and German Cuisine,
Choicest Wines of the Finest Vintage.
Every convenience for Gentlemen and families
wishing to dine before going on to the
Theatre or Opera.
Large and well-ventiliated Billiards Rooms,
with French and English tables.

* Guy Deghy, *Paradise in the Strand* (Richards Press, 1958).

At Christmas Hollingshead presented *Uncle Dick's Darling*, a comedy by Henry J. Byron, with J. L. Toole in the star part. Toole persuaded him to engage Henry Irving, an actor from the provinces, to play the part of Mr Chevenix, an arrogant City merchant rather like Mr Dombey. *Uncle Dick's Darling* had a good run. The critics gave excellent notices to Henry Irving, although he was so little known that some of them spelt his name wrong, and when Charles Dickens saw the piece he had nothing but praise for Irving's performance.

Nellie Farren and J. L. Toole appeared together the following year in *Thespis, or The Gods Grow Old*, a comic opera by W. S. Gilbert and Arthur Sullivan. (This was the first time Gilbert and Sullivan had collaborated.) Gilbert produced his own piece but, much to his annoyance, Hollingshead refused to give him a free hand to work out all the stage moves for the artists. The theme of *Thespis* was that the gods on Mount Olympus made a compact to change places with a band of strolling players for a year, with disastrous results. This piece was too subtle for the down-to-earth Gaiety patrons and, apart from that, Nellie Farren and J. L. Toole could not sing Sullivan's score properly. Nellie Farren as Mercury, messenger of the gods, complained that she was overworked:

Oh, I'm the celestial drudge,
From morning to night I must stop at it.
On errands all day I must trudge
And stick to my work till I drop at it.
In summer I get up at one
(As a good-natured donkey I'm ranked for it)
Then I go and light up the sun
And Phoebus Apollo gets thanked for it.

W. S. Gilbert had a biting wit. A small part actress in *Thespis*, who had good looks but no talent, rounded on him at a rehearsal and asked, 'Why should I stand here? I am not a chorus girl!' 'No, madam,' replied Gilbert. 'Your voice is not strong enough, or no doubt you would be.'*

Thespis was badly received and soon came off. Gilbert and Sullivan shook hands after their failure, without having the slightest idea they would work together again. However,

* Leslie Baily, *The Story of Gilbert and Sullivan* (Cassell, 1952).

their first comic opera had been seen by Richard D'Oyly
Carte, a concert manager who came from a musical family
and composed operettas himself. Carte thought highly of
Sullivan's score and admired Gilbert's libretto, and had a
feeling that the two men might write something remarkable
one day.

The stalls at the Gaiety were monopolised by wealthy young
men about town, the 'mashers' or 'stage-door Johnnies', who
spent a great deal of time and money in trying to win the
favours of the chorus girls. They all wore tight trousers, carried
crutch sticks and had fashionable affectations, which accounted
for their nickname of the 'Crutch-and-Toothpick Brigade'.
F. C. Burnand of *Punch*, who wrote some of the best Gaiety
burlesques, hit them off in his lyric 'The Mashers':

Then as mashers there are plenty
Of the sort at three-and-twenty,
Their shirt-front is immaculately got up.
Though their look is somewhat vapid
They are living rather rapid
And there isn't much in town to which they're not up.
In the afternoon at five
They begin to be alive
And they call each other 'Chappie' or 'Sonny'.
And they wear a curly hat
And there isn't much in that,
And the set that they belong to are 'Johnnies'.

The Crutch-and-Toothpick Brigade could laugh at themselves,
and when Nellie Farren sang about them they always joined
in the chorus:

How do you like London, how d'you like the town?
How d'you like the Strand, now Temple Bar's pulled down?
How d'you like the la-di-da, the toothpick and the crutch?
How did you get those trousers on, and did they hurt you
much?

In one of the Gaiety burlesques Nellie Farren came on dressed
as a masher, carrying a crutch stick and waving her golden
toothpick, and sang:

I'm a swell, you can tell,
And I have, of course, as such,
Close cut hair, elbows square,
With my toothpick and my crutch.

Nellie Farren was the finest burlesque artist of her time. She
was petite and had a piquant face; by no means a beauty, she
was described as 'cheeky in tone and manner, but not in the
least offensive'. She usually appeared in a wig of yellow curls
and had a pink and white complexion. Her blue eyes changed
expression constantly with her mobile face, and the secret of
her appeal was her great personal magnetism. When she made
her entrance at the Gaiety in the seventies and eighties, she
had only to give one glance upward and the whole house
was under her sway—and yet she suffered agonies from first-
night nerves. The galleryites and pittites called her 'Our Nellie'
and worshipped her, while on her side Nellie Farren loved 'the
boys of the gallery' for their loyalty and devotion to her.
Graham Robertson, the painter and author, who had a very
poor opinion of the Gaiety burlesques, only went to them to
see Nellie Farren. He loathed their puns, thought the productions were tawdry and the costumes hideous. 'Only the genius
of Nellie Farren held together these feeble extravaganzas.'*
    John Hollingshead used to boast that he gave his patrons at
the Gaiety every kind of entertainment under the sun, but
burlesques were always the main attraction. The early ones
had been built round Nellie Farren, but in 1876 he engaged
Edward Terry, Katie Vaughan and Edward Royce. These three
with Nellie Farren established themselves as the 'Gaiety
Quartette'; whenever the four of them appeared on the stage
together they used to break into their signature tune:

We are a Merry Family,
We are, we are, we are!

Edward Terry was a brilliant and inventive comedian with a
perky style which blended perfectly with Nellie Farren's
Cockney humour. He had a whimsical face and his eccentric
vocal inflections delighted the audiences. He and Nellie Farren
regularly introduced topical jokes which they based on items
in the current evening papers.

* Graham Robertson, *Time Was* (Hamish Hamilton, 1931).

Katie Vaughan, one of the outstanding dancers of the period, had been discovered by Hollingshead on the music halls. She had a slight figure and a delightful presence and was the first dancer to wear long, graceful skirts instead of the tights and tu-tu ballet skirts of the old burlesque artists. Her black gloves and stockings and her svelte figure fascinated the public for a decade. It was a pleasant change to watch this slim woman on the stage after a succession of girls with full bosoms and enormous thighs. Katie Vaughan had a pensive face and dreamy eyes and her admirers found poetry in every movement of her dancing.

Edward Royce, fourth member of the Gaiety Quartette, was a sound actor, a good singer and a first-rate dancer. He was Katie Vaughan's partner and they made a splendid combination.

When the Merry Family appeared in *Dom Caesar*, Nellie Farren and Edward Terry did a skit on Za-Zel, the man who used to be shot out of a cannon at the old Westminster Aquarium. Nellie climbed into a cannon and Edward Terry appeared to ram her down with a big ramrod, but she really went into a trap which opened underneath the stage. One night the prompt man had deserted his post, so the trap did not function. Suddenly Edward Terry realized he was ramming the rod into a human body. He said impromptu, 'Are you in?' After a pause he yelled, 'Are you Far-in?' And then, 'Are you Nellie Far-in?'* The audience were convulsed; the noise brought the prompt man back to his post and he worked the trap for Nellie Farren to escape underneath the stage. But the gag had gone so well that they always used it afterwards in *Dom Caesar*.

This burlesque had been written by Henry J. Byron, a prolific author who hated rehearsals and used to escape from the theatre as soon as possible and seek refuge in the nearest pub. Edward Royce once found he needed some extra lines after his dance and managed to locate Byron at his pub. Byron worked like lightning. Within a few minutes he told the actor, 'End your dance by disappearing through a vamp. And then pop up a star trap and say these words:

I've cut sly passages and secret doors,
Panels that slide and traps let in the floors,
So that my movements are eccentric—very:
One moment deep below myself I bury

* Pope, *Gaiety*.

And ere you say I'm there with words emphatic,
I'm that erratic,
I'm in that there attic!'*

This doggerel type of verse was fairly typical of the lines the artists had to put over in Gaiety burlesques. Audiences tolerated them, and found them quite entertaining. But as soon as W. S. Gilbert presented the public with his marvellous lyrics in *H.M.S. Pinafore*, the Gilbert and Sullivan operas led the way in musical plays and the burlesques sounded puerile and old fashioned, though the artistry of Nellie Farren and the three other artists carried these pieces to success for a few more years.

One of Nellie's most popular numbers was 'I'll Strike you with a Feather!' This rather feeble ditty only became a hit because of the charming way in which Nellie Farren put it over. As she sang she skipped all over the stage and made great play with her fan. She used to throw her head back so far that audiences got quite alarmed, fearing she would dislocate her neck.

Nellie Farren, the first 'Queen of the Gaiety', was in a class of her own. She could not compete with Katie Vaughan as a dancer and had only a tiny voice, but no woman ever came near her natural genius for broad caricature and her subtle, entrancing devilry.

* J. G. Hibbert, *A Playgoer's Memories* (Grant Richards, 1920).

2 A Job for George

*I have never regretted the day I went down to
Leicester to take over that acting manager's job,
and I have never ceased to be grateful for the
chance that sent me out on my eventful career.*

GEORGE EDWARDES,
quoted by D. Forbes Winslow, *Daly's*

Seven years after the opening of the Gaiety, Richard D'Oyly
Carte was still a concert manager, with offices at Craig's
Court off Shaftesbury Avenue. One of his clients, Madame
Selina Dolaro, had taken the Royalty Theatre, Dean Street,
for a season of operas, and asked D'Oyly Carte to be her
manager. Madame Dolaro, though talented, was very far from
being a Melba or a Tetrazzini. After producing various operas
at the Royalty, she decided to appear in *La Périchole*, a light
opera by Offenbach. As its playing time was too short for a
full evening's entertainment, she needed a curtain-raiser. She
consulted D'Oyly Carte.

It occurred to Carte that W. S. Gilbert might have a suitable
libretto, and he asked Gilbert to call at the theatre as soon as
possible. Gilbert mentioned that *Trial by Jury*, one of his
Bab Ballads, had already been set to music by Carl Rosa.
It was a gay and extremely witty send-up of the law, and
Carte's reaction to Gilbert's verses was most enthusiastic, but
there was one snag: he objected to using the score by Carl
Rosa. He remembered some delightful numbers Arthur Sullivan
had written in *Thespis* and insisted on getting Sullivan to write
a new score for *Trial by Jury*.

Gilbert hailed a cab and drove off in the snow to Sullivan's rooms in Victoria Street, where he read *Trial by Jury* to the composer. For some strange reason Gilbert suddenly found himself bored with his piece, but Arthur Sullivan was so enchanted with it that he agreed at once to set the verses to music. Three weeks later he delivered the complete score to D'Oyly Carte.

Trial by Jury, a one-act comic opera, was produced by W. S. Gilbert, who was given a free hand, and presented at the Royalty on 13 October 1875 as a curtain-raiser to *La Périchole*. The *Daily Telegraph* reported next morning:

W. S. Gilbert's *Trial by Jury* goes better than ever . . . and seldom has applause been so spontaneously bestowed. The merit of this most original and subtle eccentricity does not depend on Mr F. Sullivan (as the Judge) or on the sound singing of Mr Courtnay and Mr Campbell . . . but the excellence of the whole thing consists in the appreciation of the fun shown by every juryman, attendant and bridesmaid in the court. The outside juryman, with the dolefully solemn face, and the most gushing bridesmaid are as entitled to compliment as the clever principals.

Here, in fact, is the happiest idea, caught to perfection by Arthur Sullivan, and faultlessly executed by the company. It is a good bit of fun, and the actors seem to think so as much as the audience. The true enjoyment of laughter has not yet been discovered by those who have not seen *Trial by Jury*.

The public strongly endorsed this verdict and D'Oyly Carte kept *Trial by Jury* at the Royalty for a year in support of Madame Dolaro's season of operas.

While Londoners were scrambling to get seats for *Trial by Jury*, a tall, handsome Irish youth sat in his room at Bloomsbury cursing himself for being so lazy. George Edwards had just been officially notified that he had been ploughed in the Army examination for Woolwich. His parents, who lived in Cleethorpes, Lincolnshire, had sent him to London to be crammed for the Army by Forest Fulton, Q.C.; but instead of studying for his exam at nights he had gone off to the West

End and enjoyed himself to the limits of his small allowance. His favourite entertainment was going to the music halls; they were great fun and a good seat cost him less than in a theatre. His regular companion on these forays to the West End had been Edward Marshall Hall, a fellow pupil at Mr Fulton's establishment. Marshall Hall, who was then studying for the Bar, later became one of the greatest criminal advocates of the twentieth century.

George Edwards was the youngest of the seven children of Captain James Edwards, an Irishman who had settled in Lincolnshire with his wife and family and worked as a senior Customs officer at Cleethorpes. Every allowance had been made for George because he was the baby, and he had been spoilt. Whilst his three brothers had all done well at school, George had idled away his time and never minded being bottom of his class at St James's Catholic College, Cleethorpes. However, he had been good at games and very popular and he made several lifelong friends whose families were in the fishing business at Grimsby. At home his mother, Eleanor, had ruled the roost; George Edwards adored her, although he was terrified of her. Eleanor came from Yorkshire and had been a Miss Widdup; the Widdups were a wealthy family and she had her own private income. In fact, Eleanor had provided George with his allowance in London.

George Edwards was lodging at the house of Mr Isaacs, a diamond merchant. Isaacs had no need whatsoever to take in paying guests, but he liked having young men staying in the house. He appreciated their company and, even more important, so did his five unmarried daughters. George Edwards, who had abundant Irish charm, soon became Isaacs's favourite lodger. He was dreading the thought of going back to his parents in Cleethorpes, who would be furious with him for failing in his exam; he had a horror of getting involved in scenes. So he decided not to break the bad news to them yet and to stay on in London instead and try and find a job.*

Mr Isaacs had a talk with George Edwards in his private sanctum that evening. After listening sympathetically to George's tale of woe the diamond merchant said he had known all along that he was not cut out for the Army. Isaacs invited him to stay on in his house as his guest for as long as he liked

* Ursula Bloom, *Curtain Call for the Guv'nor* (Hutchinson, 1954).

while he looked around for a job, and also offered him the
chance of starting on the ground floor in the diamond trade.
But George felt Hatton Garden was not the place for him, even
though he had not the least notion of what he really wanted to
do.

He took a temporary job as a clerk in the City, but found the
work extremely dreary. After that experience of commerce, he
could find nothing congenial although he kept trying. He was
walking down the Strand, temporarily unemployed, when he
happened to meet his cousin Michael Gunn, who owned the
Gaiety Theatre, Dublin, in partnership with his brother John.
They also ran touring companies. Michael Gunn was a good
deal older than George and had always liked him. By a coincidence, he had just sacked the acting manager of one of his
touring companies for absconding with the takings of the
last tour; hearing George's story, he offered him the chance to
go out in his place as acting manager of the Gunn Company's
No. 3 tour of *The Lady of Lyons*, which was just about to
start at Leicester.

Young Edwards knew precisely nothing about the theatre
and had never been remotely interested in it. However, he
thought the tour sounded like a great adventure and would
give him a wonderful chance to visit famous English towns
and cities he had never seen in his life. And, apart from that,
if he went off on tour now he could avoid seeing his family
for a few months. He hated getting involved in scenes, like
all the Edwards family. So he gladly accepted Michael Gunn's
offer. He packed up at Bloomsbury and took the first train to
Leicester, where he met the rest of the company.

He had no idea of what a No. 3 tour of *The Lady of Lyons*
was going to be like. His first shock was the discovery that the
Gunn Company were playing at the worst theatre in the town.
It turned out that most of the 'dates' were at minor towns in
the provinces, and wherever it went the company was certain
to be booked at the smallest theatre. They were paid so little
that everybody had to put up with weekly digs in squalid
back streets; yet they all had to butter up the landlady, call
her 'Ma' and praise her cooking—although some of their
landladies were drunken sluts who could not be trusted to
boil an egg. It took a fastidious youth like George Edwards a
long time to get used to these digs.

When Seymour Hicks was on tour with a theatrical company in Staffordshire he once had the temerity to ask his landlady for a bath at nine o'clock every morning. 'A bath every morning, lovey!' she exclaimed. 'You must get mighty dirty at theatre every evening to want a tub every day. Eh, lad, theatre must be worse than coal mine!'*

Most of the provincial theatres they played at had a staff consisting of a gas man, who fixed the elementary stage lighting, a property man, two stage hands and a carpenter. A competent stage manager was almost unheard of in 1875!

Edwards found that, in order to get reasonable co-operation from the theatre staff, one had to give the stage hands plenty of beer money: unless they were absolutely satisfied with their beer money they could easily wreck the show. Jessie Millward, who toured in the provinces before joining Henry Irving's company, once found herself at the mercy of some thirsty stage hands in a small town. As the heroine of a Victorian melodrama she had to wring the hearts of the audience as she proclaimed her virtue to a lecherous squire. As she played her scene on a stage about the size of a billiard table, she felt the hot and onionated breath of the machinist and the limelight man almost pouring down the back of her neck through the 'hole of observation' in the front cloth. Then, during her speech in which she protested she would never lose her virginity at any price, the stage hands called out, 'That's the way—get rid of it, get rid of it!' Then there was an actress playing in *A Woman's Cross Roads* who refused to give a gas man his beer money and always regretted it. He took an old duster up with him to his perch. In her big scene she had to stoop down and take the key to the town mortuary from the villainous doctor's surgery. As she bent down the gas-man tore the duster *cr-r-ck*, and in the most ghastly apprehension the actress rushed through the rest of the scene holding herself fore and aft with both hands.†

George Edwards soon found that an acting manager of a No. 3 tour had to work seven days a week. Every Saturday night after the show he had to supervise the striking of the sets at the theatre and to see that all the costumes were packed into

* Seymour Hicks, *Twenty-four Years of an Actor's Life* (Alston Rivers, 1910).

† J. B. Booth, *Sporting Times* (Werner Laurie, 1931).

B

stage baskets. And on Sundays, when the company had to travel from one date to the next, he had to organize their railway transport and to ensure that every item of scenery and all the costumes arrived safely at the next town. Their train usually left at eleven in the morning and stopped at every little halt and junction on the way, so that it might take all day to do a journey of only thirty miles. There were even occasions when the company arrived at a strange town, quite exhausted from travelling, only to find that owing to a mistake no accommodation had been reserved for them.

One of the most unpleasant things about Edwards's job was having to cope with actors who went on to the stage dead drunk on Saturday nights. Many actors got into the fatal habit of going to the local pub every night and getting tight because they dreaded going back to their sordid digs. Fortunately, Edwards hardly drank at all and had a most diplomatic way of handling actors who were in an alcoholic haze.

The Lady of Lyons, an old play by Bulwer Lytton, had some speeches which were so stilted and unreal that only a great actress like Ellen Terry could get away with them. So no wonder the No. 3 Gunn Company sometimes got 'the bird' at a performance.

The worst ordeal for George Edwards was when he had to face an audience who demanded their money back. On these occasions Edwards would go up on to the stage and exert all his Irish charm to persuade them to calm down. For the first few months he hated the life on tour, but something made him stick it out. He had a natural affection for other people and a sense of humour which enabled him to see the funny side of a crisis in the theatre. But his greatest asset was his unflappable temperament.

As he gradually picked up the rudiments of the business he found himself enjoying the experience of managing a No. 3 tour. He took great care never to quarrel with the actors and actresses in the company, most of whom were years older than himself. He also evolved a technique of coaxing artists into a reasonable frame of mind until they did what he wanted. He became very popular with the company and, after he had proved himself, Michael Gunn received excellent reports about his cousin. When *The Lady of Lyons* ended its tour Gunn brought him to Dublin to work in the box office at the Gaiety

Theatre in Grafton Street. He did so well there that he was promoted to be box-office manager.

Michael and John Gunn, apart from their theatrical interests, were leading musical publishers and were known as the 'Chappell's of Ireland'. Some months earlier Richard D'Oyly Carte had presented a season of opera at their Gaiety Theatre, Dublin, with a company headed by two prima donnas, Madame Selina Dolaro and Bessie Sudlow. D'Oyly Carte, who already had the instincts of a showman, had sailed up the Liffey with his artists in a specially chartered steamer with a flag at her mast bearing the words *D'Oyly Carte's Opera Company*. Michael Gunn and Richard D'Oyly Carte got along like a house on fire and their new friendship was to have an important sequel.

At the beginning of 1878 Michael Gunn summoned George Edwards to London and gave him a slap-up lunch at Romano's. Throughout the meal he was singing the praises of D'Oyly Carte. The success of *Trial by Jury* had helped to convince Carte that in the light musical field British composers, like Arthur Sullivan and Fred Clay and others, could beat the Continental composers at their own game. He resolved to found a school of English comic opera and had managed to form a syndicate of £6,000 to finance the future works of Gilbert and Sullivan and, possibly, other composers and librettists. Tom Chappell, the music publisher, had taken shares in it and so had Charles Lukey Collard, the pianoforte maker. And Michael Gunn had such faith in Carte's flair for musical plays that he had immediately taken shares in the Comic Opera Company. D'Oyly Carte had recently presented their first venture, the production of *The Sorcerer* by Gilbert and Sullivan at the Opéra-Comique Theatre.

At the end of their lunch Gunn told George Edwards that he was sending him round to see D'Oyly Carte at the Opéra-Comique. Edwards set off to meet London's new impresario with a note from Michael Gunn in his pocket:

This is to introduce George Edwards. Pay him £1 a week and see that he earns it.

M.G.*

* Conversations with David Sherbrooke, grandson of George Edwardes.

3 The D'Oyly Carte School

George Edwardes was inspired by the tireless energy and the never-ceasing care which D'Oyly Carte lavished on his work and by the amount of polishing which Gilbert and Sullivan gave to their operas.

W. MACQUEEN POPE and D. L. MURRAY,
Fortune's Favourite

'We will have no ridiculous travesties of dress and manner in our pieces. No star shall be allowed to spoil the balance of the play. Sullivan and I intend to produce comic operas to which any man may safely bring his mother and his aunts. We will have no improper jokes. And we have agreed that no lady in the company shall be required to wear a dress which she could not with absolute propriety wear at a fancy dress ball.'*

W. S. Gilbert addressed these remarks to a gentleman of the Press who had asked him for information about the policy of the new Gilbert and Sullivan operas. William Schenk Gilbert was a tall, good-looking man of forty with a prominent moustache and a military bearing. He was a martinet in the theatre, who often reduced actresses to tears and sometimes gave actors nervous breakdowns, yet he was a kind man at heart. He dominated his charming partner, who was six years younger. In contrast to Gilbert, Sullivan treated all the artists with great courtesy. As a rule Gilbert worked out the librettos and roughed out the lyrics of their operas before Sullivan began

* Baily.

to write the scores. Gilbert had produced *Trial by Jury* with such a masterly touch that D'Oyly Carte left him in complete command of the stage; before he called his first rehearsal he made scale models of all the sets and decided all the entrances and exits of his characters.

Besides producing the operas, Gilbert also drew the original designs for the sets and supervised the costumes. Having planned exactly how his artists should play their scenes, he would keep them rehearsing for hours till he was satisfied that every role in the piece was being correctly played. Edwards was full of admiration for this remarkable man of the theatre, who invariably succeeded in drilling his company into a perfect team by the first night.

After his lunch with Michael Gunn, George Edwards went straight to the Opéra-Comique Theatre, where he was shown in to D'Oyly Carte's office. Gilbert and Sullivan's manager was an alert-looking man of thirty, of medium height, who wore a short black beard. He made quick judgements about people and seldom made a mistake. He took an instant liking to George Edwards and engaged him as box-office manager. Carte introduced him to Helen Lenoir, his brilliant secretary, with whom Edwards worked in close harmony from his very first day.

A Scotswoman, who had taken a first-class degree in mathematics, she had an extraordinary aptitude for work and a gift for diplomacy. After a hard day's work at the office she would still be ready at midnight 'for the very sharpest consideration of a business proposal or the terms of a contract'.* Richard D'Oyly Carte was a man of ideas and sudden impulses, who alternated between violent bursts of work and hectic periods of recreation. Helen Lenoir, with her sweet nature and gentle efficiency, was just the person he needed to complement him.

The Sorcerer was playing to such poor houses at the Opéra-Comique that D'Oyly Carte had nearly taken it off on several occasions. This Gilbert and Sullivan opera, handicapped by a feeble plot and an uninspired score, had never caught on with the public and was now in its final weeks. The box office was so slack that Edwards had plenty of opportunity of escaping into the auditorium to watch W. S. Gilbert rehearsing the

* *Sporting Times*, 1906.

company in his new comic opera, *H.M.S. Pinafore*, which poked fun at the Royal Navy.

The little Opéra-Comique, in Wych Street off the Strand, was probably the worst-designed theatre in London. It had four different entrances from four different streets near the Strand and, in order to reach the auditorium, audiences had to make their way through a series of dismal underground tunnels. *H.M.S. Pinafore* opened on 26 May 1878, to a most enthusiastic reception. George Grossmith gave a magnificent performance in the principal part of Sir Joseph Porter, First Lord of the Admiralty, a pompous ass who knew absolutely nothing about the 'Queen's Navee'. D'Oyly Carte had no doubt that this was the best work Gilbert and Sullivan had yet done and was sure of its ultimate success; but at first the public failed to support it.

Gilbert and Sullivan's operas were a novelty and it took time for people to appreciate the humour of Gilbert's topsy-turvy world. There was a very hot summer in 1878, and the badly ventilated theatre was stifling inside, which did not help to bring in the public. D'Oyly Carte began to get worried when receipts went down in June, and one day in July George Edwards reported that they were taking only £40 a night.

The Comic Opera Syndicate, who were backing the venture, included a coal merchant and another hard-headed business-man. Convinced that *Pinafore* was doomed to failure, they persuaded their partners to put up a fortnight's notice. Carte, who retained his faith in *Pinafore*, was determined to 'nurse' it into a success, and as fast as the syndicate put up the notices he went and persuaded the directors to cancel them. The principals and the chorus agreed to take half salaries until business picked up, which was a great help, but the constant battle with his syndicate was wearing Carte's nerves to shreds.

Suddenly the tide turned. Arthur Sullivan, who was best known as a serious composer, conducted Promenade Concerts at Covent Garden; at one of them he played a selection from *H.M.S. Pinafore* and was encored five times. Next day George Edwards found hundreds of people at the box office, all clamouring to get seats for *Pinafore*. On the strength of this D'Oyly Carte planned that he would buy out the Comic Opera Syndicate—who had put up £500 each—and then go into partnership with Gilbert and Sullivan to produce all their future operas.

By August it was said that England was suffering from *Pinafore* mania. 'A hundred thousand barrel organs have been constructed to play nothing else,' said Arthur Sullivan. Touring companies were performing it all over the country, and amateurs were writing in by every post for licences to perform it. D'Oyly Carte was furious when reports came in that *Pinafore* was being produced throughout the United States by pirate companies: in New York alone there were eight theatres playing pirate versions. Carte decided he would show the Yankees how Gilbert and Sullivan operas ought to be produced. Towards the end of 1878 he sent over a strong company to the States; then, accompanied by W. S. Gilbert and Arthur Sullivan, he sailed off to New York to supervise the production.

George Edwards remained at the Opéra-Comique with increased responsibility in Carte's absence. Helen Lenoir had been put in sole charge of all business at the theatre. George Edwards was most impressed by her efficiency: Miss Lenoir fixed up all Gilbert and Sullivan's provincial tours, engaged new artists for them and also supervised D'Oyly Carte's concert tours. 'The whole fabric of the Gilbert and Sullivan business rested on Miss Lenoir's shoulders,' said Edwards years later. Helen Lenoir took him under her wing and explained to him in detail how the operas were sent out on tour all over Britain and to the United States and the other English-speaking countries.

George Edwards was soon on the best of terms with George Grossmith, Rutland Barrington, Rosina Brandram and the rest of the company. All of them succumbed to his charm, appreciated his tact and found him very useful in an emergency. Whenever W. S. Gilbert produced a new piece he was liable to be rude to the artists and upset them. When a crisis blew up at a rehearsal somebody generally said, 'Just send for George Edwards.'*

Gilbert, accustomed to being kowtowed to by everyone in the theatre, disliked Edwards for standing his ground if he was called in to pour oil on troubled waters. Gilbert became most hostile to George Edwards after he returned from the States and even complained to D'Oyly Carte about him. By this time Carte thought so well of Edwards that Gilbert's

* Baily.

attempt to get him the sack completely failed. Carte had soon realized that though W. S. Gilbert had a genius for writing comic operas, he could be maddening in real life.

Sometimes Gilbert brought his pretty young wife, Lucy, to rehearsals. One day he noticed she had disappeared from the stalls just when he wanted her opinion about some costumes. So he demanded to know where she had gone. 'I have no idea where she is, sir,' said an assistant stage manager. 'Then go and find her—I want her here immediately!' shouted Gilbert. The assistant hurried out of the auditorium and returned, looking most embarrassed, and said, 'She's round behind, sir.' 'I know she's round behind,' retorted Gilbert, 'but where *is* she?'*

Richard D'Oyly Carte bought out the Comic Opera Syndicate and under a new arrangement he went into partnership with Gilbert and Sullivan for the exclusive production of their operas. He gave George Edwards a rise, which enabled him to move into better rooms in London and to go out to supper sometimes at Romano's or the Gaiety Restaurant, both of which adjoined the Opéra-Comique.

At the Gaiety he often met John Hollingshead and had supper with him. Though Hollingshead was old enough to be his father, they shared a love of the theatre. 'Practical John' liked to hear the latest news about D'Oyly Carte's musical pieces, while George Edwards always took an interest in Hollingshead's productions at the Gaiety. The two men soon became firm friends.

The Gaiety had continued to flourish, thanks mainly to the great drawing-power of Nellie Farren, Katie Vaughan, Edward Terry and Edward Royce. They played there most of the year round, appearing in a mixture of burlesques and pantomimes. At times it was very hard to tell the difference between the two: in both cases an actress in tights always played the dashing hero, and actors in fantastic disguises generally impersonated females. John Hollingshead had a blind spot about Gilbert and Sullivan operas, which he dismissed as 'burlesques in long clothes'. He never dreamt they were about to become the outstanding light musical entertainment of the era.

H.M.S. Pinafore ran on at the Opéra-Comique until 1880.

* George Bancroft, *Stage and Bar* (Faber, 1939).

It was followed by *The Pirates of Penzance* in which Gilbert lampooned the Army and the police force. Presented on 3 April 1880, it had a wonderful reception. George Grossmith played 'a modern Major-General', but Rutland Barrington made the hit of the evening as the Sergeant of Police. His number 'The Enterprising Burglar' was encored time and again:

> When a felon's not engaged in his employment
> Or maturing his felonious little plans,
> His capacity for innocent enjoyment
> Is just as great as any other man's.
> Our feelings we with difficulty smother
> When constabulary duty's to be done,
> Ah, take one consideration and another—
> A policeman's lot is not a happy one.
> When the enterprising burglar's not a-burgling,
> When the cut-throat isn't occupied in crime,
> He loves to hear the little brook a-gurgling
> And listen to the merry village chime.
> When the coster's finished jumping on his mother
> He loves to lie a-basking in the sun.
> Ah, take one consideration and another—
> A policeman's lot is not a happy one.

Gilbert's superb lyrics were again enhanced by Sullivan's delightful score. The public had now decided that the comic operas were exactly to their taste, and *The Pirates* took possession of the theatre for over a year. By the time D'Oyly Carte withdrew the piece there was a successor ready for production: *Patience, or Bunthorne's Bride*. It was a satire on the follies of the Aesthetic Movement, its main butt being a poet who was a mixture of Oscar Wilde, Algernon Swinburne and Walter Pater. George Grossmith revelled in the part of Bunthorne, the aesthetic poet, who sang:

> If you're anxious for to shine in a high aesthetic line
> As a man of culture rare,
> You must get up all the germs of the transcendental terms
> And plant them everywhere.
> You must lie upon the daisies and discourse in novel phrases

Of your complicated state of mind.
The meaning doesn't matter if it's only idle chatter
Of a transcendental kind.
    And everyone will say,
    As you walk your mystic way,
If this young man expresses himself in terms too deep for *me*,
Why, what a singularly deep young man this deep young
man must be!

Later in the song he mentioned walking down Piccadilly with a
lily in his hand. Oscar Wilde, who was said to have done this,
attended the fashionable first night with James McNeil Whist-
ler, the painter, and other prominent aesthetes. Consequently,
the audience divided their attention between the stage and the
aesthetes, anxious to see how they were reacting to Gilbert's
devastating dialogue and lyrics.

Gilbert and Sullivan operas had now become a British
institution— their enormous public knew all the songs by heart
—and every day George Edwards had to turn people away from
the box office because the little Opéra-Comique was full up.

Richard D'Oyly Carte had already bought a large site
down the Strand and was building a much larger theatre on it.
Since the palace of the Princes of Savoy had stood there three
hundred years earlier, the obvious name for it was the Savoy.

George Edwards meanwhile had fallen in love with Julia
Gwynne, an exceedingly pretty actress who played a small
part in *Patience*. She had nut-brown hair and dark blue eyes
and had collected a host of admirers since making her debut
in *The Pirates of Penzance*. Her real name was Julia Putney,
and her parents kept a pub at Hampstead called the Black
Boy. Although Julia Gwynne was fond of George Edwards,
and quite willing to accept his invitations to lunch or supper,
she made it clear that they could only be platonic friends
because she was unofficially engaged to a young man named
Vere Campbell.

Julia had been madly in love with Vere Campbell for five
years; the pages of her diaries are full of Vere, whom she generally calls 'my boy' or 'my darling boy'. He was a West End
doctor's son who held a minor position on the Stock Exchange,
so minor that he earned very little and often had to pawn his

watch or borrow from his friends, or even from Julia. Vere thought himself very superior to Julia because her family kept a pub. He had seduced her and was regarded as her fiancé, but he often humiliated her and made her terribly unhappy.

Julia Gwynne kept a diary, which reveals a great deal about her stormy romance with Vere and the vicissitudes of her relationship with George Edwards.

25 July 1881. I did not go out all day, had a row with Vere. I went to supper with George and he came home with me.
26 August 1881. Vere came down with me [*to the theatre*]. I went to supper at the Gaiety with George and the gentleman who is going to give George a diamond ring.

There is no doubt that Julia was referring in this entry to Mr Isaacs: George Edwards had kept in close touch with Isaacs since his return to London and his old friend took a keen interest in George's progress in the theatre.

10 Sept. 1881. I went to tea with George at his rooms. Vere came too, with a friend. George gave me the ring he promised me. I went to supper with George at the Gaiety.

So George Edwards gave the diamond ring to Julia.

20 Sept. 1881. I went down to see George and met Moore who took me to lunch at the Gaiety where we met George. I afterwards had a long conversation with him and he gave me a ring as a peace offering.

George had quarrelled with Julia Gwynne, but he always came back to her. They quarrelled again a few days later because he had grown jealous of her obsession about Vere Campbell. He was also angry with her for the way she encouraged other admirers and let them take her out to supper and see her home.

On 10 October Richard D'Oyly Carte transferred *Patience* to the Savoy Theatre. He made a new agreement with Gilbert and Sullivan under which the three of them became joint partners and joint owners of the Savoy Theatre; henceforth the Press called them the Triumvirate. The Savoy, an extremely elegant playhouse, was one of the first to be constructed on the cantilever principle which enabled the audience to obtain a perfect view of the stage from any seat in the house. It could accommodate 1,292 people and had entrances and exits on all four sides. Julia's diary for the 10th is quite interesting:

10 October 1881. The first night we played at the Savoy Theatre. We sang 'God Save the Queen' in our *Patience* dresses. Vere took me down in a cab. George took me to Rules to supper and drove me home.

Edwards was promoted to be acting manager at the Savoy and Carte raised his salary to £3 a week. He was twenty-seven he had recently grown a moustache, which suited him, but had also put on a lot of weight. He decided he would spell his name 'Edwardes' because the extra *e* made it seem more unusual and also because another George Edwards had recently joined the staff at the Savoy. He and Julia often went to the Gaiety Restaurant, where they met John Hollingshead, who complained bitterly because business was so bad since the Merry Family Quartette had broken up. Edward Royce had been the first to go: it was given out that he had left for health reasons, but the real reason was that he had been hitting the bottle too hard. Katie Vaughan and Edward Terry followed him, both determined to leave burlesque pieces to make their names in the legitimate theatre. Luckily for Hollingshead he still had the inimitable Nellie Farren under contract; the Gaiety patrons were as devoted to her as ever.

By the end of the year there was a change in George Edwardes's attitude to Julia Gwynne. Her attachment to Vere made him furious, particularly as he had discovered that Vere was a drunkard and a wastrel. How could Julia throw herself away on such a rotter? He asked her to marry him and warned her that if she turned him down all was over between them. But nothing would make Julia give up Vere! Yet within a few weeks George was dancing attendance on her again, taking her out to supper and giving her presents. It was exactly the same situation as before, with Julia still adoring Vere, although he often treated her abominably, and George in his old role of odd man out.

However, Julia's romance with Vere Campbell was approaching a climax.

6 April 1882. Vere met me after the play and blackguarded me in the Strand, calling me the most fearful names. I ran up one of the quiet streets, he followed and bruised my arm again. He forced me to the omnibus, and all because he thought I had been drinking.

At the end of the month she has a 'very serious conversation with my darling boy which makes me very sad'.

9 May. Vere came [to the Savoy theatre] and was drunk. . . . We came home in a cab. Vere shook me and I struck him in the face. He tried to cut my throat and almost knocked my head off. He also bruised my arm most fearfully.

On 12 May Vere told her he was going to America to make a fresh start and was sailing the following Tuesday. He asked her to forgive him for his bad behaviour and made the excuse that he had been drinking to drown his sorrows. Julia was utterly wretched because he was going off to America and she might never see him again. She met Vere on 15 May at Somerset House where they inquired about the possibility of getting married; but it was too late because he was leaving England the following day.

15 May. Vere is going to America without any money or influence and does not know whether he will ever come back.

She went home with Vere to his lodgings and stayed there all night, 'walking about until the morning'. She helped him to pack next day and sent a message to the Savoy that she was too unwell to go in the evening. George Edwardes met Julia and Vere after the performance of *Patience* and they took a cab to Euston Station, where she and George saw Vere off on the midnight train to Liverpool.

16 May. I am in despair and utterly wretched. If my dear boy had some definite appointment it would be different but he has gone with only a few pounds and one or two letters of introduction and does not know what he will do when he gets there. George has done everything for him.

George Edwardes had obviously paid Vere's fare to the States and had probably lent him a few pounds as well because Vere was now penniless—in fact he owed money all over the town. But in June Vere cabled George from New York, saying everything had gone wrong, and would he send him twenty pounds for his return fare to England? As Edwardes knew that Vere Campbell was being sued in the courts for swindling various tradesmen, he put his foot down and refused to help him. Julia had only heard once from her 'beloved boy' and treasured his letter although it brought her little comfort. Eventually, George told her he had decided not to send Vere the money to come home.

8 June 1882. I was very rude to poor old George and he was very angry. We afterwards made it up. George gave me a little turquoise and pearl ring.

This was probably the decisive moment in George Edwardes's courtship of Julia. He was already on very friendly terms with her sister Emma, with whom she was now sharing rooms in Boscobel Gardens: it was important to have Emma as an ally because Julia paid far more attention to her sister than to her erratic mother, Mrs Putney, or to her father. In the following months he exerted himself to woo Julia, although there was still competition from one or two other admirers. At the end of the year, after nothing more had been heard from Vere, she consented to become engaged to him. But it was agreed that there was no point in getting married in a hurry.

The next Gilbert and Sullivan opera was *Iolanthe*. Julia Gwynne had a small part in it, but confided to George that, although she liked being at the Savoy, she felt her career was standing still. The best parts for young actresses always went to Jessie Bond, the most popular soubrette who ever appeared in the comic operas. Julia had been encouraged by W. S. Gilbert, who had once reduced her to tears at a rehearsal. He made up for his rudeness by giving her some coaching in acting and getting her a part in one of his short plays. In fact,

Gilbert seems to have had a crush on Julia. After the company had had a party to celebrate an anniversary of *Patience*, he had taken her home in a cab and she had noted in her diary: 'Mr Gilbert was very attentive.'

She was determined to prove herself as an actress and gave an audition to Mr and Mrs Bancroft at the Haymarket Theatre. They offered her £8 a week to play in their company and she accepted at once. She told George Edwardes about it afterwards, stressing that it was far more than D'Oyly Carte was paying her after all this time.

Meanwhile everything had gone wrong for John Hollingshead at the Gaiety. In 1883 the theatre had shown a loss for the first time. Something drastic had to be done in order to bring back his old patrons to the playhouse; but before he could attempt to work out a new plan he caught typhoid fever and was out of action for several weeks. When Hollingshead returned to the Gaiety his nerves and will power had been seriously impaired—and he needed all his faculties if he was ever going to get on top of his difficulties.

Convinced that he had to keep the sacred lamp of burlesque burning, he continued to present Nellie Farren in the same kind of pieces. But even Nellie Farren was unable to carry every one of them on her shoulders. George Edwardes saw him as much as ever and sympathized with his tales of woe. Business was still booming at the Savoy, but it made little difference to Edwardes because D'Oyly Carte ran the show and he knew that if he stayed on there he would be an underling all his life. He yearned to become a theatre manager in his own right and was only waiting for an opportunity to realize his ambition.

He had already formed the Edwardes Menu Company to give himself an outside interest, and had obtained a contract to supply food to the Empire Theatre, Leicester Square, and to other London theatres. Having gained an entrée to the Empire, he determined to edge his way into the management side. Edwardes had acquired a flair for spotting a clever artist or a novel turn, and in 1884 he persuaded Augustus Harris and the other directors to let him book most of their variety acts.

Princess Ida made her debut at the Savoy at the beginning of 1885. But this Gilbert and Sullivan opera, based vaguely on

Tennyson's well known poem, lacked Gilbert's usual humour and made little appeal to the public. The failure of *Princess Ida* was soon forgotten when *The Mikado* arrived at the Savoy later in the year. It was the greatest success of all the comic operas.

Rutland Barrington, who played Pooh Bah superbly, sometimes sang out of tune. A lady sitting in W. S. Gilbert's box at the first night remarked that Rutland Barrington was singing very well. 'It is only first night nervousness,' quipped Gilbert.*

As George Edwardes reported the record takings at the Savoy every night, it only whetted his appetite to become a theatre manager in his own right. Hollingshead had been laid up again with a very painful attack of rheumatic fever and felt the effort of trying to break even at the Gaiety was becoming too much for him. Business had slumped so badly that he owed four weeks' salary to Nellie Farren, who told one of her friends, 'John is really impossible now. He not only owes me my salary, but he has just sold me the old green room piano!'†

George Edwardes received a note asking him to call on John Hollingshead, who offered to take him into partnership if he would pay an agreed sum for a half share in the Gaiety. Edwardes, who was still on the best of terms with Mr Isaacs, went off to Hatton Garden to see him in his office. Isaacs had always believed that he would make good and regarded him almost as a son. He sat down and wrote out a cheque in favour of Hollingshead without even bothering to ask for details of the partnership.

Edwardes arranged to join Hollingshead at the Gaiety in the autumn. Then he hurried round to the Haymarket Theatre to tell Julia Gwynne the good news, and promised her that one day he would make the Gaiety the most popular theatre in London.

* Hicks.   † Booth, *London Town.*

4 The New Broom

*Since I opened the Gaiety Theatre in 1868, it
has only been closed eighteen months. . . . If
the Gaiety has done less for the cause of art
than one or two houses . . . it has done more for
the pockets of the 'profession' and those who
live by theatres.*

JOHN HOLLINGSHEAD; last Manifesto—
19 December 1885

Julia Gwynne had already agreed to go on tour with the
Bancrofts at the end of July when she heard the exciting news.
Now that George Edwardes had attained his goal and was
about to become joint manager of the Gaiety, he wanted to
marry her before she went on tour. But a religious difficulty
stood in their way: the Edwards family were staunch Roman
Catholics while Julia was a rather unenthusiastic Protestant,
and George was very keen that she should change to his
religion. Her mother, Mrs Putney, was violently opposed to the
idea of Julia going over to the Romans when she got married.
She loathed Catholics and for some weeks bombarded Julia
with tracts and long letters to try to dissuade her from leaving
the Protestant faith. There were constant arguments for
several weeks before Julia finally consented to become a Roman
Catholic.

They arranged the wedding for 9 July and Julia's diary
throws an interesting light on the proceedings.

8 July 1885. McNamara came up with some presents, and he brought me a paper from the priest to sign, saying the children of our marriage were to be Catholics. I signed it. I felt very nervous and worried.

9 July 1885. My wedding day. I was married to George Edwardes at nine o'clock in the morning at the Catholic Church, Maiden Lane. . . . We went to Folkestone from Charing Cross immediately . . . George and I stayed at the West Cliff Hotel and enjoyed ourselves very much all the time we were there. Beautiful weather.

Julia's diary has nothing more to say about their honeymoon, except she records that she and George had a little tiff at breakfast their first morning because she put sugar in her porridge; salt, he told her, was correct. They returned to London at the end of a fortnight because Julia had to leave for the Bancroft tour. One of the letters awaiting George Edwardes came from Mr Bayles, who owned Rules Restaurant, where Edwardes often went with Julia before their marriage.

1, Queen Victoria Street, E.C.

20 July 1885

MY DEAR FRIEND EDWARDES,

I learned by accident that you had become the fortunate husband of Miss Julia Gwynne whose charms of person and talents have captivated so many susceptible hearts and eyes. Knowing you as I do, I venture to assert that there is good fortune also on her side in securing so worthy and excellent a husband.

May I ask you to kindly beg her acceptance of the accompanying case [of champagne] . . . it carries with it my sincerest felicitations and belief that the married state will prove for you as it has for me, one of comfort and blessedness unspeakable.

Yours most cordially,

J. CLOWES BAYLES

Having seen her train depart for the North of England, George Edwardes returned to the Savoy to complete his engagement with D'Oyly Carte.

He stayed on at the Savoy till the autumn, but even after he had left to join Hollingshead he remained on the warmest terms with Carte. He always kept in close touch with him and Helen Lenoir, and sometimes wrote to Carte for advice about his new ventures in the theatre.

He kept a letter he received from Arthur Sullivan, who had recently been knighted for his services to music:

1, Queen's Mansions,
  Victoria Street, S.W.   *23 September 1885*
DEAR MR EDWARDES,

I was much gratified by your kind note. Your departure from the Savoy Theatre is a matter of very great regret to myself and I am sure to my colleagues also, since we lose in you a faithful and loyal adherent.

And I need hardly say that you carry with you into your new undertaking our heartiest good wishes for your success and welfare. I am sending you a little souvenir which I hope you will accept in remembrance of our connection.

            Yours sincerely,

                    ARTHUR SULLIVAN

It almost goes without saying that Edwardes never received a word of thanks from W. S. Gilbert. The two men hardly ever met again, which was just as well because the cantankerous Gilbert made no secret of his dislike of Edwardes. In October George Edwardes joined Hollingshead at the Gaiety and they got down to work on a new burlesque entitled *Little Jack Sheppard*. Nellie Farren impersonated the famous highwayman and Fred Leslie, a versatile and brilliant light comedian, played Jonathan Wild, the villainous thief-taker.

Fred Leslie's family had a prosperous Army outfitting business at Woolwich, but Fred had been stage-struck from his childhood. He went into the family business, but acted with amateur dramatic societies at night. Despite family opposition, he went on the stage at twenty-three and with his natural gift for acting made swift progress. He had become a star through his performance in the name part of *Rip Van Winkle*, a drama at the Comedy which drew the town.

Leslie was a first rate actor, an excellent singer and a superb mimic who could imitate the sounds of birds and humans equally well. Although Nellie Farren was over forty, she still cavorted about the stage like a young girl and never spared herself. The regular patrons remained just as loyal to the Gaiety queen as they had ever been.

During his years with D'Oyly Carte and W. S. Gilbert at the Savoy, George Edwardes had learnt a great deal about the production of musical plays. He persuaded Hollingshead to spend more on the sets, and to dress the principal actresses and chorus girls in attractive clothes instead of tights and scanty costumes from the theatre wardrobe. Henceforth the Gaiety girls appeared on the stage in long dresses with abundant petticoats underneath them, and, just as Edwardes expected, the men in the audience got terribly excited if a girl showed her legs; even the sight of a trim ankle was enough to whet their appetites. He also took over the musical side of *Little Jack Sheppard*; Meyer Lutz was commissioned to write a special score for it and excerpts from Continental composers were never used again.

Moore, the first Gaiety stage doorkeeper, had died in the previous year. Edwardes arranged for Tierney, a retired sea captain, to take on this responsible job. Tierney was the husband of Edwardes's old nurse, whom he also engaged as the new housekeeper at the theatre.

Tierney was a gruff character: he wore a beard and had a strong and rather irritable voice. If a stage-door Johnnie called without an appointment with a Gaiety girl, Tierney pocketed a tip from him—it was generally a sovereign—and would say, 'I can't promise anything, but I'll see what I can do.'* He generally succeeded in making an appointment for the masher to meet the girl he fancied: in fact Tierney did so well at the stage-door that he eventually owned a street of London houses.

Described as a 'Burlesque-Operatic-Melodrama', *Little Jack Sheppard* opened on 26 December and was received with tremendous enthusiasim. Fred Leslie played Jonathan Wild with a twinkle in his eye, to the hearty applause of the audience. Besides being a consummate artist, Leslie formed a wonderful rapport with Nellie Farren. Marion Hood made an extremely decorative heroine and Sylvia Grey, the *première danseuse*, proved herself a worthy successor to Katie Vaughan.

* Pope, *Carriages at Eleven*.

'Nellie Farren is back again and now adds Jack Sheppard to
the list of her successful parts,' said the *Daily Telegraph*
next morning, adding, 'It cannot be needful to say how the
favourite was received by a Boxing Day audience after a
prolonged absence from the stage that knows her so well.
There was heartiness in every cheer and enjoyment in every
laugh raised by Miss Farren's well-remembered tricks of
voice and manner.'

The *Sporting and Dramatic* singled out Fred Leslie's performance: '. . . His conception of Jonathan Wild is altogether
grotesque, whimsical and eccentric. . . . The idea of a thief-
catcher who surrounds his grim task with elements of drollery
is not altogether an impossible conception, and the licence
permitted in burlesque gives the artist almost unlimited
scope for fun. . . .' At the end of the profitable run, Nellie
Farren and Fred Leslie toured the provinces in *Little Jack
Sheppard* and were feted in every town. Afterwards they went
out on a highly successful tour of Australia. John Hollingshead
had been devoted to the Gaiety tradition of burlesque, but
George Edwardes had other ideas. He realized that burlesque
pieces appealed only to a limited section of the public; very
few women came to the Gaiety. But at the Savoy he had
watched the middle classes queuing up to see the wholesome,
clean-limbed Gilbert and Sullivan operas. They never patronized
the Gaiety because respectable married women refused to go to
a theatre where brazen, well endowed females disported
themselves on the stage while the mashers in the stalls trained
their opera glasses on them. Moreover, these respectable
matrons found the suggestive innuendoes in burlesque pieces
were too shocking for words.

Edwardes, confident that he had found a musical play that
would bring the family audience to the Gaiety, had a straight
talk with Hollingshead. Though 'Practical John' was only
fifty-eight his hair had gone snow white and his mouth drooped
as a result of several attacks of rheumatic fever; he had never
completely recovered from his illness in 1884. George Edwardes
outlined the plot of *Dorothy*, a sentimental light opera that
took place in eighteenth-century England. It had a score by
Alfred Cellier, who had conducted for Gilbert and Sullivan.
He believed the middle classes would flock to see this show
and make them both a fortune.

Hollingshead heard him out, then declared that the regular Gaiety patrons would never stand for such a tame and sugary piece. However, the ailing Hollingshead was no match for a dynamic young man like Edwardes. Despite his protests, it was settled that *Dorothy* would go into production at the Gaiety in the autumn. Julia was expecting her first baby. For weeks George could talk of nothing but the progress of *Dorothy*, they agreed that if Julia had a girl she would be called Dorothy, and in the summer this duly took place.

In the meantime, Edwardes and Hollingshead had been at loggerheads about the Gaiety's new piece. After 'Practical John' had seen some early rehearsals he told Edwardes it was madness to put on *Dorothy* at the Gaiety. Hollingshead wanted to wash his hands of the whole production and Edwardes was delighted to take him at his word and to assume responsibility for *Dorothy*. First, he made sure there was nothing in the piece that could offend the susceptibilities of a maiden aunt, then he proceeded to spend far more on the costumes and scenery than he had originally intended.

He decided that Marion Hood, who had made her name in Gilbert and Sullivan and been acclaimed for her singing of 'Poor Wandering One' in *The Pirates of Penzance*, should play the key role of Dorothy. Tall, fair, slight and graceful she was a typical 'English rose'. The hero was played by Hayden Coffin, a handsome American actor with a magnificent singing voice.

Dorothy took place in an English country village. Dorothy's father was the popular squire, they lived at Chanticler Hall, and she was supposed to marry her cousin, Wilder, whom she had never seen in her life. The latter and his friend, Sherwood, came down from London to escape from the Sheriff's Officer, who was trying to arrest them for debts. Lurcher, the Officer, caught up with them in the village, but they got round him by a cunning ruse. Dorothy fell in love at sight with Sherwood—instead of cousin Wilder—but everything worked out satisfactorily in the end.

The main set in this comic opera represented the exterior of an English country house and had to be big enough to allow horses and hounds to pass through its doorway on their way to a meet. During a rehearsal the 'gallery' of the set collapsed, injuring several of the cast. The stage hands began to murmur

that there was a jinx on *Dorothy*. George Edwardes was so
upset that as soon as the 'gallery' had been repaired he made
the chief carpenter put twelve men on it to make sure it was
safe.

That was not the end of his worries: a week before the first
night he sensed that Marion Hood's voice might not be strong
enough for the score, but decided to take a gamble on her as
there was no time to put another actress into the role. He had
great faith in Hayden Coffin as Sherwood and felt that he
could carry the piece to success on his own.

But nothing went right on the first night of *Dorothy* on
25 September 1886. Hayden Coffin was so nervous that he
'dried up' in his first duet, and although Marion Hood looked a
perfect picture in eighteenth-century costume, her voice
proved too weak for the music.

George Edwardes paid little attention to the stage, since
he almost knew the piece by heart, but spent the evening
watching the fashionable audience in the stalls. He could sense
they were bored with *Dorothy*, while the boys in the gallery
made it clear that they had no time for this eighteenth-century
opera. The press gave it poor notices, and John Hollingshead
wagged his finger and told George to stick to Gaiety burlesques
in future.

But George Edwardes refused to accept the public's verdict
on *Dorothy*; he had the entire opera reconstructed, and decided
to retain Marion Hood, Hayden Coffin and the rest of the
original cast. Needing a special solo for Hayden Coffin, he
hunted out an old number by Alfred Cellier and had a new
lyric written to it by H. C. Stephenson. It was called 'Queen
of my Heart', and Hayden Coffin sang it as a serenade to
Dorothy outside her bedroom. The sentiment of 'Queen of
my Heart' appealed greatly to the romantic natures of
audiences:

> For from daylight a hint we must borrow,
> And prudence might come with the light.
> Then why should we wait till tomorrow?
> You are queen of my heart tonight!

The Gaiety audience warmed to the song immediately and
encored it—but the house remained half empty.

After *Dorothy* had been playing to poor business for some weeks, Edwardes transferred it to the Prince of Wales's, a much smaller theatre. *Dorothy* languished there for a few more weeks, then he decided to cut his losses and sold the piece lock, stock and barrel to Henry J. Leslie, the Gaiety accountant. Leslie immediately sacked Marion Hood and brought in an unknown actress with a wonderful stage presence and the voice of a prima donna—Marie Tempest. She transformed *Dorothy* into a success overnight and made an ideal partner for Hayden Coffin who became the most popular matinee idol of the day and got encored regularly for 'Queen of my Heart'.

George Edwardes had once tried in vain to persuade Hayden Coffin to change his name. The actor had been asked to a party at the Edwardeses' new house, 6, Park Square West, Regent's Park, and at the end of the evening a nervous parlourmaid had said to the actor, 'Excuse me, Mr Cab, your coffin is waiting!'*

Dorothy ran for three years and made a fortune for Henry Leslie. He built the Lyric Theatre in Shaftesbury Avenue out of its profits and transferred the piece there. Edwardes cursed his luck, and for many years after that it upset him if anybody even mentioned *Dorothy* to him.

He was suddenly faced with a critical situation at the Gaiety: poor Hollingshead had succumbed to another attack of rheumatic fever and found it impossible to attend to any business; also, he was on the brink of bankruptcy. He had lost money on his investments in the Holborn music hall and other halls and, in an effort to put things right, had speculated in businesses in Manchester which had failed. People in the theatre world said that if 'Practical John' had only concentrated on his interest in the Gaiety he would never have got into financial difficulties.

In a painful interview with George Edwardes, he offered him the other half-share in the Gaiety at a very fair price. Edwardes could not raise such a large sum himself after his losses on *Dorothy*, but he knew where to find the balance. He took the first train up to Grimsby and called on some of his old school friends in the fishing trade. They were all flourishing and only too pleased to have a flutter in the theatre by giving him the

* Hibbert

rest of the money. George Edwardes went straight back and clinched the deal with Hollingshead, and thus became Guv'nor at the Gaiety at the age of thirty.

In order to try to recoup his losses on *Dorothy*, Edwardes went back to burlesque pieces and produced *Monte Cristo, Junior* at the Gaiety on 23 December 1886. Nellie Farren was Edmond Dantes, the hero, and Fred Leslie played his deadly enemy, Nortier. 'Nellie Farren and Fred Leslie, by sheer force of cleverness and with the aid of innumerable disguises, carried the play high on their shoulders to victory,' said one critic. The *Era* went a lot further:

> We couple Miss Farren and Mr Leslie together because they are inseparable on stage, where they play into each other's hands . . . as only two such artists can. . . .
>
> As for Mr Leslie, grotesque singing and dancing are among the least of his resources. He takes a 'header' through the walls of Dantes's cell as though he were a Harlequin born. His fertility of invention is inexhaustible . . . to lighten his narrative of his swim to the Isle of Monte Cristo, he wrings . . . about half a bucket of water out of his beard.

In 1887 George Edwardes produced a second edition of *Monte Cristo, Junior* at the Gaiety. Nellie Farren and Fred Leslie took the piece on a tour of the provinces afterwards, then went off on a Gaiety tour of Australia and the United States. While his two biggest stars were out of England the Guv'nor formed a second Gaiety company and presented *Miss Esmerelda*, a burlesque of *The Hunchback of Notre-Dame*. Lovely Marion Hood played the heroine most charmingly, but E. J. Lonnen, as Claud Frollo the monk, scored the triumph of the evening. A most inventive comedian and a fine dancer, Lonnen made a great hit with his Irish song 'Killaloe'. However, *Miss Esmerelda* had only a moderate run.

Julia Edwardes had retired from the stage since her marriage. Naturally enough, she took, a great interest in George's theatrical activities, and he encouraged her to come to the Gaiety and watch rehearsals whenever she liked. But her superior attitude soon began to irritate him: she had a blind admiration for the Savoy operas, comparing them with the Gaiety burlesques to the detriment of the latter. She constantly

nagged George for 'lowering his artistic standards'. Though
he always avoided scenes if he could possibly help it, Julia
made such carping remarks about *Miss Esmerelda* that one
day he rounded on her. 'You don't know and you won't learn
about these sort of pieces,' he barked. 'You give your opinion
unasked and it won't do.'* As a matter of fact, Julia was only
trying to be helpful when she made criticisms, and sometimes
her acid comments on certain artists were perfectly justified;
but it was a great pity that she never learnt when to keep
quiet.

There is no room for a tactless woman in the hothouse
atmosphere of a theatre, particularly if she happens to be the
manager's wife. At one rehearsal she made disparaging remarks
about artists in the cast; somebody overheard her and the
gossip went all round the Gaiety. George Edwardes lost his
temper and told her not to come to any more rehearsals.

* Bloom.

II

GOOD OLD GUV'NOR
(1887–1896)

5 Fred Leslie and Our Nellie

A night at the Gaiety; ah what a time we had!
Those were the days of old-fashioned burlesque
When in each line some six puns and a rhyme we had
And Nellie was shapely and Fred was grotesque.

AUGUSTUS MOORE

The Gaiety tour of Australia and the United States was a great success and made a handsome profit. The Americans thought Fred Leslie the finest light comedian they had seen for years, but Nellie Farren's Cockney humour failed to get across very well. When Fred Leslie returned home he looked very ill and was suffering from an attack of gastritis. 'I feel done up, voiceless and altogether out of sorts,' he told his friend W. T. Vincent, the journalist.* The Guv'nor sent him off for a holiday to give him a chance to convalesce. As soon as Leslie was fit again he began rehearsals with Nellie Farren for the next burlesque, which was a send-up of *Frankenstein*. A journalist asked George Edwardes what on earth had made him choose this story about a monster made in a laboratory as a subject for burlesque. Edwardes said it was bound to be a success. Since Nellie Farren and Fred Leslie had given him two big 'winners' in succession, he believed the Gaiety patrons would come to see their two favourites even if they played *Hamlet*.

The first night of *Frankenstein* at the Gaiety on Christmas Eve 1887 was a complete fiasco. The trouble started when the

* W. T. Vincent, *Recollections of Fred Leslie* (Kegan Paul, 1894).

pittites discovered that George Edwardes had converted the front rows of the pit into stalls and was charging 7s. 6d. for them instead of 2s. The pittites began bellowing at the top of their voices and hadn't stopped when Nellie Farren made her first entrance as Frankenstein. The loyal gallery boys greeted her with a great shout of welcome and managed to drown the pittites for a time; but the noise was indescribable and the artists on the stage soon became inaudible.

Fred Leslie, who played the Monster, took off his polar bear's make-up and came forward and politely asked the audience to stop making such a row, but they ignored his appeal and went on shouting. Clement Scott wrote in the *Daily Telegraph*:

Hisses on Christmas Eve! Groans and gibes instead of good-will! Clamour and cat-calls from a surly and discontented minority....

We never remember to have observed in a theatre at Christmas-time such an exhibition of ill-tempered surliness, such a fit of childish petulance as that which was within an ace of wrecking the fortunes of the new melodramatic burlesque, *Frankenstein*.

It was a bad experience for George Edwardes, but one consolation was that Julia was not with him in his box to say 'I told you so'. She was resting at home at Park Square after the recent birth of their son and heir, D'Arcy Edwardes.

After Christmas the Guv'nor called in the authors of *Franken-stein* and they all got to work and revamped the piece. But he had made a mistake in attempting to burlesque such a horrific subject: the Victorian wouldn't laugh at the ghoulish humours of *Frankenstein*; the piece never caught on, and was withdrawn after a run of four months. The Guv'nor sent the company off on a tour of the provinces with some of the earlier Gaiety burlesques. Then he arranged for Nellie Farren and Fred Leslie to go on a second tour of Australia and the United States with *Monte Cristo, Junior* and *Miss Esmerelda*.

It was an understood thing that artists always received a higher salary for overseas tours. Edwardes offered Marion Hood £100 a week for the tour, the same salary that he was paying Nellie Farren, but she wanted £200. He explained to Marion Hood that their tour of Australia would include a tour of India and added meaningly, 'Rajahs, Jams and Nabobs are in the habit of presenting stage favourites with ropes of pearls and rubies.' She promised to think it over, and next day she wrote to him: 'Dear Mr Edwardes, If you accept my terms, you can have the Rajah's rubies.'*

The Gaiety company's tour of Australia and America was another triumph. Fred Leslie had written in collaboration a new burlesque of *Ruy Blas*; the title role had been written specially for Nellie Farren and he intended the part of Dom Caesar de Bazan for himself. *Ruy Blas, or the Blasé Roué* had its première in New York and got a wonderful reception.

The Guv'nor went to Liverpool to meet his company on their return; he was in high spirits because the tour had been such a success. He had grown very fond of Fred Leslie and was most upset to find him down with gastritis again. Leslie's doctor ordered him to go and convalesce at Bournemouth for a few weeks before going back to work.

The Gaiety was packed to the rafters for the first night of *Ruy Blas* on 21 September 1889. It was eighteen months since Nellie Farren and Fred Leslie had appeared there and the regular patrons were determined to show them how greatly they had been missed. Marion Hood, playing the heroine, looked so beautiful on her first entrance that she stopped the show, and the audience cheered and cheered again.

Nellie Farren came on later as Ruy Blas, the love-lorn lackey, wearing a little Lord Fauntleroy suit. She was greeted by round after round of cheering and stood there looking incredulous. Then a long, elaborate streamer was hung out from the railing of the gallery with the words: THE BOYS WELCOME THEIR NELLIE. This was followed by more affectionate demonstrations—until Nellie Farren felt she had to say something to the gallery boys: 'Boys, I'm so nervous. Really my heart's too full. I have been longing for this night, and now it's come I'm frightened. I thank you and I can say no more.'†

The performance proceeded normally again until Fred Leslie came on in a suit of rags and tatters as Dom Caesar de

* James Jupp, *The Gaiety Stage Door* (Cape, 1923).
† Vincent.

Bazan. There were loud cheers and yells and the whole house rose to its feet and sang 'For He's a Jolly Good Fellow'. Victor Hugo's play was used merely as a peg on which to hang all kinds of topical fun. Our Nellie sang 'I'm Glad to be Back Again' and brought the house down. And Fred Leslie rendered his number 'Stick to the Whisky You're Used To' wearing a coat that was half Scotch and half Irish, and had them rolling in the aisles.

Later, Fred Leslie appeared with Charles Danby, Fred Storey and Ben Norman and did a take-off of the old 'pas de quatre' which the chorus used to dance in Hollingshead's day. The four men wore ballet skirts and Fred was made up as Henry Irving: the others depicted J. L. Toole, Wilson Barrett and Arthur Roberts. Fred Leslie's brilliant imitation of Irving was tremendously popular.

Ruy Blas received rave notices and George Edwardes knew that he had a big winner. Bernard Shaw, then drama critic for the *Saturday Review*, was so impressed by Fred Leslie that he wrote:

> . . . Mr Leslie is an accomplished vocalist, a comedian of original gifts and excellent training, a dancer of infinite sprightliness and grace, daring, masterful, possessed of a superbly keen and nimble intelligence. He over-brims with by-play. . . . When he darkens the stage by blowing out the moon at a breath, or when he recalls the light by the daring device of a safety match, he shows the admirable quality of his fooling.

> . . . His mimicry of Mr Irving . . . is perfect: the stride, the muttered phrase, the oblique pathetic look flashed over the shoulder, under the acute angle of the heavy eyebrow, are simply irresistible. . . .

However, Fred Leslie's caricature of Henry Irving had an unfortunate sequel two days later. Weedon Grossmith, brother of George Grossmith, the Gilbert and Sullivan star, stirred up trouble by telling Irving that he had seen Fred Leslie take him off at the Gaiety and considered it a disgusting exhibition. Irving was most sensitive about anybody imitating him on the stage; now established as England's greatest actor at his own theatre, the Lyceum, he had lost his sense of humour. He once saw Ellen Terry, his leading lady, sliding down the banisters from her dressing-room, and she felt she had been caught laughing in church.

Without even going to see the Gaiety skit for himself, he wrote to Fred Leslie:

DEAR MR LESLIE,

I see that in your new burlesque I am put by you into woman's clothes, and I hope you will at once withdraw such an exhibition. . . . Whether or not you are doing this by your manager's desire, I cannot tell but it seems to me no consideration should tempt an artist to such an act.

HENRY IRVING.*

Fred Leslie showed the letter to George Edwardes, who was most annoyed that Irving had not written to him instead. 'I don't wish to wound any man, least of all an artist of Mr Irving's position in the profession, but he should have written to me,' said Edwardes. 'I am perfectly willing to take the responsibility of anything done on my stage.' Fred Leslie agreed. 'Why, Irving has been burlesqued time out of number and never objected before. . . . The public like imitations of him—it's one of the penalties of fame.'†

Edwardes refused to take the Irving skit out of *Ruy Blas*. But when Henry Irving heard that Fred Leslie was still imitating him every night, he reported the matter to the Lord Chamberlain's Office. Edwardes was informed by Sir Ponsonby Fane, the Comptroller, that 'unless the offensive personality was dropped' his licence at the Gaiety would not be renewed. This was a very serious threat for the Guv'nor: in Hollingshead's time there had been several complaints to the Lord Chamberlain about the revealing tights and 'scandalous' garments worn by burlesque actresses on his stage, and some of the suggestive puns had offended a few people.‡

However, the Guv'nor stuck to his guns and defied the Lord Chamberlain, and Fred Leslie continued to convulse the public with his Irving imitation. Then Edwardes received an ultimatum from the Lord Chamberlain, Lord Lathom, and

* Laurence Irving, *Henry Irving* (Faber, 1912).
† Jupp.   ‡ Irving.
C

was forced to withdraw the skit: but it made him very angry. Nevertheless, Fred Leslie managed to get the last laugh. He made his entrance the following week in a ballet skirt with his head completely bald, carrying a masked head wrapped in folds of gauze. Then he mimed every detail of Irving's peculiar gait and gestures without speaking a single word. . . .

The Lyceum stood in Wellington Street, a turning off the Strand, only a short distance away from the Gaiety. In 1871 Irving had made his reputation there as a great tragedian when he appeared in *The Bells*, an old melodrama adapted from the French by Leopold Lewis. Irving played the principal role of Mathias, an Alsatian burgomaster who had murdered a Polish Jew fifteen years earlier and stolen his money to save his family from starving. Instead of portraying the burgomaster as a villain, Irving played him as a good man overwhelmed with remorse for his crime.

Irving's powerful acting was a revelation to the audience, although on the first night the theatre was half empty; he mesmerized them into believing in the character of Mathias. *The Bells* received wonderful notices next morning and Irving's performance drew every serious playgoer to the Lyceum.

Henry Irving entered into management at the Lyceum and produced *Hamlet*, with Ellen Terry, his new leading lady, in the part of Ophelia. Ellen Terry was then thirty-one, ten years younger than Irving. People called her the most beautiful woman of her time, and everybody agreed that she had overwhelming charm. At the end of the performance the two stars stood together on the stage and received an ecstatic welcome. 'Irving and Ellen Terry could not have wished for a more popular coronation as together they entered their theatrical kingdom.'*

The *Daily Telegraph* said:

> Mr Irving has played *Hamlet* before . . . but never so well as last night. . . . It must be granted that Mr Irving had at his side Miss Ellen Terry, who from first to last more than confirmed the pleasant anticipation made beforehand of her Ophelia, and in every accent, every movement and every expression satisfied and gratified the most exacting taste. Miss Ellen Terry's Ophelia may be termed, without exag-

* Irving.

gerating, a poem in action and . . . this charming realization
of Shakespeare's imagination gave to the revival a new
interest and a fresh grace.

Londoners queued up to see Irving and Ellen Terry in their
first season at the Lyceum: the intellectual public came back
in force to the theatre, which they had deserted for years.
Irving produced all the plays himself, cutting them ruthlessly
to his requirements. Whenever he appeared in a play he towered
over the rest of the company and commanded every corner
of the stage. He was a tall, handsome, clean-shaven, ascetic-
looking man. Being very short sighted, he wore pince-nez in
private life but never in the theatre, where he felt his way
about the stage by instinct. He wore his hair long and had a
very deliberate walk; his manner gave people the impression
that he was an important person. The play of his features was
so mobile that he could register every phase of a mental struggle:
he always had a lime-light ray following his face with a small
'pin' light of blue steel.

In 1886 Henry Irving produced an adaptation of Goethe's
Faust at the Lyceum, in which he played Mephistopheles to
the Marguerite of Ellen Terry. This version of *Faust*, by
William Gorman Wills, was by no means a work of art and was
said to resemble the 'book' of an infernal pantomime. Though
eminent critics damned it, the public adored it and Irving
made the success of his lifetime, retaining *Faust* at the Lyceum
for a second season.

When Arthur Pinero was a young man he played small
parts in Henry Irving's company: at twenty-two he was
already trying his hand at plays and Irving encouraged him
and produced two of his one-act plays as curtain-raisers. One
day Irving noticed him sitting on some jagged scenery. 'Get
up, my boy, you will cut yourself!' cried Irving in alarm.
Arthur Pinero, who was never afraid of Henry Irving like
most of the company, replied, 'Mr Irving, we are accustomed
to having our parts cut in this theatre!'*

Arthur Pinero knew very well that he would never be a great
actor, and he retired from the stage on leaving Irving's company
and settled down to writing plays. Working for the theatre
came so naturally to him that by the end of the 1880s he had

* Booth, *London Town*.

become the leading British playwright. His first outstanding play was a farce entitled *The Magistrate*, which was produced at the Court in March 1885. Taking a leaf out of Gilbert's book, he poked fun at a magistrate who married a gay widow with a son of nineteen whom she passed off as a schoolboy. The magistrate got led astray by the lad, was nearly arrested in a police raid, and then had to try his wife and his best friend in court. Arthur Cecil and John Clayton, actor-managers of the Court Theatre, were in fine form in the principal parts and Mrs John Wood appeared as the widow.

Pinero wrote *The Schoolmistress* for the Court the following year, and in January 1887 his farce *Dandy Dick* was produced there. In *Dandy Dick* his butt was a pious Dean who got involved in backing horses, and was unjustly locked up in the village jail. His horsy sister, a wonderful comedy character who was the life and soul of the piece, finally came to his rescue. John Clayton as the Dean and Mrs John Wood as his sister both gave splendid performances. Both *The Magistrate* and *Dandy Dick* hold the stage to this day.

Arthur Pinero led the renaissance of the British drama almost single-handed. Before he came on the scene most London theatres presented revivals or melodramas or adapatation from the French. His closest rival was Henry Arthur Jones whose first important play, *The Silver King*, was a melodrama written in collaboration with Henry Herman and produced at Drury Lane in November 1882. Wilson Barrett starred in it as a ne'er-do-well who got drunk on Derby Day and was tricked into believing he had committed a murder. He skipped the country and returned home years later a millionaire, having found silver in Nevada. After two more acts he cleared his name, exposed the real murderer and was reunited with his wife and family. Wilson Barrett's acting carried this melodrama to success; *The Silver King* became his favourite part and was revived many times.

A farce entitled *The Private Secretary* was first produced at the Prince's Theatre (later the Prince of Wales's) in March 1884. Adapted by Charles Hawtrey from the German, it had little wit or characterization, but depended entirely on its gags. The piece hinged on the trials and tribulations of a timid curate engaged as secretary to a fox-hunting squire. After being forced to change places with a young rip, he was arrested for debt, kicked into corners, hidden under a table and bundled into an old oak chest.

Beerbohm Tree played the Rev. Robert Spalding effectively in the original production, but it was very badly directed. When the farce was about to come off W. S. Penley took it over and presented it in May 1884 at the old Globe Theatre. He played the Rev. Spalding, and produced the piece with such expertise that it ran for 785 performances.

George Edwardes and Augustus Harris were the joint managing directors of the Empire, Leicester Square. Harris presented a grand spectacular ballet on the theme of Spring in May 1888. Mlle Adele Rossi danced as the Queen of the Flowers, but Signor Cechetti took the honours as the Demon, who seemed to have been gifted by nature with india-rubber limbs and bounded about the stage to the audience's delight.

Both the Empire and its neighbour, the Alhambra, had a 'promenade' at the back of the circle where ladies, dressed up to the nines and looking from afar like duchesses, walked up and down until some man hailed them. They were high-class prostitutes and for three decades men of all ages used to make a beeline for the Empire and find the ladies of the promenade far more interesting than the corps de ballet on the stage.

The sirens of the Empire walked with the slow gait of caged tigresses and hardly ever accosted a man. A man was expected to invite his favourite girl to his table for a drink, where he could discuss her terms for the night. This extraordinary procession of glorified vice became world famous, and many Englishmen regarded the Empire as a club where they would meet their friends on returning from abroad.

Empire audiences generally behaved quite well, but on Boat Race Night the undergraduates invaded London and monopolized the theatre, and it was always the rowdiest night of the year. One burly Empire manager devised a technique for dealing with the worst offenders from the Varsities. He would pick out a ringleader, put his arm round his shoulder in a friendly fashion and politely request him to make a little less noise. The offender would walk off, never suspecting that the manager had put a chalk mark on his jacket; as soon as one of the bouncers spotted a youth with this mark, they seized him and threw him out of the Empire.

At the Adelphi Theatre William Terriss had a corner in melo-dramas and in July 1888 he presented a prime specimen entitled *The Union Jack*, written by Henry Pettit and Sidney Grundey, who were old hands at the game. Its hero, Jack Medway, was an honourable petty officer who discovered his sister had been seduced by a villainous naval officer and promptly knocked him down. Just before his court martial, he escaped through the porthole of his ship. On the run he was befriended by a sweet girl, and eventually he redeemed his character and married her. Bill Terriss played Jack Medway as if he believed every word of it; he was regarded as the ideal Adelphi hero.

Arthur Pinero had a remarkable success with his sentimental comedy, *Sweet Lavender*, which was produced at Terry's Theatre in March 1888. Dick Phenyl, the main part, was played by Edward Terry, who had once appeared with Nellie Farren in the Gaiety Quartette. Dick Phenyl was a broken-down barrister addicted to strong drink who suddenly became a reformed character and sorted out the problems of the other main characters. Clement Scott, the leading theatre critic, went overboard about *Sweet Lavender* and said he would like to see it all over again. Edward Terry was reputed to have produced it for £66 and it had a wonderful run of 684 performances.

Pinero's rival, Henry Arthur Jones, had several plays produced in London after *The Silver King* but, though he had a better ear for dialogue than Pinero, there was always a touch of melodrama in his plays. The best of them was *The Middleman*, a drama produced at the Shaftesbury in May 1889. It had a strong part for its hero, Blenkam, a porcelain worker with an inventive genius whose ideas had enriched his firm but not himself. But when he found that his daughter had been seduced by his employer's son, his character changed and he took his revenge. A. J. Willard gave a fine performance in this one-character play.

The Weaker Sex, another Pinero play, was produced by Mr and Mrs Kendal at the Court in March 1899. Tall, stately and awe-inspiring, Mrs Madge Kendal was known as the matron of the British drama. This accomplished actress played the principal role of a widowed lady whose daughter returned from America and announced her engagement to the man the widow had once jilted and was still in love with. The play ended with the man in the middle departing, leaving mother and daughter broken-hearted. It was a daring theme for that period: Madge Kendal had never done anything better than her portrait of the society widow and W. H. Kendal played the man.

Pinero's last triumph in the eighties was *The Profligate*, a drama produced at the Garrick in April 1889. The hero was a reformed rake; he married an innocent girl who worshipped him until one fatal day when—by a wild coincidence—she met the woman he had seduced long ago. The revelation of his sordid past ruined their idyll. The play owed its success to a superb performance by Johnston Forbes Robertson in the main part. At this time Pinero had three plays running concurrently in London.

The Drury Lane pantomime opened according to tradition on Boxing Day 1889. Augustus Harris presented *Jack and the Beanstalk* with Dan Leno and Herbert Campbell leading the company. Big, fat Herbert Campbell was Fanny the Flirt, the Queen of Nomanland, and Dan Leno played Jack's mother, whose dairy was in the doldrums, with his usual grim and genuine humour. After Jack had slain the giant there was a final scene at Mount Olympus with one of the most spectacular tableaux ever put on the stage. Harris was said to have spent the earth on the magnificent costumes of the gods and goddesses of ancient mythology.

A Pair of Spectacles was produced by John Hare at the Garrick on 22 February 1890. Adapted by Sydney Grundey from a farce by Labiche, it was an extremely competent piece which revolved round two brothers as different as chalk from cheese. Benjamin Goldfinch, played by John Hare, was open, trusting and benevolent, whereas his brother Gregory was mean, misanthropic and grasping. Gregory came from Yorkshire on a visit and poisoned Benjamin's mind with his cynicism, making him look at everything from a jaundiced point of view and suspect his wife and all his acquaintances of deceiving him. But Benjamin ended by having his faith in human nature restored and even managed to change his brother's character for the better.

John Hare, 'by some subtle art of his own', gave a masterly performance as Benjamin Goldfinch and was admirably supported by Charles Groves as the cynical brother. *A Pair of*

Spectacles had such a resounding success that John Hare revived this farce time and again.

This period was the golden age of the actor—manager—from Henry Irving, the high priest of tragedy, at the Lyceum to W. S. Penley, the past master of farce, at the Royalty. The successful authors of the day, including Pinero, always wrote their plays with one or other of the actor–managers in mind.

The Gilbert and Sullivan operas remained the principal attraction at the Savoy Theatre. After George Edwardes had left, Richard D'Oyly Carte had presented *Ruddigore* and *The Yeomen of the Guard*. But although Sullivan had composed some of his finest music for them and Gilbert had written some of his best lyrics, they broke away from the established comic opera pattern and lacked the topsy-turvy humour that the public expected from W. S. Gilbert. The pieces only did moderately well at the box office, to the deep disappointment of Sullivan, who resented Gilbert's autocratic regime at the Savoy, complaining to Carte, 'I am only a cipher in the theatre,' and threatening he would never write another comic opera.*

However, D'Oyly Carte managed to bring about a reconciliation between the two great collaborators, which resulted in *The Gondoliers*. Produced on 14 December 1899, it was one of Gilbert and Sullivan's outstanding successes. It was a good-natured satire on the notion that in the ideal community everyone should be absolutely equal. This beautiful theory, of course, broke down in practice. Clement Scott had nothing but praise when he reviewed *The Gondoliers* in *Theatre*: 'Mr W. S. Gilbert has returned to the Gilbert of the past and everyone is delighted. We welcome the Gilbert of whimsical conceit, subtle satire and playful paradox . . . this is the Gilbert the public want to see and this is the Gilbert who on Saturday night was cheered till the audience was weary of cheering any more.'

Ruy Blas played to packed houses at the Gaiety for ten months and broke the theatre record: some people saw it twenty or thirty times. George Edwardes was naturally elated by its success, but Julia continued to sneer at his burlesque pieces. Her tactless comments annoyed him so much that he told her not to come to his first-night parties in future. This was a most unfortunate state of affairs because by now his

* Baily.

theatre meant more to Edwardes than anything in the world. Consequently from this time onwards he and Julia began to drift apart.

George Edwardes had always been susceptible to a pretty face, and at the Gaiety he was surrounded by attractive young women, each one prepared to go out of her way to keep on the best of terms with the Guv'nor; also he was a charmer and one of the best-looking managers in London. It was almost inevitable that he began to carry on discreet affairs with one or two actresses in his company. Julia stayed at home at Park Square and turned a blind eye to his peccadillos; her chief concern was helping to bring up her daughter, Dorothy, and baby D'Arcy, the son and heir. She spent a great deal of time with the children, but, like most women in her position, left the hard work to their Nannie.

The Guv'nor had arranged another Australian tour for Nellie Farren and Fred Leslie after *Ruy Blas* came off. But as Fred was suffering from gastritis and Nellie was laid up with twinges of rheumatism, he had to postpone the tour until they were fit again. When the company eventually left for Australia they took with them a new burlesque, *Cinder Ellen up-too-Late*, which Fred Leslie had written in collaboration with his friend W. T. Vincent. Nellie and Fred made a great hit in *Ruy Blas* all over Australia; then *Cinder Ellen* had its première at Melbourne and got a splendid reception.

Nellie Farren was one of the most courageous stars who ever trod the boards. Although plagued by her rheumatic affliction, this fabulous little woman of forty-five still capered about the stage and continued to go on as Cinder Ellen until she was utterly prostrate; then she was forced to let her understudy replace her. Nellie consulted two Australian doctors who told her to have a complete rest when she got home, but when she returned to London her condition seemed to improve.

The Guv'nor had announced *Cinder Ellen up-too-Late* as the Christmas attraction at the Gaiety. He was shattered when the London doctors told him Nellie Farren was crippled with rheumatism and could not possibly be fit to act again at Christmas; in fact they doubted if she would ever be able to resume her career. Edwardes decided to go ahead and produce the new burlesque without Nellie, knowing only too well that it was courting disaster.

Cinder Ellen opened on Christmas Day 1891, with Kate
James, a comparatively unknown actress, in the title role. No
actress could possibly have replaced Nellie Farren at the
Gaiety, and Kate James never stood a chance. Despite the
heroic efforts of Fred Leslie, the public remained lukewarm
about the piece. The Guv'nor decided to reconstruct it and
started by cutting out an entire act, which greatly improved
it. Then the Duke of Clarence died suddenly, which led to
lengthy Court mourning and a slump in theatre business. At
the end of the mourning period *Cinder Ellen* was still in the
doldrums.

The Guv'nor had an inspiration and signed up Lottie Collins,
a music-hall artist who was enjoying a fantastic success with
her 'naughty' number 'Ta-ra-ra-boom-de-ay'. Its words are
worth quoting in full:

> A smart and stylish girl you see,
> The Belle of High Society,
> Fond of fun as fond can be—
> When it's on the strict Q.T.
> Not too young and not too old,
> Not too timid, not too bold,
> But just the very thing, I'm told,
> That in your arms you'd like to hold.
> > Ta-ra-ra-boom-de-ay,
> > Ta-ra-ra-boom-de-ay, *etc.*
>
> I'm a timid flower of innocence,
> Pa says that I have no sense—
> I'm one eternal big expense.
> The boys say that I'm immense,
> Ere my verses I conclude
> I'd like it known and understood,
> Though free as air, I'm never rude,
> I'm not too bad and not too good.
> > Ta-ra-ra-boom-de-ay, *etc.*

The late Walter Macqueen Pope saw Lottie Collins when he
was a boy and retained a vivid memory of her performance.
She wore a big Gainsborough hat and a red dress and her
blonde hair came right down to her shoulders. She sang her
first verse rather timidly and made great play with her lace

handkerchief. Then the chorus rang out. The first 'boom' was accompanied by a terrific cymbal crash and a bang on the drum. Lottie Collins waved her handkerchief and seemed to go mad as she broke into a wild Bacchanalian dance. 'The hair streamed, the hat bobbed, the short skirts whirled and she showed a positive foam of petticoats.'*

Lottie Collins shook the Gaiety patrons off their feet; George Edwardes paid her £200 a week and his box-office receipts shot up like a rocket. At last *Cinder Ellen up-too-Late* had become a winner.

When *Cinder Ellen* came off, the Guv'nor sent out Fred Leslie and the company on a provincial tour which did extremely well. He presented a second edition of the burlesque in October. But a month later Fred Leslie fell ill again, and knew instinctively that it was something much more serious than a gastric complaint. Fred made his last appearance at the Gaiety on 25 November, feeling so ill that he told W. T. Vincent in his dressing-room, 'I don't know how I shall get through my work tonight. I hope I shall not break down.'†

Vincent and his wife, sitting in the stalls watching the show, could see that Fred Leslie was in distress on the stage. But the audience, in fits of laughter at his antics, had no idea anything was wrong. After the performance Fred Leslie's doctor ordered him to go straight to bed. It was only discovered then that he was suffering from malignant typhoid, probably caught in a dressing-room in the provinces.

A few days later Fred Leslie became delirious. George Edwardes, who thought the world of him, sent his own doctor to see him—but it was too late. His previous attacks of gastritis had left a chronic weakness of his constitution and he had no resistance left to fight with. Fred Leslie died on 7 December, aged thirty-seven.

The Guv'nor closed the Gaiety Theatre 'in consequence of the sad death of Mr Fred Leslie'. Clement Scott wrote this moving obituary in the *Daily Telegraph*:

It is seldom possible in these days to describe an actor's death as 'eclipsing the gaiety' of the public. There is a sense in which the loss of Mr Fred Leslie may be said . . . to have produced that effect. In him the very spirit of modern

* Pope, *Gaiety*. † Vincent.

burlesque with its lightness, its effervescent quality, its restless variety of appeal to the eye and ear of the audience, appeared to be incarnate.

As the funeral cortege passed the Strand on its way to the cemetery all the traffic came to a standstill. The Gaiety Theatre was entirely draped in black. Old Tierney, the stage doorkeeper, had broken down and was in tears. Nine miles of the road from London to Blackheath was kept clear and they buried Fred at Charlton Cemetery.

Amongst the chief mourners were George Edwardes and Arthur Roberts. Roberts, who had been one of Fred Leslie's best friends although they were rival burlesque comedians, was to play a leading part in the next phase of the Gaiety.

6 The Invention of Musical Comedy

> *Musical comedy was . . . originally invented by*
> *George Edwardes as a happy combination between*
> *the Continental operas of Offenbach and Lecoq, the*
> *comedy burlesques of the old Gaiety Theatre, and*
> *the healthy, clean-limbed but melodious high jinks*
> *of Gilbert and Sullivan.*
>
> SIR NOËL COWARD
> Raymond Mander & Joe Mitchenson,
> *Musical Comedy*

> *Musical comedy is a clever concoction, having*
> *neither beginning, middle or end, and therefore*
> *admirably adapted for an after dinner audience*
> *who want to hear a song or see a dance or stare at a*
> *particular young lady through a double-barrelled*
> *opera glass.*
>
> JOHN HOLLINGSHEAD, *Gaiety Chronicles*

After the tragic death of Fred Leslie and the permanent
retirement of Nellie Farren, George Edwardes produced a few
more burlesques at the Gaiety, but they were never the same.
He had already launched a new form of entertainment, which
became known as musical comedy. These pieces had catchy
and melodious music and a light-hearted and inconsequential
plot, strung together with the object of keeping the audience

amused between the song or dance numbers and designed to
give the comedians scope for putting in their individual gags.
There was always a romance going on between the hero and
heroine: half-way through the show they would have a bust-up
and the heroine would break off their engagement or under-
standing and down would come the curtain. But it was odds
on that they would be reconciled at the very end of the show.
The chorus girls were dressed in the very latest fashions, which
was a complete innovation. Musical comedies took something
from the Gilbert and Sullivan operas, had a good deal in
common with the Continental operettas, and derived some of
their comedy ideas from the old Gaiety burlesques.

The Guv'nor became famous for his musical comedies and
developed his own individual style at the Gaiety. He had
produced *In Town*, the first musical comedy, at the Prince of
Wales's Theatre on 5 October 1892. Its star was Arthur Roberts,
a light comedian often compared with Fred Leslie and one of
the most inventive artists of all time. It was said that if Arthur
Roberts was given a bottle of champagne, a table, paper and a
pencil, and told the rough plot of a show, he could entertain
any audience for half an hour with his gags. Arthur Roberts
played Captain Coddington in *In Town* and carried the piece
on his own.

The *Sunday Times* called it 'a curious medley of song, dance
and nonsense . . . and the very vaguest attempt at satirizing
the modern masher'. And the paper added, 'Mr Roberts is a
host in himself and kept the whole house in a roar.' The *Sunday
Sun* was far more enthusiastic and said, 'Of all the light and
musical entertainment in town just now, Mr Edwardes may
congratulate himself that he produced last night the brightest,
raciest and spiciest.'

Every actress in the cast, from the principals to the chorus
girls, was dressed in Bond Street creations in the height of
fashion, whilst the men looked as if they had just walked in
from Savile Row. Arthur Roberts as Captain Coddington wore
a curly-brimmed topper that was hailed as *le dernier cri*. A
hat named the Coddington was introduced into the West End
and the mashers were soon wearing it. Roberts's coats and
spats and buttonholes were copied by all the mashers in town
and his witticisms were repeated everywhere. His most popular
song was almost up to the standard of W. S. Gilbert:

I'm a terrible swell it is easy to tell
From my dress and my general deportment:
And I wish to declare that of qualities rare
I've a large and a varied assortment.
I'm at dinners and balls and suppers and halls,
I'm never at home for a minute,
And a 'Tableau Vivant' would be sure to go wrong
If they hadn't included me in it:
For I'm the chief and the crown
Of the Johnnies who stroll up and down:
The affable, chaffable, cynical, finical, typical
             Man about Town.

Florence St John, who played opposite Arthur Roberts, had a fine voice and had sung in opera; she was a sweet woman, but rather unworldly and naïve. Captain Coddington was supposed to be a bit of a rip, and Arthur Roberts played the part so well that she really believed he had gone to the dogs. During the piece she had to say to him, 'Arthur, why don't you go straight?' and he replied brazenly, 'Because I can't!' He put so much conviction into this line one night that Florence St John burst into tears on the stage.*

In Town ran for several months at the Prince of Wales's. Then the Guv'nor sent it on tour, and brought it back to the Gaiety in 1893.

Ever since Gilbert had parodied Oscar Wilde in *Patience*, Wilde had been regarded as the wittiest man in London. He had said that 'to get into the best society nowadays one has either to feed people, amuse people, or shock them'. Since he couldn't afford to feed society, Wilde amused and shocked it. The aristocracy had taken him up and, finding that he was the most wonderful conversationalist they had ever heard, they spoilt him. Oscar Wilde was lionized; at the height of his fame people would receive invitation cards *To meet Oscar Wilde.†*

In 1892 he showed that he was also a gifted playwright when *Lady Windermere's Fan* was produced by George Alexander at the St James's. It depended on its brilliant dialogue, which was vastly superior to anything written by Pinero or Henry

* Arthur Roberts, *Fifty Years of Spoof* (John Lane, 1927).
† Hesketh Pearson, *Beerbohm Tree* (Methuen, 1956).

Arthur Jones. *Lady Windermere's Fan* was such a resounding success that Oscar Wilde was commissioned to write a play for Beerbohm Tree, the brilliant actor-manger who had never had a drama lesson in his life.

Herbert Beerbohm Tree was a born actor with very little technique who relied on inspiration. He was a tall, slim young man with red hair and intensely blue eyes; he had a vague manner, but missed nothing of importance. A very witty man and a bon viveur, he had a lot in common with Oscar Wilde and they were great friends. Oscar Wilde once said; 'Tree is a charming fellow and so clever—he models himself on me!'

Wilde called his new comedy *A Woman of No Importance* and Tree put it into rehearsal at the Haymarket Theatre. Though Wilde knew very little about stage production, he kept interrupting rehearsals with amateurish suggestions and became such a nuisance that Tree gave orders that he was not to be admitted to the theatre. Two days later Beerbhom Tree met Wilde just outside the Haymarket. Tree was wearing a frock coat and carrying his top hat in his hand. Oscar noticed that his hat had a bright red lining and said: 'My dear Herbert, what a charming lining you have in your hat!'

'My dear Oscar, do you really like it?'

'Yes, I think it is perfection.'

'Then it is yours', said Tree, plunging his hand into his hat and ripping out the lining. He handed it to Wilde and hastily disappeared into the theatre, having avoided the subject of *A Woman of No Importance.'*

Arthur Roberts was very flattered when Beerbohm Tree and Oscar Wilde invited him to supper with them at the Carlton Grill; Oscar Wilde had asked to meet Roberts so that he would explain the meaning of a new word he had invented: *spoof*. At supper Roberts gave Wilde and Tree a little lecture on 'spoofing', which he said was the knack of persuading people to believe that something wildly improbable is gospel truth.

'I love spoofing people,' said Arthur Roberts.

'I am afraid, my dear Roberts, that some of us have been playing "spoof" all our lives without knowing the name of the game,' remarked Oscar Wilde.

He informed Arthur Roberts at the end of the evening that

* Pearson.

he was really one of the most delightfully impossible people who ever happened.*

While *In Town* was at the Gaiety, George Edwardes travelled down on the train to Brighton with Jimmy Davis, an improvident solicitor who was drama critic of the *Sporting Times* or the 'Pink'un'. Jimmy Davis upset Edwardes by calling *In Town* a damn dull show.

'Could you write a better?' demanded Edwardes.

'I'd go and boil my head if I couldn't!' retorted Jimmy.

'A penny to a pound you don't!' said Edwardes.

Jimmy Davis immediately accepted the challenge. The Guv'nor never expected much of a piece from Jimmy Davis, a Bohemian who lived from hand to mouth. He had once been advised that the only way to get free from his many financial crises was to go and face his creditors. 'My dear good man, my sole object in life is to avoid them,' said Davis.†

A few months later Jimmy Davis sent Edwardes the book of a musical comedy called *A Gaiety Girl*. The Guv'nor was astonished to find it extremely entertaining; he accepted it for production and commissioned Sidney Jones to write the score. Jimmy Davis needed a nom-de-plume and, as he was so often in debt and 'owing all', he hit on the name of Owen Hall.

A Gaiety Girl was produced by George Edwardes at the Prince of Wales's in 1893. The slight plot centred round a Gaiety actress who won the love of a young aristocrat despite the unscrupulous opposition of her rival, a society girl. The story hardly mattered; Owen Hall had laced it with plenty of witty lines, some of which had difficulty in passing the censor, and Sidney Jones had composed a charming score. The Guv'nor took the opportunity of putting the Gaiety girls on the stage most of the time, and whenever they appeared they wore different dresses, each change more ravishing than the last.

The Guv'nor picked his chorus girls carefully so that each girl stood out as an individual type: all of them were statuesque creatures who knew exactly how to wear their clothes. The mashers flocked to the theatre, drawn by the magnet of the Gaiety Girls.

A Gaiety Girl did so well that the Guv'nor transferred it to

* Roberts.

† Ada Reeve, *Take It for a Fact* (Heinemann, 1954).

Daly's Theatre in 1894. In the meantime he had taken off *In Town* at the Gaiety and presented a burlesque of *Don Juan*, starring Arthur Roberts. But even the drawing powers of Roberts failed to bring in the public, which confirmed Edwardes's belief that burlesque pieces had had their day. He therefore planned to produce nothing but musical comedies at the Gaiety.

The heroine of *A Gaiety Girl* was played by Marie Studholme, whose much admired picture postcards were sold in thousands all over the country; for some time she held the title of number one pin-up girl. Hayden Coffin, the hero of *A Gaiety Girl*, had been a leading matinée idol since the days of *Dorothy*. The small part of Alma did not require an actress who could sing, and George Edwardes engaged Miriam Clements from the legitimate stage. She was an extremely attractive brunette and before long Edwardes started an affair with her. All his other mistresses had meant very little to him, but he fell deeply in love with Miriam Clements.

While *The Gondoliers* was still playing to capacity at the Savoy, Gilbert and Sullivan had a serious dispute over the small matter of paying for new carpets in their office at the theatre. Gilbert went to law about it, Sullivan sided with D'Oyly Carte against him, and at the end the two collaborators refused to speak to each other and vowed they would never write another opera together. So after D'Oyly Carte had taken off *The Gondoliers* he had to rely on producing new musical plays, none of which ran very long, and he was forced to fall back on revivals of the old Gilbert and Sullivan operas. Thus George Edwardes became the leading impresario of musical plays.

The Guv'nor was preparing to produce a musical comedy entitled *The Shop Girl* at the Gaiety. H. J. Dam had written the book, which was far better than *In Town* and *A Gaiety Girl*, and the excellent score was by Ivan Caryll, a Belgian composer who became the mainstay of the early musical comedies. The additional numbers were composed by Lionel Monckton. Ivan Caryll used to drive up to the theatre every night to conduct the orchestra in a pair-horse Victoria with two men on the box, and used to walk on to the stage looking like a fashion plate in his dress clothes, with his black beard parted on both sides of his chin.

The Guv'nor engaged Ada Reeve from the music halls to play Bessie Brent, the shop girl. She acted well and sang well and had enough vitality for ten ordinary women. She had been a child actress in the East End and been brought up in a hard school in Whitechapel. She was married to an actor and was pregnant when she took this part, though she did not tell Edwardes of this. Seymour Hicks, cast as the hero, was a light comedian with hardly any singing experience, and quite different from the usual light operatic hero: he had a large pointed nose and few pretensions to good looks.

Hicks was an irrepressible practical joker. When he and Ada Reeve did the Perambulator Duet together in *The Shop Girl*, he used to push the pram at her at such speed that she nearly tripped over her long skirt. One night she did trip up, and the pram passed over her. Feeling that the joke had gone too far, she confided to Seymour Hicks that she was pregnant.*

Edmund Payne, the principal comedian, played a shop-walker at a big department store. A small Cockney with pop eyes, Edmund Payne had an extraordinary lisp: he wore his hair across his forehead and had very quaint mannerisms. He was a most inventive low comedian who excelled in eccentric disguises. George Grossmith Jr, the son of the Gilbert and Sullivan star, made his début in *The Shop Girl*, in the role of Beautiful Bounding Bertie, a masher. He had an odd, rather cadaverous face, dressed immaculately and wore a monocle. Young Grossmith inherited his father's skill at putting over a point number and also his unctuous humour.

The Shop Girl, presented at the Gaiety on 24 November 1894, received outstandingly favourable notices. *The Times* said, 'The performance was a triumph for all concerned.' And the *Daily Chronicle* critic wrote:

Mr Edwardes never had a body of vocal comedians more determined to do their best for a novelty. . . . Miss Ada Reeve, the representative of the shop girl, speaks her lines and sings free from suspicion of the music hall twang. . . . Mr Seymour Hicks takes pains with the delivery of his words, he knows what to do, and he is a capital dancer. To him falls one of the most effective songs in the piece . . . concerning a shrewd beauty with golden hair. . . . Mr Edmund Payne

* Reeve.

is grotesquely funny as the shopwalker and has a couple of very original dances with Miss Katie Seymour. Their exceedingly quaint Japanese dance had to be twice repeated. . . .

The Shop Girl had a marvellous run of 546 performances and broke all the records at the Gaiety. Ada Reeve had to leave the show early in the run as her baby was due in three months. The Guv'nor replaced her with Ellaline Terriss, who had recently been married to Seymour Hicks. Being very much in love, they welcomed the chance of playing opposite each other. She was the daughter of William Terriss, the actor. She had flaxen hair and the delicacy of a Dresden figurine. Ellaline Terriss was a talented little actress whom audiences always found enchanting.

Seymour Hicks had made a big hit with his song 'Her Golden Hair was Hanging down her Back' which was considered rather daring. He was invited to a party at Cadogan House, at which the Prince of Wales and Princess Alexandra were to be present, and was specially asked to sing this number. But at the last moment an equerry had some doubts as to whether the song was fit for the ears of royalty; so Seymour Hicks was asked to recite it beforehand to Princess Alexandra. The Prince of Wales, noticing that Seymour Hicks looked very apprehensive, said, 'I believe you're nervous, Hicks.' 'Sir, I'm shaking all over,' replied Hicks.* He recited the words of the song to Princess Alexandra and waited anxiously for her verdict. This famous song told how Flo, a country girl whose golden hair was hanging down her back, left her village pure and innocent, and came back years later a 'ruined' woman.

> Oh Flo! what a change you know,
> When she left the village she was shy.
> But, alas and alack,
> She came back
> With a naughty little twinkle in her eye.

Hicks was most relieved when Princess Alexandra gave him a dazzling smile and said the song was charming. He only found out years later that the Princess was stone deaf!

The Guv'nor took the final responsibility for every show, but

* Hicks.

at the Gaiety he had a few men working under him whom he called his lieutenants. His right-hand man was 'Pat' Malone, a handsome Irishman who had resigned from the Army and graduated to stage production. Pat Malone and Sydney Ellison produced the Gaiety pieces up to the final rehearsals, then the Guv'nor took over. Edwardes used to sit in the stalls, wearing a monocle in his critical eye, and if he wanted to raise a point he would interrupt the rehearsal and say, 'No, that's wrong!' and rush on to the stage. 'You can't do it that way, don't you see? Do it this way!'* He would proceed to show an artist just how he wanted him to play the scene. George Edwardes was not an actor or a singer, and certainly not a dancer, yet he could always give a thumbnail impression of what he wanted. The Guv'nor had such an endearing personality that he drew out the good will of his artists and they didn't mind the criticisms he would make in his low, rather plaintive voice with traces of an Irish accent. If he called a late rehearsal he gave the small-part actors and the chorus an extra week's pay. No wonder many of his staff stayed on with 'the good old Guv'nor' for so long.

Ellaline Terriss described George Edwardes as 'a large man with an indolent manner, a sleepy petulant voice and two brilliant blue eyes which missed nothing at all'. He used to pick out the glamorous girls in his chorus and put them in a special category which he called 'the Big Eight'. All the chorus had to work much harder than they did in Hollingshead's day. Constance Collier was one of the original 'Big Eight'; in *The Shop Girl* there was a fortune-telling scene in which she had to hold out her hand for Seymour Hicks to read. Noticing that Constance Collier had a very beautiful arm, Hicks used it as a razor strop and said, 'Shave or haircut?' and kept in this gag throughout the run.†

Max Beerbohm often visited the Gaiety and wrote about the chorus girls in his delightful way.

As always the surpassing joy is the chorus. The look of total surprise that overspreads the faces of these ladies whenever they saunter on to the stage and . . . behold us for the first time, making us feel that we have taken rather a liberty in being there: the faintly cordial look that appears

* Jupp.   † Terriss.

for the fraction of an instant in the eyes of one of them who happens to see a friend among us . . . the splendid nonchalance of these queens, all so proud, so fatigued, all seeming to wonder why they were born, and born to be so beautiful.*

Hundreds of girls used to apply to join the Gaiety chorus. When the Guv'nor picked a girl he groomed her thoroughly and arranged for her to be given lessons in elocution, singing, dancing and fencing. The chorus girls were taught dancing by Mr Bertrand, the ballet master of the Empire corps de ballet. The Empire girls were showered with presents from the mashers, some of whom were young men with titles, and once a girl had accepted jewellery from them she was expected to accept an invitation to supper at the very least.

Mr Bertrand's pretty daughter was sent a diamond ring on coroneted notepaper with a note:

DEAR MISS BERTRAND,
Will you accept the enclosed little present as an appreciation of your artistic ability, by an admirer?
Yours faithfully, X

Mr Bertrand returned the ring to the sender with this scathing reply:

MY LORD,
Will you accept the enclosed 'present' back as an appreciation of your damned impertinence.
From
HER FATHER†

George Edwardes sent *The Shop Girl* over to America in 1895 with a young company headed by Seymour Hicks and George Grossmith, Jr. Ellaline Terriss was also acting in New York in *His Excellency*, a comedy by W. S. Gilbert, so she and Seymour Hicks were able to stay together in the States.

Hicks had discovered 'Her Golden Hair was Hanging down Her Back' in New York, and had also 'borrowed' some of his jokes and gags from American shows. Although this was a

* Sir Max Beerbohm, *Around Theatres* (Hart-Davis, 1953).
† James Glover, *Jimmy Glover and His Friends* (Chatto & Windus, 1913).

two-way practice, and American comedians often filched material from British pieces, the show-business papers in New York made a dead set against Seymour Hicks, whom they called 'Stealmore Tricks'. *Variety* came out with the headlines: 'Comedians Beware! Stealmore Tricks is in town—Padlock your Gags! Lock up your Jokes!' And another theatrical journal told its readers, 'Nail everything you have: Hicks the real live bunco man is among you.' When Hicks went to a matinée of a Broadway show, the leading comedian appeared in the interval and said, 'Sorry, folks, we're not doing all the next scene today—Hicks is listening!'*

During the tour George Edwardes's manager took a party of Gaiety chorus girls for a ride on the elevated railway in New York and lost them for a while. He found them waiting at the original station, huddled together like a flock of frightened sheep. 'But why didn't you ask the way?' he inquired. One of the chorus girls replied angrily, 'Why, there isn't one of us can speak the language!'†

In 1895 there was a serious dispute between the United States and Venezuela because the Americans claimed some territory from the Venezuelans, and it nearly led to a war. Britain stated that she thought America was in the wrong, which was extremely bad for Anglo–American relations: all the British shows running on Broadway were boycotted and *The Shop Girl* had to close. Another casualty was *His Excellency*, so Ellaline Terriss packed her bags for England at the same time as her husband.

Ellaline Terriss and Seymour Hicks were young and resilient and so was George Grossmith; they soon got over their disappointment and resumed their parts in *The Shop Girl*. This trio, with Edmund Payne, became regular members of George Edwardes's Gaiety company. Hicks thought the Gaiety was a wonderful school for a young actor or actress and said no theatre in England kept you in closer touch with the public. On a first night the gallery didn't take a minute to make up their minds if they liked a show or not and always made their feelings clear to the rest of the house. A first night at the Gaiety was charged to the utmost with electricity.

* Hicks.

† Conversations with Mrs Barker, daughter of Margaret Fraser, a Gaiety actress.

7 Queen Maria

*I was a self-important little baggage who was
more disliked than liked by managers in those
days.*

MARIE TEMPEST

George Edwardes had already decided that he needed a second
theatre for his musical plays, and in 1890 he had bought an
excellent site in Cranbourne Street, Leicester Square, from the
Marquess of Salisbury. But when the time came to start
building he had run out of money owing to the failure of the
last Gaiety burlesques. Fortunately he heard that Augustin
Daly, a leading American impresario, who had brought his
company to London several times in the eighties, was looking
for a theatre where he could present Ada Rehan in a series of
classic plays. Edwardes undertook to build Daly a theatre on
his site in Cranbourne Street and to lease it to him for £5,000 a
year, at a profit to himself of £1,000.

The new theatre was built right on schedule and called
Daly's. An extremely elegant playhouse, it was built in the
Florentine style of the Italian Renaissance and the auditorium
was constructed on the cantilever principle. The *Daily Graphic*
called it a pleasing relief from the unimposing architecture of
most of the London theatres. The general scheme of the decor
in the auditorium was a mixture of red, gold, silver and bronze.
The dress-circle fronts and boxes had been amusingly designed
as boat-loads of sea-nymphs and Cupids blowing bubbles,

The auditorium of Daly's Theatre in the 1890s

which were converted into electric lights of all colours of the rainbow.*

Augustin Daly and Ada Rehan, the famous American actress, had a unique relationship: he dominated her like a Svengali, telling her exactly how he wanted her to play every scene, and she obeyed all his instructions blindly. Daly had rather vulgar taste and sometimes, by following his interpretation, Ada Rehan spoilt her performance. Daly was an autocrat in the theatre who regarded his artists as puppets. His voice was harsh and his manners atrocious and people often disliked him on sight, but he was a decent man if people took the trouble to get to know him.

Daly opened his theatre with *The Taming of the Shrew* on 27 June 1893. After the orchestra had played 'God Save the Queen', two artists sang 'The Star Spangled Banner', and then the audience joined heartily in the chorus. Ada Rehan repeated her former triumph in the role of Katherine with Arthur Bouchier playing Petruchio. *The Shrew* received excellent notices; but Daly, sticking to his rigid policy, took it off after only two weeks. All his subsequent plays similarly only ran for a fortnight, which was a big mistake. Ada Rehan was greatly praised for her Rosalind in *As You Like It*, and Henry Irving came along to see her play the role one evening. Irving hardly ever praised another artist; his only comment was, 'How long d'you suppose those silk tights of hers would have lasted in the Forest of Arden?'†

Augustin Daly's first season did only moderately well and his second lost money. His most expensive production was *The Foresters*, a play by Lord Tennyson on the Robin Hood theme. Though it had been popular in New York, London gave it a very cool reception. At the end of the year Daly decided to terminate his lease of the theatre and notified George Edwardes. As *The Shop Girl* was then playing to capacity at the Gaiety, the Guv'nor jumped at the opportunity of getting a second theatre at last.

He started to prepare the production of *An Artist's Model*, a new musical play by Owen Hall and Sidney Jones. He sent a cable to Marie Tempest in the United States, asking her if

* Raymond Mander and Joe Mitchenson, *The Lost Theatres of London* (Hart-Davis, 1968).

† Robertson.

she would come back to England to be his leading lady at Daly's. Marie Tempest had been starring in America but, knowing that George Edwardes had become the leading producer of musical plays, she accepted his offer at once and sailed home in a luxury suite which Edwardes had thoughtfully filled with the most exquisite flowers.

When Marie Tempest was shown into his luxurious new offices in Lisle Street at the back of Daly's, he greeted her effusively and handed her her new contract. 'You are to be the star of Daly's Theatre, my dear,' he said impressively as though conferring a supreme honour on her.

Marie Tempest was so mesmerized by his charm and enthusiasm that she scarcely glanced at her contract. Then he handed her a copy of the libretto of *An Artist's Model*. She looked at it quickly, then looked at it again: it seemed incredible, but there was no part in it for her!

Marie Tempest was boiling with rage as Edwardes admitted frankly that somehow he had forgotten to have her part written into the piece after he had cabled her in America. 'But you will be wonderful in it when it is written,' he assured her. She was so angry that she started to walk out of the office. 'Now, my dear, don't worry,' said Edwardes soothingly. 'You just go away for a little holiday and when you come back I promise you it will be written in for you!'*

Bewitched by his self-assurance and his promise, Marie Tempest left the office believing in George Edwardes after all. She took a holiday and when she returned to Daly's she found her part, her music and her lyrics all ready for her.

Marie Tempest was a petite brunette; not pretty or particularly attractive, she looked a little like a pouter pigeon. But an actress of her quality did not need to be a picture-postcard beauty; she had a superb singing voice, a genius for comedy and, above all, a magnetic personality. The other artists at Daly's disliked her because she was so bossy and they called her 'Queen Maria' behind her back.

The Guv'nor reunited Marie Tempest and Hayden Coffin, the stars of *Dorothy*, in *An Artist's Model*. It opened at Daly's on 2 February 1895, and the first night went very badly indeed. At the end the Guv'nor walked on to the stage and asked the audience what they thought of it.

* Hector Bolitho, *Marie Tempest* (Cobden-Sanderson, 1936).

'Half and half,' shouted the gallery.

'Well, come back again in five or six weeks and I'll have the other half put right,' he assured them.*

Next day he called in Owen Hall and Sidney Jones and they reconstructed the entire piece. They made such a fine job of it that *An Artist's Model* ran for 405 performances and did record business.

Letty Lind, the second lead, was blonde and beautiful and extremely graceful: she had made her name as a dancer in the last Gaiety burlesques, and had known the Guv'nor for a long time, and liked him very much and respected his opinions. He called Letty Lind 'a good little girl', and wished that Marie Tempest was more like her. His star often argued with him and sometimes made scenes at Daly's. Edwardes hated scenes more than anything and always tried to humour 'Maria', but found it a great strain and privately called her 'a naughty girl'.

Some nights he would return home to Julia at Park Square with a splitting headache; Julia would guess at once that he had had a row with 'Maria' Tempest. She was by far the most troublesome actress he had ever had to deal with, yet he admitted that she was also the cleverest.

The year 1895 was one of extreme contrasts for Oscar Wilde. In January Lewis Waller produced his play *An Ideal Husband* at the Haymarket and it was an immediate success. On 14 February *The Importance of being Earnest*, his masterpiece, was produced by George Alexander at the St James's Theatre. Although the first night took place in one of the worst snowstorms on record, the theatre was full. London society had turned up in force to come and laugh at Oscar Wilde's devastating epigrams about themselves; Oscar's young men friends were also present, all wearing lilies of the valley in their buttonholes.

Oscar Wilde's four comedies in the nineties had all been distinguished for their brilliant dialogue and clever situations. He invariably wrote about society and had the great advantage over his rivals of being on intimate terms with the peerage. Yet George Alexander actually lost money on the original production of *The Importance of being Earnest* because it had to be withdrawn in a hurry when Oscar Wilde, with incredible folly,

* Forbes Winslow.

brought an action for criminal libel against the Marquess of Queensberry. This led to Wilde being exposed as a homosexual later in the year, and being sentenced to imprisonment with hard labour after two trials.

It was announced in the Birthday Honours on 24 May 1895 that Henry Irving was to receive a knighthood for his services to the theatre—the first time an actor had ever been knighted in England. *The Times* said in a leader:

We have reserved the most striking Birthday Honour to the last. Lord Rosebery, in recommending that Mr Henry Irving should be knighted, has taken an entirely new departure. . . . Mr Irving has done much to raise the tone of the stage and to win public consideration for it. As an actor he represents at once the highest form of the drama and the most effective rendering of the parts in which he has appeared. . . .

It was reported that when Queen Victoria knighted him at Windsor she said, 'I am very, very pleased.' A few days after Irving had received the accolade, four thousand actors and actresses assembled at the Lyceum Theatre to present him with a congratulatory address. 'It was the sublime moment of my life,' said Irving: he had fulfilled his greatest ambition and it gave him tremendous satisfaction to know that actors would never again be regarded as rogues and vagabonds.

In the nineties George Edwardes became sole managing director of the Empire. The notorious Empire promenade was ordered to be abolished in October 1894 at the instigation of Mrs Ormiston Chant, a spoilsport who objected to the blatant way in which the 'painted hussies' were plying their trade at every performance. Announcing the temporary closure of the theatre, Edwardes said he was proud to have 'the sympathy of the London people'. When the Empire reopened in November the promenade was shut off by a screen of woodwork covered by canvas. A large crowd of men, led by Winston Churchill, then a Sandhurst cadet, attacked the screen and removed the canvas without any opposition whatsoever.*

After the Guv'nor had completed his first year at Daly's, he

* D. F. Cheshire, *Music Hall in Britain* (David and Charles, 1974).

reckoned up the cost and found it far more expensive to run
than the Gaiety. Most of the musical plays he presented there
were operettas and he had to employ an orchestra of forty
musicians. He had to take over £3,000 a week in order to 'get
out' and often found himself in the red; so he had to rely on
his provincial tours and overseas tours to make his profits.

In 1896 he arranged to produce *The Geisha*, a new piece by
Owen Hall and Sidney Jones, with additional numbers by
Lionel Monckton. The Guv'nor had a hunch from the start
that it was going to be a big winner. It had a most attractive
Japanese setting, an excellent libretto and a delightful score;
and splendid parts for Marie Tempest, Letty Lind, Hayden
Coffin and the other principals. Edwardes, remembering how
W. S. Gilbert had taken the greatest care to make *The Mikado*
look authentic, engaged Arthur Diósy, founder of the Japanese
Society, to ensure the accuracy of the costumes and scenery
and to supervise the 'japanning' of the piece.

The dances for *The Geisha* were arranged by Willie Warde, a
small-part actor and dancer who did a great deal of the choreo-
graphy both at Daly's and the Gaiety. The Guv'nor was
very fond of Willie Warde and regarded him as his mascot.
Produced on 25 April 1896, *The Geisha* was an overwhelming
success, just as the Guv'nor had hoped. Marie Tempest as O
Mimosa San, the Geisha girl, had a part which exploited her
genius for comedy; Letty Lind competed with her for the
honours as a jolly English girl far away from home. Hayden
Coffin was perfect as a sentimental Naval officer, and Huntley
Wright, the principal comedian, played the Chinese proprietor
of a tea house and soon had the town whistling his song:

> Chin Chin Chinaman
> Muchee muchee sad!
> He afraid Allo trade
> Well-ee well-ee bad!
> No-ee joke Brokee—broke
> Makee shut tee shop!
> Chin chin Chinaman,
> Chop, chop, chop!

Marie Tempest scored a big hit with her song 'The Amorous
Goldfish'. The little goldfish in love with a sailor had something

in common with the Geisha girl who was in love with a British Naval officer.

A goldfish swam in a big glass bowl,
As dear little goldfish do,
But she loved with the whole of her heart and soul
An officer brave from the ocean wave
And she thought that he loved her too!
Her small inside he daily fed
With crumbs of the best digestive bread.
'This kind attention proves,' said she,
'How exceedingly fond he is of me!'

Letty Lind as the English girl also won many admirers with her song 'The Interfering Parrot'. Clement Scott wrote in the *Illustrated London News*:

London in recent years has seen no more delightful entertainment than the Japanese *Geisha* at Daly's, which marks a new career in comic opera pioneered by Mr George Edwardes. . . . Mr Owen Hall's pretty play is a feast to the eye in colour and a delight to the ear owing to the charming music of Mr Sidney Jones and Mr Lionel Monckton. All the spirit of Japan has been captured . . . the stage has seen nothing like [the dresses]. The fashionable tea-gown of the future will surely be a Japanese kimono and a lovely obi.

. . . the musical and artistic burden of the play falls on Miss Marie Tempest and Miss Letty Lind who have never been seen to such advantage. . . . Miss Tempest is a Japanese Geisha to the life, and she sings the music allotted to her to perfection, and Miss Letty Lind personifies a merry little English girl who dresses up as a tea-house mousmee. . . .

The success of *The Geisha* started a Japanese craze in London: there were Geisha hats for women, Geisha ties for men and all kinds of goods sprang up in the night with the brand name of 'Geisha'. As a result of this triumph Marie Tempest became the uncrowned queen of Daly's: she never left by the stage door, but always had her carriage waiting at the royal entrance at the end of the performance.

Thanks to *The Geisha*, Owen Hall—still known to his friends as Jimmy Davis—became a man of substance. He started giving delightful supper parties at his little house in Curzon Street, and George Edwardes was generally one of his guests. His evening parties on Saturdays were full of clean-shirted Bohemians, and his guests never knew if they would be sitting next to a prima donna or to Bessie Bellwood, the music hall star, at supper. Jimmy Davis had friends in every walk of life, and Arthur Roberts and a duke's son were equally welcome at Curzon Street. Sometimes Signor Tosti would sit down at the piano in the first-floor drawing-room and improvise wonderful melodies in the early hours of a Sunday morning. And if a new song had been written for a play or an opera it was sure to be heard first at Curzon Street with the composer at the piano.

George Moore met Jimmy Davis when he first came to London as a young man, and fell under the spell of the ambiance of the house in Curzon Street. 'The bright, witty glance of his brown eyes at once prejudiced me in his favour,' wrote George Moore. 'It was a house of champagne, late hours, evening clothes, of literature and art, of passionate discussions. . . . I found in Curzon Street a Bohemianism of the ten sovereigns always a-jingle in the pocket, of hansom cabs, of ladies' pet names . . . and I joined in this adorable game of Bohemianism, with Curzon Street for its rallying point.'*

The Guv'nor used to have a battle royal with Marie Tempest every year on the subject of her new contract. When she came into his office he would act his head off and say, 'Are you well, my dear? Are you taking enough exercise? Are you happy in the theatre? Would it make you any more happy if I had your room redecorated?' At the end of all the affability he came to the point. 'Oh, by the way, my dear, your contract is up in a week or two. I think we ought to renew it, don't you?' Then he would hand her the new contract. Having read it very carefully, she would protest, 'But, George, this is the same salary, and you promised me a rise!'

'I know, I know, my dear.'

George Edwardes would start to wring his hands and say, 'But I've been through all the figures at Daly's, and it's impossible! It breaks my heart to refuse you, my dear.'

Marie, ignoring his appeal to her better nature, would bark out, 'It's no good, George, I'm going!'†

Then she would flounce out of his office and they started to

* Booth, *London Town*.   † Bolitho.

write letters to each other—until Edwardes suggested they ought to find an arbitrator to settle her new salary. The arbitrator was always Alfred de Rothschild, one of the Guv'nor's principal backers, and this kind gentleman always decided that Marie should get her rise.

After one of their rows Edwardes sent 'Maria' Tempest an attractive little mare, which a groom delivered to her house near Regent's Park with this note:

MY DEAR,

I'm sure this little mare will carry you beautifully. I shall be in the Row to-morrow to see how you look on her. She has perfect manners. With love, Yours,

GEORGE

George Edwardes still carried on his affairs, but Miriam Clements was the only woman who really meant anything to him. She had gone back to the legitimate stage after the tour of *A Gaiety Girl* and her career had flourished. Edwardes installed her in a house in St John's Wood. He was normally very discreet in matters of the heart, but Miriam Clements became rather an obsession with him: Walter Pallant and his cronies couldn't help noticing that he was always bringing her name into the conversation. Julia of course knew all about Miriam, but she always turned a blind eye to George's peccadilloes.

Years after Marie Tempest and the Guv'nor had parted company she said that George Edwardes was wilful and eccentric, but had the instincts of a gentleman. She noticed he was getting fat and thought one of his best qualities was his unpretentiousness; he was good company; and she admired his self-assurance. He lived dangerously and was absolutely reckless. He was extraordinarily kind to his chorus girls and he handled his principal artists brilliantly.*

It was a perceptive and very sympathetic picture of the Guv'nor in the nineties. Marie Tempest was perfectly right in saying that he treated his chorus girls very well, and he generally got his own way with his principals. But Marie Tempest might have added that in his dealings with her he nearly always met his Waterloo.

* Bolitho.

D

III

THE MUSICAL COMEDY CRAZE (1897–1903)

8 The Gaiety Style

> [George Edwardes] cast himself in every new play,
> in the part of the public, and he watched the
> production with one foot in the pit, and the other
> in the front row of the stalls.
>
> PAUL RUBENS, in the *Stage*, October 1915

The Shop Girl ran on at the Gaiety till the summer of 1896
and made the Guv'nor a very happy man. George Grossmith,
Jr, had made a reputation for himself in the role of Bouncing
Bertie, and Edwardes was sure he was a star in the making.
When walking past the Lyceum Theatre in Wellington Street
one day he met Sir Henry Irving, an old friend of his father,
George Grossmith of Gilbert and Sullivan fame. 'Are you going
to follow your father's footsteps?' asked Irving. Young Grossmith, rather embarrassed, replied, 'Well, Sir Henry, I *am* an
actor—I've been playing the other side of the road to you for
the last two years.' 'Oh, indeed yes,' said the great actor. 'I
believe there is some sort of entertainment going on there.'*

Sir Henry Irving had begun to get into a financial mess at
the Lyceum. The trouble started soon after he opened in
Richard III; he had a serious fall at his London flat and was
forced to cancel several weeks of his Lyceum season until
he was fit enough to go on again. He had no idea of economy
and spent money prodigally on his productions. 'He was the
most extravagant manager who ever put his careless signature
to a cheque,' said John Hare, his brother actor–manager. He

* George Grossmith, Jr, *G.G.* (Hutchinson, 1933).

often ordered expensive sets and cancelled them, and in one costume play he ordered a hundred suits of armour, correct in every detail, only to find all of them too small for his 'supers' to wear. Irving had hoped his second American tour would enable him to recoup his losses on his last two seasons. But though he and Ellen Terry received a wonderful welcome, the net profit on the tour was only £6,000.

Irving presented a new production of *Cymbeline* at the Lyceum on his return in September, but it was a failure. Ellen Terry, who played Imogen, had begun to feel the strain of her early days as a child actress in her father's company of strolling players. Her eyes were giving trouble and she sometimes forgot her lines. Bram Stoker, Irving's manager, tried to persuade him to cut down his overheads, but he refused.

While Irving was standing in the wings one night an old limelight man carelessly dropped one of his slides; it fell at Irving's feet, and missed him by inches. His stage manager, Loveday, dismissed the man on the spot. But a few days later Sir Henry Irving asked him: 'Er . . . by the way, Loveday, what has become of the old man with the white beard who used to work one of the limes?' Loveday told him he had sacked the man. 'Accidents happen, Loveday, and he's been here twenty years', said Irving. 'I want him back—I like my old folk round me. Please send for him.'* The old limelight man was reinstated and Sir Henry Irving gave orders for him to receive all his arrears of salary. Irving treated his staff and the little people at the Lyceum with great kindness.

The Guv'nor presented *My Girl* at the Gaiety after *The Shop Girl*. It was an inferior musical comedy with a plot about shady financiers and the Stock Exchange which was too melodramatic for the regular patrons to swallow. *My Girl* had a very short stay, but it brought stardom to Connie Ediss, a big, fleshy Cockney comedienne who sang and danced extremely well and laughed at herself for being so fat. Edwardes signed her up and she joined Ellaline Terriss, Seymour Hicks and Teddy Payne as a regular member of his company.

The Guv'nor was putting on a lot of weight; he loved good food and never took enough exercise, and liked taking his friends out to lunch at Romano's or the Savoy Grill, where he

* J. B. Booth, *Palmy Days* (Richards Press, 1957).

had his own table. His doctor said he would have to reduce and advised Edwardes to walk from his house in Park Square to the Gaiety every morning. On the first day he walked from Regent's Park to Baker Street, then remembered an urgent appointment at the theatre and took a cab. He never again attempted to walk fom his house to the Gaiety.

It happened that Connie Ediss, the lady with the outsize measurements, called in to see him at the office one morning and he asked her how she was feeling. 'I'm quite well, thank you, Mr Edwardes,' she said, 'but oh, if I could only get my weight down a bit!' 'Well, my dear, do as I do,' Edwardes told her. 'I walk to the office every morning and it's wonderful the good it does. Have one of my apples, my dear—finest thing in the world!'* Edwardes had conveniently forgotten that he had never once walked to the Gaiety. He was a firm believer in the health-giving properties of green apples and used to send Jupp, the new stage door keeper, to Covent Garden to buy fresh supplies of them every week.

Besides his permanent company of actors and actresses at the Gaiety, the Guv'nor had collected a talented team of authors, composers and lyric writers whom he kept very busy preparing his new musical comedies. This probably explains why all his shows had such an individual style. One of his little eccentricities on a first night was to sit in his box, turn his back to the stage and watch how the audience was reacting to the show.

People grew to love the Gaiety because they knew they could rely on hearing tuneful music with clever lyrics, and seeing attractive stage pictures with a bevy of pretty girls decorating the scenery. No one ever took the plot of a musical comedy seriously: audiences were quite content to let a piece get along as it pleased till the next tuneful number. In the provinces, where the Guv'nor expected to make his profits, people appreciated that the name of George Edwardes on a playbill was a guarantee of a first-class production.

This was the period of the great 'Kaffir' boom on the Stock Exchange, when men who had bought the right gold-mining shares made their fortunes in a day. Stockbrokers, merchant bankers and other City men thronged to the Gaiety because it provided them with the best light entertainment in town.

* Jupp.

Many of them trained their opera glasses on the 'Big Eight' chorus: tall, plump, voluptuous girls who sometimes sang a chorus or supported Seymour Hicks or Teddy Payne in a number, but whose main function was to look gorgeous. Each girl had her special band of admirers, some of whom would go to a Gaiety show a dozen times just for the pleasure of watching their goddess displaying her charms.

The Guv'nor presented *The Circus Girl* at the Gaiety on 5 December 1896; it had a brilliant first night, attended by the Prince of Wales, and was given a splendid reception. James P. Tanner, the leading Gaiety author, had collaborated on the 'book' and its charming score was by Ivan Caryll and Lionel Monckton. The cast was headed by Ellaline Terriss, Seymour Hicks, Teddy Payne, Katie Seymour and Connie Ediss. The scenery and costumes were as glamorous as usual; the audience raved about the scene depicting the Artists' Ball in Paris and gasped at the realism of the Circus scene.

One of the principals had to make his entrance into the circus ring on a white horse which had formerly been employed as an omnibus horse. The stage manager found the only way to get it to start was to call out, 'Charing Cross, Strand, Bank, Piccadilly Circus, Oxford Circus!' Then he had to slam the green-room door and say, 'Right behind!' and on this cue the white horse trotted joyfully into the ring.*

The Circus Girl had a run of 497 performances. Ellaline Terriss sang a Lionel Monckton number entitled 'A Little Bit of String' which was the hit of the show. The chorus went:

> Just a little bit of string,
> Such a tiny little thing
> Tied as tightly as a string could be,
> So that if I tried to play
> I could never slip away
> For they'd put me on a string, you see.

Connie Ediss scored with her comedy number 'The Way to Treat a Lady', which told how an ill-fated lady was left stranded in a pub by her husband, who never even paid for her port and lemonade.

The most popular numbers in the show had all been written
    * Hicks.

by Lionel Monckton. He used to strum away on an old cottage piano at rehearsals, and whenever the Guv'nor needed a new song Monckton always had one up his sleeve. A serious man, who wrote musical criticism for the *Daily Telegraph*, he had thrown up a career at the Bar to become a composer. He called Edwardes 'Blue-eyed George' because of the way he used to open his eyes with the bland innocence of a new-born babe. Although the Guv'nor had very little ear for music, he had a knack for knowing if a new number would be popular.

The success of *The Circus Girl*, coming at the same time as *The Geisha* at Daly's, helped to make George Edwardes a wealthy man. He bought Winkfield Lodge, a big country house near Ascot, as a week-end home; Julia always went there with the family for week-ends, and George joined them if he possibly could. But sometimes his theatrical interests kept him in town, or he had a tryst with a pretty girl.

The Circus Girl brought nothing but bad luck to Ellaline Terriss and Seymour Hicks. To begin with, Ellaline Terriss lost her first baby; she was very ill afterwards and out of the show for a long time. A far greater tragedy followed: her father William Terriss, one of the most popular actors of his generation, was struck down by a madman outside the stage door of the Adelphi Theatre on 16 December 1897.

After leaving Irving, William Terriss had gone into management at the Adelphi and produced melodramas there. In his company there was a Scotsman named William Archer Prince, playing 'super' parts, who was convinced he could be a star if only Terriss would give him a chance. Prince had a much bigger grudge against Terriss for dismissing him, with the other 'supers', at the end of the run of *One of the Best*, a play which Seymour Hicks had written in collaboration with George Edwardes.

Prince appealed to Terriss for help after leaving his company and was given a sovereign. Convinced that he had been badly treated, Prince applied to the Actors' Benevolent Fund for financial assistance, but was turned down. Prince, no longer sane, muddled up the name of their chairman, Edward Terry, with William Terriss. Frantic for revenge, Prince bought a butcher's knife and waited outside the Adelphi stage door for Terriss.

Bill Terriss had been playing chess at the Green Room Club

with George Edwardes in the afternoon. He arrived at the theatre in the evening with Mr Graves, his surveyor. As he unlocked the door of his private entrance at the back of the Adelphi, Prince ran out and stabbed him from behind, saying, 'Take that!' Terriss called out, 'You have stabbed me! Arrest him!' Mr Graves ran forward and seized Prince, who offered no resistance. Bill Terriss had fallen to the ground; he was carried into his theatre, where he died a few minutes later. His murderer had been taken to Bow Street.

When Seymour Hicks arrived at the Gaiety that evening he found his understudy ready to go on. There was a message for Hicks to go to Bow Street immediately to identify the body of his father-in-law. He was shown into a small room at Bow Street where Prince—who had now become a raving lunatic— was being held against a wall by two policemen.

'I was so distraught that had he been sane my first impulse would have been to have taken his life,' wrote Seymour Hicks. 'When, however, I was within a few feet of that savage animal —for Prince, foaming at the mouth, looked little else—I became calm.'*

When George Edwardes heard of the death of his great friend, Bill Terriss, he broke down and cried. He always kept the last letter Terriss wrote to him:

Adelphi Theatre.   *1896*
Only a grasp of the hand, dear George, and that the New Year which dawns this morning will bring you continued good fortune and happiness is the wish of your sincere friend and debtor.

WILLIAM TERRISS

Edwardes and Terriss had been regular chess opponents for many years. The Guv'nor was so sentimental that he took away the chess board on which he and Bill Terriss had played their unfinished game at the Green Room Club, and had the pieces stuck down in exactly the same positions as they had left them.†

Ellaline Terriss had to face a third blow before the end of the

* Hicks, *Between Ourselves* (Cassell, 1930).

† Conversations with Julius Edwardes, great-nephew of George Edwardes.

year when her mother died suddenly; it was a long time before
she felt well enough to resume her role in *The Circus Girl*.
On the night she returned to the Gaiety the audience gave her
a marvellous reception. Everybody in the house stood up and
cheered, and waved to her on the stage and shouted, 'Ellaline!
Ellaline!' This continued for two or three minutes and caused
Ellaline Terriss to break down completely.

Beerbohm Tree consolidated his position as Crown Prince to
Sir Henry Irving when he opened Her Majesty's Theatre on
28 April 1897. *Trilby*, in which he played Svengali, had proved
one of the biggest money-spinners of the decade and he used
the enormous profits to finance part of the costs of building
his 'beautiful theatre'. His first offering, *The Seats of the
Mighty*, was a long, pretentious play by Gilbert Parker. It
failed to draw but, in the hope that it might succeed in time,
he kept it running for several months, by the time it came off
he had incurred a heavy loss. His next piece, *Katherine and
Petruchio*, an old play by David Garrick, also failed.

By the end of the year Beerbohm Tree was on his beam
ends—yet he went ahead with an extremely lavish production
of *Julius Caesar* and staked everything on its success, mortgag-
ing his house and even raising money on his wife's jewellery.
He gave the public the most artistic and magnificent revival of
a Shakespeare play that had been seen in England for twenty
years, with scenery designed by Alma Tadema. *Julius Caesar*
opened at Her Majesty's on 22 January 1898 with Tree as
Anthony and Lewis Waller playing Brutus. Waller, an extremely handsome actor, spoke verse far better than Tree or
Irving and gave an inspired performance as Brutus. At the
end of the evening he received more curtain calls than Tree.

The Times paid tribute to Tree:

Nothing finer in point of artistic force and impressiveness
has been accomplished in Shakesperean revival than the
rendering of this noble play. . . . The busy streets of Rome,
the Senate, the assassination of Caesar, the Forum . . . the
battle of Philippi are inviting subjects for historical reconstruction. . . . Mr Tree . . . has produced a succession of
scenes of unsurpassed beauty and effect . . . the Rome of
two thousand years ago lives before us.

Berbohm Tree's production of *Julius Caesar* made him a name to conjure with; but he never became self-important, always engaged the best artists available to play the other roles in his productions, and was very accessible to his company. 'When people stand on their dignity they have no other pedestal,' was one of his aphorisms. He had a very hazy notion of the business side of the theatre and left financial affairs and the day-to-day details to Henry Dana, his business manager. Dana was a small man who wore pince-nez and looked rather like a senior civil servant; practical and businesslike, he was worth his weight in gold to Herbert Beerbohm Tree, who was frequently up in the clouds. Tree and George Edwardes were on the best of terms: in the new century Constance Collier, who had started her career with the Guv'nor at the Gaiety, was to become Tree's leading lady.

Edwardes used to say that his aim in life was simply to entertain the public and give them what they wanted, and in the nineties he nearly always succeeded at the Gaiety. 'The Gaiety first nights were things at which to marvel,' said Walter Macqueen Pope. The theatre looked like a bright jewel lighting up the London sky. Women in beautiful, elaborate dresses with jewels in their hair, on their hands and round their necks sat in the stalls and dress circle and the boxes. They all carried fans and knew how to use them, and every woman moved with grace and dignity. The men who escorted them wore perfectly tailored evening clothes.*

The moment the curtain fell on the first night of a Gaiety show there was a rush to the stage door to see the favourites come out: Ellaline Terriss with Seymour Hicks; little Teddy Payne; Katie Seymour, his dancing partner, and George Grossmith, Jr, who looked the image of a man about town. In those days people never rushed up to actors and actresses for their autographs: the tempo of life was very much slower and fans had to write in to the theatre if they wanted a star's autograph or his picture. All the London theatres used to provide a longer show for their patrons and at the Gaiety carriages were ordered for eleven o'clock.

* Pope, *Ghosts and Greasepaint* (Hale, 1951).

9 The Gaiety Stage Door

*The Gaiety stage door was one of the minor
wonders of the world. . . . The favour of Jupp was
a thing not lightly sought, or easily won. I have
seen Royal princes, but not Princes of the blood,
being bluntly refused admission.*

GEORGE GROSSMITH, JR, *G.G.*

Jimmy Jupp, who had succeeded Tierney as stage door keeper
at the Gaiety, was an ex sergeant-major with a Kitchener
moustache and a swarthy complexion acquired through years
of service in India. Jupp was quick-witted, diplomatic and had
a keen sense of humour; he worshipped the Guv'nor, who
treated him more like a friend than an employee. He had
strict instructions that no man was to be admitted to the
girls' dressing-rooms under any circumstances, and that no
actress was allowed to accept a present of money—although
there was nothing to stop a Gaiety girl receiving the finest
jewellery in London, or a town house or a yacht for that
matter. Jupp was well paid and received lavish tips from the
stage-door johnnies, yet he had the reputation of never having
any money. He probably spent most of his salary backing
horses, and as he backed them regularly was bound to pick
losers more often than winners.

On very fine mornings the Guv'nor drove up to his office
opposite the stage door in Wellington Street in a smart phaeton,
with his 'tiger' in livery sitting on the box behind; but he
usually arrived in his brougham, driven by his coachman,

Turner. On the other hand, Teddy Payne, the leading comedian, invariably turned up at the stage door on a bicycle. A thrifty man, who saved half his salary, Teddy Payne cycled straight home after the show to his wife and large family at Stoke Newington.

Musical comedies had resulted in a completely different type of girl going into the chorus. Many of them came from middle-class families; these daughters of doctors or lawyers or clergymen thought it was great fun to share a dressing-room with 'Greasy Gracie', whose father was a gravedigger at Kensal Green. The stage door was besieged at nights by the gilded youth, all waiting to take a Gaiety girl out to supper. The girls were generally escorted to Romano's or Rules or Gatti's, or they went a little further to the Café Royal or Oddenino's in Regent Street. Most of the girls left the stage door still wearing their silk stockings and long gloves from the show, and as they departed some of them would give a little wave and say, 'God bless George Edwardes.' The gilded youth had excellent manners and drove the girls home after supper if they lived in London. The Gaiety girls put a high value on themselves and young men respected them for it.

The Guv'nor promoted the most talented and attractive girls to the 'Big Eight' and raised their salaries: chorus girls earned only £2 10s. a week, but some of the 'Big Eight' got £15; they were well worth it, because some of their admirers bought stalls at the Gaiety for every night of the run. These elite females were generally taken to the Savoy Grill or the Carlton. Gaiety girls regarded the Savoy as full dress parade and went there for supper wearing the best dresses in their wardrobes and with all their diamonds on. Society ladies, sitting at tables in between at the Savoy, kept ogling them and feeling green with envy.* Ada Reeve said her escorts used to wait for her at the stage door in a hansom cab and generally greeted her with a bunch of orchids. When they took her to the Savoy Grill she had a light supper of pâté de foie gras or plovers' eggs, followed by roast chicken, and they always drank champagne.†

Sometimes young men took a party of Gaiety girls to a

* Conversations with Mrs Mirabel Topham and Miss Trixie Hope, who were Gaiety girls.

† Reeve.

Covent Garden fancy dress ball. These balls, which started about midnight after the opera had finished, were a most charming feature of London life in the nineties. Augustus Harris, who managed the Opera House, had a special dancing floor built which covered the entire auditorium. The nobility and the plutocrats hired boxes for the night and gave elaborate supper parties in retiring rooms adjoining their boxes. The ordinary revellers, all in masks and fancy dress, thronged the Grand Foyer where supper was served to them by a host of waiters. Champagne popped and they tucked in to chicken or salmon mayonnaise. The young ones ran up and down the staircases in mad chases, and raced in and out of the dancers on the floor, sometimes getting tangled up with the musicians in the orchestra.*

Everybody was supposed to keep a mask on till after supper, and it was understood that all the nice girls went to the ball with a male escort. Any girl who came on her own got picked up smartly by one of the gay sparks out for a bit of fun. At Covent Garden balls people let themselves go and danced all through the night. Young men in the boxes kissed their girls ardently, and all sorts of romantic vows were exchanged in the course of the night.

Seymour Hicks, an habitué of the balls, liked to look down on the floor from a height when the dancing was in full swing. 'It was a sight which for sheer beauty and riot of colour has seldom been equalled in London,' he said.† After the ball was over, the revellers tumbled into hansoms at six o'clock in the morning and were sometimes charged ten times the legal fare.

The mashers adored taking the Gaiety girls out for a day on the river. The usual plan was to rendezvous at Skindles Hotel, Maidenhead, and then to take a punt out from Skindles lawn. Mayfair and the theatre world thoroughly enjoyed spending their Sundays on the Thames; the eleven o'clock train from Paddington to Maidenhead was always full of attractive young women, dressed up to perfection, escorted by dashing young men in well creased flannels and straw boaters with Varsity ribbons on them, looking like the last word from Savile Row.

Seymour Hicks affectionately recalled the pleasures of the riverside in the nineties. Hours on the river sped by unnoticed

* Pope, *Carriages at Eleven* (Hutchinson, 1947).
† Hicks, *Vintage Years* (Cassell, 1943).

by the amorous couples in their cushioned punts, safely moored in silent Thames backwaters. In the evening all the boats cast off and people went to dinner at Skindles, where the food and wines were excellent but the bill could be excessive.

Most of the couples took the train back to London after dinner. But any man who had a carriage and pair would drive his sweetheart to the Star and Garter at Richmond, which welcomed them beneath fairy lights that made its balconies an enchanted place.*

Ada Reeve, who had played opposite Seymour Hicks as the Shop Girl, and knew George Edwardes very well over two decades, said he was like the father of a big family. He took a great interest in the welfare of the Gaiety girls: when he discovered some of them could not afford a proper lunch, he arranged with Romano's that any girl from the Gaiety could get her lunch there at half-price. Edwardes was a big spender and there was a great rapport between him and the 'Roman'. Romano never minded if his customers wanted to put their bill 'on the slate'; the only thing he forbade was for anyone to query his bill!

A dapper little Italian, Romano dressed faultlessly and had a fine crop of hair which was greying at the temples. He could never master the English language. On one memorable Derby night he stood up on a chair and made a speech which went roughly: 'Shellman, I am very 'appy. My 'orse 'e win! I win tree, four tousand pound! [*Much excitement.*] I 'ave no more ticks! [*Consternation.*] I 'ave no more slates! [*Deep gloom.*] . . . Wot I mean is that those who owes me anything owes me nothings. I watch slate off! [*Immense cheering.*] Next Saturday I stands free breakfast and lunch from ten o'clock. And I am done speaking . . .'†

The right time to go to Romano's was for supper. It had the most mixed clientele in London; apart from the theatre world, you saw peers of the realm there, country squires, racing men, journalists, legal luminaries, businessmen, soldiers, sailors and even explorers. Horatio Bottomley, popular journalist and prince of con men, had his regular table there until he was found out at the Old Bailey in 1922. John Corlett and the staff of the 'Pink 'un' also had their table.

* Hicks, *Vintage Years*.   † Booth, *London Town*.

Nellie Farren, first Queen of the Gaiety, as 'Little Jack Sheppard'

'Practical John' Hollingshead, first
Manager of the Gaiety

The Old Gaiety Theatre in the Strand, 1894

Not Henry Irving, but Fred Leslie as Noirtier in *Monte Cristo Jr*

The famous Gaiety Quartette— Nellie Farren, Edward Terry, Katie Vaughan and Edward Royce—in *The Forty Thieves*

A record-breaking partnership at the Savoy—Richard D'Oyly Carte, the dynamic impresario (*above*), and W. S. Gilbert, autocratic author and producer

'Queen Maria'—Marie Tempest in unusually gentle mood as the Geisha at Daly's

Seymour Hicks and Ellaline Terriss
in *The Circus Girl*

Six delightful Gaiety Girls, as seen through the mashers' opera-glasses
in *The Runaway Girl*

'Just a little bit of string'—Ellaline Terriss's hit song from *The Circus Girl*

Henry Irving in his most famous
role, as Mathias in *The Bells* at the Lyce[um]

Ellen Terry as Portia

George Edwardes 'the Guv'nor' in the nineties, when he had become London's leading impresario of musical plays

George Edwardes's family—his parents (*above*), his daughter Dorothy (*below*) and his wife Julia

The junction of Aldwych and the Strand, showing the New Gaiety
Theatre on the right

Auditorium of the New Gaiety

Gertie Millar as Prudence in *The Quaker Girl* at the Adelphi—'the epitome of musical comedy', said Sir Noël Coward

Connie Ediss in pursuit of her husband (Teddy Payne) in *The Spring Chicken*

Gabs Ray (*left*) dancing her way to stardom in *The Orchid,* and Gladys Cooper starting a long and illustrious career in *Havana*

Lily Elsie as Sonia and Joe Coyne as Prince Danilo in *The Merry Widow*

The 'Merry Widow Waltz', the most popular single number of the era

George Bernard Shaw, the leading apostle of the New Drama, which reacted against the old melodramatic style

. . . typified here by Beerbohm Tree as Fagin

Everybody who went to Romano's seemed to know each other: J. B. Booth, a pillar of the 'Pink 'un', said that Romano's 'had the merriest gatherings of good fellows—and that included ladies—that ever came together in a mere eating establishment'.

There was a great kudos about getting into the Gaiety chorus; hundreds of girls used to turn up at the stage door every week to audition for the Guv'nor's London shows and touring companies. Constance Collier had arrived there one day, desperate to get a job: she was only fifteen, but was trying hard to look older in her mother's dress. Jimmy Jupp at the stage door was so impressed by her dark beauty and charm that he broke a rule and introduced her to the Guv'nor, who happened to come through the swing doors just at the right moment.

George Edwardes, very taken with Constance Collier, invited her to have tea with him. Discovering that she was under age, he arranged to meet her again with her mother, a touring actress, who gave her consent to Constance going to the Gaiety. But George Edwardes would not let her appear on the stage until he had 'groomed' her, which meant she was given an intensive course of lessons in elocution, singing, dancing and fencing. George did his utmost to glorify the Gaiety girls; years later his example was followed by Flo Ziegfeld on Broadway when training his girls for the Ziegfeld Follies.

Constance Collier had started in the chorus of *The Shop Girl*, but the Guv'nor at once spotted her talent and promoted her to the 'Big Eight'. One evening Constance and the other girls in the 'Big Eight' were invited to a party at the Savoy by some South African magnates. She was too poor to afford a party frock and the right accessories, but waited till the very last moment before refusing such a glamorous invitation. At the end of the performance she returned to the 'Big Eight' dressing-room to find laid out for her an evening dress, petticoats, silk stockings, gloves and a fan—a present from the other girls. 'It was the most wonderful present I ever had,' she wrote.*

The Guv'nor, always on the lookout for new talent for the Gaiety and Daly's, used to send his lieutenants periodically

* Constance Collier, *Harlequinade* (John Lane, 1929).

to see shows in the provinces. If one of them recommended that a certain actress in the provinces should be given a chance in London, he would say in his slow, plaintive voice, 'But would you want to sleep with her?' Unless his lieutenant replied in the affirmative the Guv'nor would not engage her at the Gaiety; he knew from experience that a newcomer would have to be an absolute stunner to bring in the 'carriage trade'. Whenever George Edwardes brought an artist into London he gave her three chances to make good; nearly all of them managed to pass the test.

Although Edwardes was a great showman, his general knowledge was abysmal. Once, when he needed a new number for the Gaiety, he sent for Paul Rubens, the composer, and said, 'Paul, I want you to write something for Miss so-and-so—something sweet and dainty—something like Tolstoy's 'Good-bye'.* His staff had to keep making allowances, too, for his appalling memory. When he needed a new duet for Teddy Payne and Katie Seymour he ordered his stage manager, Dodson, to send for Eustace Miles, who ran a vegetarian restaurant and had no connection whatsoever with the stage. Dodson, very surprised, said, 'Excuse me, sir, do you really want to send for him?'

'Certainly I do—at once—it's about this restaurant scene . . . I want him at once!'

The assistant manager was then sent off in a cab to Eustace Miles's restaurant in Chandos Street. Miles was astonished to see him and protested, 'But I don't know Mr Edwardes at all!'

After the assistant had explained it was something to do with a restaurant scene Eustace Miles consented to go back to the Gaiety with him. Having arrived there, he sat in the stalls while the Guv'nor carried on rehearsing and ignored him.

'Does Mr Edwardes want me or does he not?' Eustace Miles asked impatiently.

The assistant went up to George Edwardes and said, 'He's here, Guv'nor.'

'Who's here?' asked George irritably.

'Eustace Miles.'

'Eustace Miles? What's he doing here?'

'You said you wanted him, Guv'nor.'

* Jupp.

'I said so? I said so? I don't want Eustace Miles. I want
Leslie Stiles to write me a new number for Teddy Payne.'*

He apologized to Eustace Miles, who saw the funny side of it.

The Guv'nor was much too kind for his own good. He was
an 'easy touch' for a hard-luck story and had to stop answering
personally all the begging letters he received, or he would have
given away a fortune. He could never bear to dismiss an
artist and left this unpleasant chore to Pat Malone, his chief
lieutenant. Every year he had to sack chorus girls who had
become too 'old' for the exacting standards of the Gaiety
patrons. George Edwardes would go to the back of the stalls
and put his opera glasses on the girls on the stage to make
sure that they all remained worthy of his chorus line. If a
girl looked past her prime, he would shake his head sorrow-
fully and say to Pat Malone, 'We can't keep so-and-so any
longer!'

But the superannuated chorus girls were crafty females:
after Pat Malone had given them their notice they used to
waylay George Edwardes in the street outside the stage door,
cry on his shoulder and convince him that it would break
their hearts to leave the Gaiety. This upset Edwardes so much
that he would summon his secretary and say, 'Tell Malone
to cancel those girls' notices. Why did he sack them? I've
never said so—it's all a mistake!'† Consequently Pat Malone
had to reinstate the girls in the chorus and, by means of this
ruse, they generally managed to get a year's reprieve.

At the end of every production the Guv'nor gave his principals expensive pieces of furniture which were no longer required. And when a show came off the chorus boys were
entitled to keep the smart suits they had been wearing in it;
these gradually became known as 'God bless you George
Edwardes suits', or simply 'God bless suits'.

George Edwardes had a way of magnifying the importance
of a part when he wanted an artist to play it. He once tried to
persuade George Grossmith, Jr, to play a small part and
started off: 'He's a young man down from Oxford who has
inherited a million and a half from his father. He has a palatial
town house, a château in France, and everything that mortal
man could wish for. He comes through the South African
war and hurries home. He is engaged to a girl in India, but

* Forbes Winslow.   † Pope, *Carriages at Eleven*.

gets involved with one in London. To escape from his troubles he goes off on a Sunken Treasure Expedition——'

'But just a minute, Mr Edwardes, does he do all this in the play?' asked Grossmith.

'Well, not exactly. To tell you the truth I haven't read the piece properly yet, but I think he only comes on at the end of the first act.'*

George Grossmith, Jr, who was generally called Gee-Gee, had little in common with Teddy Payne, although they always sang a duet together at the Gaiety. Teddy Payne was a Cockney of mature years, while Gee-Gee looked and behaved just like a masher; off the stage Gee-Gee was a bon viveur, while Teddy Payne was as sober as a judge. However, they sometimes had a glass of port and a bun together at Shorts in the Strand.

One day Teddy Payne told Gee-Gee he was going to take him to the Athenaeum for a glass of port. Gee-Gee was amazed; the Athenaeum was considered the most exclusive club in London and he could not imagine how Teddy Payne became a member.

'Do you mean the Club?' he asked incredulously.

'Thertainly,' lisped Payne, 'they have the betht glath of port in London there.'

Gee-Gee followed the little man cautiously into Pall Mall, but instead of entering the noble portico of the Athenaeum Club, Teddy Payne led the way down some steps into the basement area. Then he said to Gee-Gee with a perfectly straight face, 'The head waiter is a particular fwiend of mine and always thaves me a glath of port.'†

Gee-Gee laughed his head off—it was the only time Teddy Payne had ever made him laugh off the stage!

The Guv'nor started a new interest in 1898 when he registered his racing colours: turquoise blue and white chevrons and turquoise cap. He had his horses trained at Ogbourne Maisey near Marlborough by his brother, Major John Edwardes, and ran them at first in the name of Mr George Widdup, using his mother's maiden name. But within a year he was racing under his own name and had acquired a big string of racehorses at Ogbourne. Horse racing, which had been one of Edwardes's favourite sports for a long time, became the most important interest in his life, apart from the theatre. He would bet heavily

* Grossmith.   † Grossmith.

on one of his horses if he thought it stood a fair chance, and also had big wagers on other horses. Julia caught the betting fever from him and got into the habit of putting £5 each way on a horse in every race at the principal meetings. Since she picked most of her horses with a pin she rarely had a winning week. However, one Monday morning she received a cheque for £2,000 from Douglas Stuart, the bookmakers. George pocketed it absent-mindedly, thinking it was for him.*

If the Guv'nor thought one of his horses was 'a good thing' he always passed on the tip to his artists at the Gaiety and Daly's and to Jupp and the staff. A friend once asked him why he ran his horses so often on Saturdays. George replied, 'Saturday is the only day when my people have any money and I always like them to have a bit on and win.'†

---

* Conversations with David Sherbrooke.   † Jupp.

10 Sporting and Dramatic

He did not try to belong to any life but his own, and this lay between the Theatre and horses. I once remarked to him that he should be called 'sporting and dramatic'.

ADA REEVE, talking about George Edwardes

All Irishman are supposed to have an affinity with horses, which was certainly the case with George Edwardes. An accomplished horseman, he might have become a champion show jumper like his brother Major John Edwardes—but he could never afford the time. There was nothing he liked better than getting up on a horse and, since his theatres kept him in London so much of the time, he often went out for a canter in Rotten Row. In the summer he enjoyed taking the reins and driving out of town in his phaeton, and generally managed to go over to Ireland for the Dublin Horse Show, his usual procedure being to take one of his touring companies to the Gaiety Theatre, Dublin, for the appropriate fortnight in August.

No power on earth could have stopped him going to the Derby. His old friend, Chance Newton of the *Referee*, once made an appointment to see him on the first Wednesday in June, but Edwardes cancelled it at the last moment, saying, 'My dear boy! I am so sorry! But they tell me that tomorrow's the Derby and do you know they want to *make* me go racing!' Chance Newton dined out on the story of anybody having to make George Edwardes go to the Derby!

* H. Chance Newton, *Era*, October 1915.

Half the people in London seemed to go to the Derby in those days. The aristocrats and the gentry took the road to Epsom, and so did the clubmen and the dashing young guardsmen; stockbrokers and other City men took the day off, and one could be sure of meeting hundreds of artists and journalists and members of the theatrical profession, besides costermongers and tramps and a good assortment of acrobats and nigger minstrels.

All ranks and conditions of men mingled together on the racecourse, and all kinds of vehicles travelled down from London. G. A. Sala, the well-known journalist, noticed the regimental drag of the 90th Hussars behind the cart of a little East End tradesman driving down with his 'missus'. An open landau, with four spanking greys and postilions in blue jackets, buckskin and white silk hats, was closely followed by a costermonger and his pal, who were piloting a 'shallow' cart through the seething throng.*

George Edwardes used to drive down with a party of friends in his private coach. With typical generosity, he used to take his friends to any meeting where his horses were running. Lily Langtry was a frequent guest at his racing parties, which generally included Ellaline Terriss and Seymour Hicks, Nellie Farren, Marie Studholme, Letty Lind, Arthur Roberts, Huntley Wright and Willie Warde.

At Ogbourne Maisey, where Major John Edwards ran his racing stable, Edwardes had bought the Manor, a fine Jacobean house, and an estate of 3,000 acres. He also began to breed racehorses on a large scale at Ballikisteen near Dublin. He could never persuade Julia to come and stay at Ogbourne; she declared she couldn't bear the place—it was 'full of stable boys and pewter skies'. She preferred to spend her weekends with the children and her own circle of friends at Winkfield Lodge.

Edwardes followed the progress of his racehorses with an enthusiasm which never flagged. He made regular tours of the stables with his brother, and sometimes got up at six o'clock in the morning and went out in his pyjamas to watch the horses in a special training gallop.†

Santoi, the best horse he ever owned, was entered for the

* G. A. Sala, *London Up to Date* (A. & C. Black, 1896).
† Conversations with David Sherbrooke.

Kempton Jubliee on 11 May 1901 after he had won some good races. The Jubilee was over a mile and a quarter, and Santoi was being specially trained for the Ascot Gold Cup, a race of two and a half miles; so Edwardes was afraid a mile and a quarter might be too short for him. On the day of the race the Guv'nor was rehearsing a show at Daly's, but had arranged to leave the theatre before lunch to go to Kempton and watch Santoi run. Before leaving the theatre, he spoke to his staff and the artists.

. . . 'Now, boys and girls, ladies and gentlemen, I expect you want to know about Santoi in the Jubilee. . . . Well, all I can tell you is that he is trying . . . I don't say he'll win, but he is out to try . . . I think we shall get a place. So, if you like, back it both ways. I don't think you'll lose. Good morning.'*

The rehearsal broke up the moment the Guv'nor left, and everybody started to scribble out their bets on Santoi. Pat Malone, the producer, the actors and actresses, musicians, carpenters, stage hands, electricians, firemen—all of them had a flutter. A shower of betting-slips was handed to Alfred, the call boy, who hurried off with them to the nearest bookie.

There was no rehearsal at Daly's at the time of the race that afternoon because all the leading lights were in the office upstairs, clustered round the tape machine. Pat Malone was there with Emilie Reed, George Edwardes's invaluable secretary, and so was G. Edwards minor, his namesake, who had joined the Guv'nor after leaving the D'Oyly Carte management. E. Biggs, the accountant, and H. W. Anderson, the box-office manager, had also taken a little time off. Everybody in the theatre was agog to know how Santoi was faring in the Jubilee. The news came through on the tape that Santoi had won at 25-1, and a great cheer went up that could be heard outside in Leicester Square.

On the day Santoi won the Jubilee Handicap, Julia was away at the seaside. But she had wired George Edwardes at Kempton, asking, 'Do we back ours today?' He had replied cautiously, 'No, on no account.' However, Julia was convinced he was pulling her leg, put a fiver each way on Santoi and had a good win for a change.†

The *Sporting Times* often chronicled the activities of George Edwardes. This piece, which appeared in the pink paper the

* Winslow.   † Conversations with David Sherbrooke.

week after the Jubilee, gives one an insight into his London life:

> There was nothing but luck for the Gaiety manager all last week. He won every night at 'solo', he bought for a third of its value a big picture of tigers that will presently be seen at the Gaiety Theatre and he was given a cob . . . that you will presently see him cavorting on in Rotten Row. . . . On top of all came the Great Jubilee Handicap and now he is on the look-out for the Ascot Gold Cup.

Santoi was made favourite at 11–10 for the Ascot Gold Cup, the most famous race for staying colts in the racing calendar. The Gold Cup of 1901 took place in heavy rain. Santoi was ridden by F. Rickaby, his regular jockey; Kilmarnock II, an American horse, was made second favourite and seemed to be the principal danger to Edwardes's horse.

Santoi started at the back of the field. At the Bricklins he began to improve his position, and as they rounded the bend he took second place. Soon after they started going uphill Kilmarnock II began to creep up on the outside, and many people began shouting him the winner. In the straight Santoi and Kilmarnock II battled it out, neck and neck. Then Rickaby called on Santoi for a final effort; his horse responded gallantly and passed the post a length in front of Kilmarnock II.

Julia was standing behind George Edwardes in his box at Ascot as Santoi sailed home. Hundreds of delighted punters shouted, 'Good old Guv'nor! He's done it!' A large contingent of the theatrical profession joined in the chorus of cheering. Edwardes was surrounded by a multitude of friends and well-wishers and smothered with congratulations. 'Mr Edwardes is a good sportsman and bore the laurels of a victor with imperturbable serenity,' reported the *Sporting Life*.*

Sometimes there was a clash between the Guv'nor's sporting and dramatic interests. He decided he must go to Ascot one Friday, and instructed Jimmy Jupp, the stage door keeper, to take the train down from Waterloo and meet him by Tattersall's on the racecourse. Jupp travelled down with a suitcase full of cheques for the Gaiety staff and the artists. As soon as the Guv'nor had signed them, Jupp hurried off and caught the next train back to town.

* *Sporting Life*, June 1901.

The Gaiety had now become a limited company with George Edwardes as managing director and Walter Pallant, a Stock Exchange man, in the chair. The principal shareholder was Alfred de Rothschild, the youngest of the three Rothschild brothers who had also helped to finance Sir Henry Irving at the Lyceum. 'Mr Alfred' was rather short; he dressed in perfect taste and wore vivid scarlet carnations in his buttonhole. Alfred de Rothschild was also the principal backer of the Empire Theatre, Leicester Square, which George Edwardes managed jointly with Augustus Harris.

During the nineties the Guv'nor's productions at the Gaiety, Daly's and elsewhere kept him busy till all hours of the night; sometimes he would make an appointment to see his dentist at one o'clock in the morning. He often made changes in a show that was still running at the Gaiety or Daly's. He would tell all the people concerned, 'Come to the office after the show,' which meant a meeting at his big office in Lisle Street. He held conferences there any time between 11.30 p.m. and 2 a.m. with his stage manager and his authors, composers and lyric-writers.

The Guv'nor used to stroll up and down the office, alternately smoking a cigar, a pipe or a cigarette. He listened to what everyone had to say, but gave himself the casting vote on any suggestion. If he disagreed with anyone he never said so directly; but he would suddenly change the subject and tell an author or composer about an exciting horse race or a first night in Vienna or a new cure for insomnia. Another of his ploys was to tell the author—or composer—that he was not looking his best and brightest, and be recommending him to take Malvern water right away and to eat a pound of green apples every day.*

His liaison with Miriam Clements had come to an end when she married a Guards officer. It was no problem for Edwardes to find another woman to console him: before long he was having an affair with Florence Collingbourne, Marie Tempest's attractive understudy.

The Runaway Girl, his next production at the Gaiety, was by Seymour Hicks and Harry Nichols; Hicks also produced it, but did not appear in it, and the score was again by Ivan Caryll and Lionel Monckton. Produced on 21 May 1898 *The*

* Forbes Winslow.

Runaway Girl was another big winner. This notice appeared in the *Era*:

> *The Runaway Girl* has an ingenue role for Miss Terriss, a low comedy part for Miss Connie Ediss; and a character in which Mr Edmund Payne can disport himself to the delight of the audience, assisted by Miss Katie Seymour in duet and dance. Without these necessaries no musical play at the Gaiety would be considered complete . . . the story is garnished with musical numbers and dances and served up in chef Edwardes's best style. . . .
>
> Mr Edmund Payne's gifts of talent and person are always sufficient to create ecstatic merriment at the Gaiety. Miss Connie Ediss . . . is unrivalled in giving full point to the lines of a song. Miss Terriss, ever sweet, and fascinatingly fresh and dainty, exercised her usual spell on the Gaiety audience.

Lionel Monckton composed a number entitled 'The Boy Guessed Right' for Ellaline Terriss, which was a big hit. But his most popular song was 'Soldiers in the Park', whose chorus is still being played:

> Oh, listen to the band
> How merrily they play!
> Oh, don't you think it grand?
> Hear everybody say:
> 'Oh, listen to the band.'
> To the shout of 'Here they come'
> And the banging of the drum,
> Oh, listen to the soldiers in the Park.

This number was put over with great panache by Grace Palotta. Inspired by a typical London scene, it conveyed the feeling of the great trees and the green lawns in Hyde Park when the season was in full swing. While a Guards band played it, the soldiers marched on to the stage in their red coats and bearskins with all the Victorian pride in military pomp.

Lionel Monckton had a rather supercilious manner and a sarcastic tongue. This grave, sombre bachelor seemed a fish out of water at the Gaiety, yet he wrote some of the most melodious stage music since Sir Arthur Sullivan. He had an odd habit of standing near the pit or the gallery doors of the theatre with a little counting machine in his pocket which registered the number of people who came in for the matinées and evening performances. Perhaps he was trying to check up on his weekly royalties from the Guv'nor.

Seymour Hicks had left the Gaiety to join Charles Frohman, the American impresario, as an actor-producer. Though still in his twenties, Hicks was already a brilliant man of the theatre: he was a light comedy star, a producer, and had written dramas, comedies and musical comedies. Later on, the Hicks Theatre in Shaftesbury Avenue was named after him.

It was obvious that Nellie Farren would never be able to resume her career on the stage. She had put up money for an ill-fated theatrical venture and fallen on hard times, and when this became known the profession organized an all-star charity matinée of *Trial by Jury* at the Savoy for her benefit. Arthur Roberts was amongst the stars who appeared as members of the Jury. W. S. Gilbert was invited to produce his own piece and made a bad start by keeping all the artists waiting at the first rehearsal and not apologizing for being late.

Gilbert spotted Arthur Roberts among the jurymen and said arrogantly, 'I must tell you, Mr Roberts, we don't allow any gagging in this theatre.' 'I quite understand, sir,' said Roberts meekly.* Gilbert had no inkling that Arthur Roberts might be 'spoofing' him. The comedian was as good as gold at rehearsals and all went smoothly up to the day of the matinée.

When the curtain rose on *Trial by Jury* the audience were intrigued to notice a revolting pair of old boots hanging up outside the jury box with a message chalked up, 'Call me at 7.' They belonged, of course, to Arthur Roberts, who seemed to be asleep in the box. In fact, he was snoring so heavily that he almost drowned the words of Gilbert's witty verses.

Suddenly Arthur Roberts woke up and started to eat a bag of whelks. The audience, already distracted by his behaviour, gazed in fascination as he started to juggle with the whelk shells. All the house were in fits of laughter—not at Gilbert's piece, but at Arthur Roberts! Behind the scenes W. S. Gilbert had gone white with anger, and shouted at Roberts to stop

* Roberts

it at once and leave the stage. But the comedian took no notice of him and continued to gag in the jury box right up to the moment when the jurors made their exit, which was almost at the end of the opera.

In the summer of 1899 the Guv'nor had a very busy time rehearsing *San Toy* at Daly's with Marie Tempest in the name part. The piece bore some resemblance to *The Geisha*: in the former a British officer had philandered with a Japanese girl and in this one a British officer made a pass at a Chinese girl, San Toy. The libretto was by Edward Morton, the score by Sidney Jones and the amusing lyrics by Adrian Ross and Harry Greenbank.

Adrian Ross wrote most of the lyrics for the Guv'nor's shows at the Gaiety and Daly's. He had once been a Cambridge don, and still looked like one when he peered through his spectacles. He was a solemn individual and, like Lionel Monckton, seemed to live in a different world to the Guv'nor's. When he first came to the Gaiety he had been so shy that if a chorus girl spoke to him at a rehearsal he ran away into a corner.

During rehearsals for *San Toy* the Guv'nor's difficulties with 'Maria' Tempest reached their climax. First, she insisted on wearing a red wig when all the other actresses were wearing black ones. Then she upset the other artists by telling them where they should stand and when they should exit, and behaving as if she was the producer. Ada Reeve, who had signed a new contract with the Guv'nor, had hoped to play San Toy; she was most disappointed when Edwardes gave her the secondary role of Dudley, a pert ladies' maid. It made matters worse when Marie Tempest started to order her about at rehearsals and she decided to go and see the Guv'nor.

'My dear Ada, you look tired and ill!' he exclaimed before she had a chance to say a word about Marie. 'You're not taking enough care of yourself, are you? Now you mustn't lose your looks, you know.'

'But I came here——' she began.

Edwardes interrupted and doled her out a box of his wonder pills; then he politely showed her out of the office before she could register her complaint.*

In the last weeks of rehearsals Marie Tempest declared that

* Reeve.

she would *never* wear the correct long Chinese trousers as San Toy. She took her trousers home with her, cut them down overnight, and appeared at the dress rehearsal in short trousers. When she made her first entrance the Guv'nor lost his temper and shouted: 'If you won't wear the costumes you are given, you must leave Daly's!'

'All right, I'll go,' she said calmly.*

George Edwardes was shattered that she had called his bluff. But Marie Tempest had made up her mind to leave Daly's, mainly because she couldn't bear acting any longer with comedians like Huntley Wright, who chopped up musical plays to suit their own ends, and often ruined the effect of the music. Another reason was that her husband, Cosmo Gordon Lennox, had convinced her that she ought to quit the musical stage at this point and then concentrate on establishing herself as a legitimate actress.

San Toy had a most unlucky first night on 2 October 1899. London had a pea-souper and consequently Daly's Theatre was half empty when the curtain rose: the fog was so fierce that it penetrated the auditorium and made it impossible for the audience to see half the stage. However, the performance went without a hitch and was very well received. It was undoubtedly one of the finest spectacles the Guv'nor had ever produced, although Joseph Harker's gorgeous Chinese settings and the marvellous costumes were partly obscured by the fog.

Everyone connected with the show feared it would be a failure because the house had only been half full, but George Edwardes remained unperturbed. One of his staff asked him next morning if he intended to revamp *San Toy*.

'Certainly not,' he replied. 'It is perfect as it stands and will be a big success.'†

Edwardes proved to be right: the notices were first class and *San Toy* went on to run for two years. The *Daily Chronicle* said:

For the stage on which it is produced there are all the elements of success in *San Toy*. The patrons of Daly's require a bright story, graceful music, with a strong infusion of sentiment, and magnificent spectacle. These were all forthcoming on Saturday night. . . . Unquestionably there is considerable humour in Mr Edward Morton's neatly-

* Forbes Winslow.   † Forbes Winslow.

written book. . . . The thick yellow mist of course prevented the delicate tints of the costumes being seen to proper advantage, though it was manifest that in this respect the Chinese piece excelled its predecessors at Daly's. . . .

The lyrics (by Adrian Ross and Harry Greenbank) are quaint and always thoroughly singable. They have been excellently treated by Mr Sidney Jones, who is quite as much at his ease penning a refined ballad as in increasing the effect of a song intended to make the audience laugh. . . .

Considerable fun resulted from the appearance of Yen How, the mandarin, with his six little wives . . . Mr Rutland Barrington made the most of a song 'Six Little Wives' constructed in 'The Ten Little Niggers' pattern. . . . Altogether the comedian is well suited, and he has capital support in the . . . representatives of the wives. Their scenes together are funny enough to live in the memory. As Li . . . a very amusing Chinese attendant, Mr Huntley Wright sang, acted and danced with a spirit that was speedily communicated to the audience. He was droll throughout, and, as usual, worked indefatigably. To their respective tasks Miss Marie Tempest and Mr Hayden Coffin brought experience and perfect vocal fitness. They had duets together . . . which the patrons of Daly's always expect. . . .

Rutland Barrington, who had left the Gilbert and Sullivan revivals at the Savoy to join George Edwardes, revelled in the part of Yen How and sang:

Oh, my name is Yen How—
I'm a mandarin great
And this is my famous umbrella of State,
And these are the robes that my office contrives,
And *these*, if you please, are my six little wives.

Marie Tempest left the cast of San Toy a few months after its première. This consummate actress soon mastered the transition from musical plays to legitimate ones, and she became a leading comedy actress in the new century. The Guv'nor decided to replace her with Florence Collingbourne, her understudy, who made a great hit as San Toy. His affair with Florence Collingbourne had come to an end because she was getting married. But Edwardes had a shock when she told him she intended to retire from the stage as soon as she was married.

He decided that the new San Toy should be Ada Reeve, who was already playing in the show; this entailed a certain risk, because though Ada Reeve could certainly act the part, he was not certain if she had the voice to do justice to Sidney Jones's light operatic score. Ada Reeve felt as nervous as a kitten on the first night, particularly as the Guv'nor was watching her from his box. But she gave a wonderful performance which captivated the audience, and sang almost as well as her predecessors.

The Guv'nor was so pleased with her that he sent round this note to her dressing room after the show:

MY DEAR ADA REEVE,
    I can't leave the theatre without letting you know how delighted I am with your performance to-night. I only hope you are as pleased as I am.
                                    GEORGE EDWARDES.*

When *The Runaway Girl* came off at the Gaiety, Ellaline Terriss told the Guv'nor that she was leaving his management because she was going to join her husband, Seymour Hicks, in his theatrical ventures with Charles Frohman. The Guv'nor took this very badly indeed: she was not only his favourite leading lady, but also the daughter of his great friend Bill Terriss. Edwardes believed—quite wrongly—that Seymour Hicks had put pressure on her to leave the Gaiety. The truth was that Ellen Terry, who had appointed herself godmother to Ellaline ever since she lost both her parents, had persuaded her to go.

Ellen Terry had put the case in her own unique way. 'Ella, my child, this form of entertainment [*musical comedy*] when you have achieved all you can—as you have—only means standing on top of a ladder, with a hundred young women pulling at your pretty petticoats. Make an end of it.'†

During the run of *San Toy* George Edwardes noticed that one of the chorus girls looked ill. He called her into his office

* Reeve
† Ellaline Terriss, *Just a Little Bit of String* (Hutchinson, 1955).

and said, 'You are not up to the mark, my dear. You must go and see a doctor.'

The doctor informed Edwardes that the girl was in an advanced state of consumption, and a long sea voyage was the only chance of saving her life. Edwardes told her he would pay for her trip to Australia.

'That's awfully good of you, Mr Edwardes,' she said sadly, 'but Mother's sick and I can't leave her at home.'

'Oh, that's all right—you shall both go,' replied Edwardes.

He ordered two return tickets and sent the chorus girl and her mother off to Australia.*

San Toy ran till 1902 at Daly's, and was followed by *The Country Girl*. Evie Greene, its star, had been brought into London by Edwardes after making her name in the provinces. A lovely brunette with the full figure so much admired then, Evie Greene was a talented actress who sang like a prima donna. But she had poor health and, believing that *The Country Girl* could make or break her, she grew increasingly nervous as the first night approached.

On the first night 16 January 1902, she took a stiff drink on an empty stomach to give her confidence before the performance. Rutland Barrington called at her dressing-room to wish her luck and found Evie Greene out for the count. It was impossible to know how long it would take to bring her round! The Guv'nor heard of Evie Greene's collapse just as another crisis blew up: a big staircase set which had been sent back for alterations had not yet arrived at Daly's.

The result of this was that a full house waited in their seats for over an hour before *The Country Girl* began, by which time the pittites and the gallery boys had grown extremely restless and uncomplimentary. The staircase set had turned up at about eight o'clock and behind the scenes the Guv'nor had taken off his coat and worked with the stage hands to make sure they got the set in the right position.

Evie Greene recovered just before nine o'clock. The Guv'nor went straight round to her dressing-room and managed to cheer her up. Then he assured her that everybody in the show was depending on her tonight and he knew she would never let them down; this had a wonderful effect on Evie Greene. After that Edwardes walked calmly on to the stage and made a

* Forbes Winslow.

E

winning little speech in which he apologized for the unfortunate
delay, and this coaxed the audience out of their ugly mood.

The Country Girl was wonderfully received at the end of the
long evening. Although Evie Greene had shown a few signs of
nervousness, her magnificent voice saw her through the
performance. All the principals took their bows, then the
audience yelled: 'We—want—Edwardes!' The Guv'nor walked
on, holding Evie Greene and Hayden Coffin by the hand, to a
storm of cheers.

Within a week Evie Greene had settled down to the part of
Nan, the country girl, and was regularly encored when she
sang 'Molly the Marchioness', her comedy number. Hayden
Coffin had a typical role as a susceptible Naval Commander who
came ashore to stand for Parliament. Huntley Wright played
his more or less trusty servant and scored a hit with 'Yo ho,
little girls', a light-hearted warning to the village girls to
beware of men.

Rutland Barrington pleased the public as the Rajah of
Bhong, an Eastern potentate who travelled everywhere with
his numerous wives. This was a sort of reprise for Barrington, as
he had already appeared with six little wives in *San Toy*.
Barrington felt that perhaps it might be bad for his reputation if
he got type-cast as a bigamist, so he went and had a talk
with the Guv'nor about it. He had known George Edwardes a
long time—ever since he had joined D'Oyly Carte as a young
man in 1878—and regarded him as an expert on the psychology
of the British public.

Edwardes soon put his mind at rest. 'They don't give a
damn what you do, Rutty, as long as they just see you!' he
explained.*

* Rutland Barrington, *Rutland Barrington* (Grant Richards,
1908).

11 Farewell, Old Gaiety

In a few minutes Mr Edwardes will close the doors of the old Gaiety for ever . . . and in a few weeks he will open the doors of the new Gaiety to a flood of popularity and prosperity.

SIR HENRY IRVING,
speech at the last night of the old Gaiety,
4 July 1903

By the turn of the century the Gaiety Theatre had become out of date; in any case the old playhouse in the Strand was under sentence of demolition by the London County Council on account of a scheme to widen the Strand and to build a new road from Kingsway to the Strand, which was to be called Aldwych. The London County Council scheme provided fair compensation for the theatre and granted permission for a new Gaiety Theatre and restaurant to be built on the corner of the junction of the Strand and Aldwych.

The Toreador, which had opened at the Gaiety in the summer of 1901, was still playing to crowded houses in its second year so the Guv'nor decided to wait until the end of its run before pulling down the theatre. James P. Tanner had written a 'book', with situations as far-fetched as ever, but the tuneful songs and fantastic dances easily carried *The Toreador* to success. Teddy Payne had a marvellous part as a 'tiger', the name given to a footman who used to sit on the box of a phaeton wearing full livery. Payne got mistaken for a famous toreador and was forced to go into a Spanish bull ring, then got embroiled in a Carlist plot and was ordered to throw a lot of bombs. The delectable Marie Studholme played a Ward in Chancery who persuaded her best friend (Ethel Sidney) to dress up in men's clothes and masquerade as her husband in order to keep fortune-hunters at bay.

George Grossmith, Jr, distinguished himself as Sir Archibald Slackitt, Bart, of the Guards, a young man about town. The lyric of his 'Everybody's Awfully Good to Me' by Paul Rubens had a flavour of early Bertie Wooster:

I'm an awfully simple fellow
As I'm sure you'll all agree,
And I really don't know what
My various friends see in me:
My acquaintances are endless
And their names I quite forget.
The one half I only know by sight
And the rest I've never met.

But everybody's awfully good to me,
Don't you know.
I'm just about as spoilt as I can be,
Don't you know.
If I go to Prince's and alone I chance to dine,
Why, it's ten to one I meet some dear old Oxford friend of mine,
Well, not only does he join me, but he orders all the wine,
Everybody's awfully good to me!

The Toreador ran for 675 performances and notched up another new record for the Gaiety. The *Daily Chronicle* said, 'There is more pleasure in a Gaiety piece—more melody for Londoners and the dwellers in our great cities . . . than in all the wretched problem and society-scandal plays that were ever hatched. . . .'

The Guv'nor's main object as a theatre manager was obviously to produce 'winners'—his name for his successes—but it was also important to discover new stars for the future. In *The Toreador* Gertie Millar played the small part of Cora Bellamy, the bridesmaid who always outshone the bride. Gertie Millar's charm and freshness crossed the footlights and she made a highly promising debut, helped by two numbers specially written for her by Lionel Monckton. One of them was 'Captivating Cora':

Cora, Cora, captivating Cora,
Just a little bridesmaid for you all,
With a little smile-ah
Walking down the aisle-ah
Captivating Cora makes the bride look small.

Her other number, which had a very catchy melody, was entitled 'Keep off the Grass'. Gertie Millar put over her songs in a tiny, reed-like voice; her strong sense of comedy and her graceful dancing made her an instant favourite with the Gaiety patrons. The Guv'nor, who desperately needed a leading lady to take the place of Ellaline Terriss, recognized that Gertie Millar had star quality.

Yet she had only been given her chance through the persistence of Lionel Monckton, who had seen her at Bradford in *The Messenger Boy* and been so impressed with the way she had sung his number 'Maisie' that he went round afterwards to congratulate her. This reserved bachelor of forty had fallen in love with her at first sight; he gave her advice about stage technique and paid for her to have lessons in elocution to tone down her strong Yorkshire accent. When Monckton returned to London he saw the Guv'nor about *The Toreador*, but spent most of the time raving about Gertie Millar. He knew that she had the makings of a big star, but it was hard work persuading the Guv'nor to bring her down to London.

During the run of *The Toreador*, Lionel Monckton proposed to Gertie Millar and she accepted him. They were married shortly after, and he composed nearly all her numbers throughout her career.

The Lyceum Theatre, like its neighbour, the Gaiety, had become old fashioned by 1900. Sir Henry Irving was faced with the alternatives of either rebuilding it or completely modernizing it, but knew only too well that he could afford to do neither. He was over sixty and tired out by forty strenuous years as an actor. He had had a crippling setback in 1898 when a fire at Southwark destroyed the scenery and properties of forty-four of the plays in his repertory. Scenery worth £30,000 had been burnt underneath the arches of the old Chatham and Dover Railway, and thus he lost all the resources on which he had been relying to support himself before he retired, for he had been counting on acting mainly in revivals of his most popular plays and producing very few new ones.

After the fire at Southwark he was persuaded by his friends, the Comyns Carrs to let them form a syndicate to relieve him of all financial responsibilities at the Lyceum. He gave the syndicate his exclusive services and in return he received a capital sum. The Lyceum became a public company and virtually took over his theatre. By this time Irving and Ellen Terry had begun to lose their drawing power and the new arrangement turned out to have been a fatal mistake.

In the Edwardian era Sir Henry Irving found it very hard to compete with Herbert Beerbohm Tree at His Majesty's. The serious playgoing public had switched their custom from Irving to Tree, and his magnificent productions of Shakespeare and of poetic playwrights like Stephen Phillips nearly always played to packed houses.

Trying to forget all about his misfortunes, Irving kept very late hours at the Garrick Club with his friend, J. L. Toole. He had always been fond of a drink, but now he began taking too many.

In the spring of 1902 Sir Henry Irving unveiled a memorial window to Richard D'Oyly Carte at the Chapel Royal, Savoy. George Edwardes's old chief had died the previous year, only a few months after Sir Arthur Sullivan. It was a bitterly cold day for the ceremony at the Chapel Royal and Irving caught a chill. Unfortunately he had been invited by Beerbohm Tree to a banquet at His Majesty's the following night, after the première of *Ulysses* by Stephen Phillips. Irving went to the banquet because he felt he couldn't possibly refuse an invitation from his chief rival at the last moment.

Beerbohm Tree delighted in entertaining his guests at the Dome, which he had built at the top of his beautiful theatre. Sir Henry Irving drank far too much champagne at the party. In the early hours of the morning, when the guests started to leave, Tree noticed that Irving was still sitting in his chair, fast asleep: the great actor was as tight as a tick. There was no love lost between Tree and Irving, but as Irving was his guest, Tree felt responsible for his welfare. He asked several people in his company to see the old man home, but all of them refused.

So he called a cab and dropped his rival in Stratton Street outside his flat.

As Tree drove away, he saw Irving striding up and down the street, declaiming, 'We must keep the oriflamme burning.' The oriflamme was the sacred banner of the Abbey of St-Denis; Irving regarded it as the symbol of his constant struggle to keep the Lyceum going.

A few days later Irving was supping at the Garrick Club when somebody mentioned Beerbohm Tree. 'Hm . . . a good fellow, Tree—clever actor, too,' said Irving. 'A pity he . . . er . . . drinks!'*

Later that year Beerbohm Tree asked Sir Henry Irving if he would temporarily release Ellen Terry from her contract so that she could appear in his all-star production of *The Merry Wives of Windsor*. Irving agreed to let her go, though it was galling to think of his Ellen Terry gracing Tree's company. However, he sent her a telegram on the first night: '*Heaven send you many merry days and nights.* HENRY.'

Although Henry Irving seldom went to see his fellow actors in a play, he made an exception in the case of his best friend, J. L. Toole, and watched him bring the house down in a light comedy entitled *Walker, London* at Toole's Theatre in February 1892. The author was J. M. Barrie, a young Scotsman who had made his name with his novel *The Little Minister*. *Walker, London* had a glorious part for Toole as a rascal of a barber who fled from his bride and took shelter in a houseboat on the Thames, where he posed as a great explorer and proposed to all the pretty girls. He had a habit of sending telegrams to himself, addressed WALKER, LONDON. The critics called Barrie a born playwright, and the public gave his play a very long run.

W. S. Penley was the shining star of *Charley's Aunt*, a farce by Brandon Thomas produced at the Royalty Theatre in February 1892. The audiences were bowled over when the little comedian impersonated Donna Luiza, the aunt from Brazil, wearing a black silk gown over his trousers. Penley was the pivot of the play, but it was a well-written piece with comic opportunities for all characters. *Charley's Aunt* gave W. S. Penley the part of a lifetime; even eighty years later one can be sure that this perennial farce is being played somewhere in the world.

* Irving.

The Second Mrs Tanqueray, Pinero's most famous play, was produced by George Alexander at the elegant St James's Theatre in May 1893. Mrs Patrick Campbell played Paula, the woman with a past, in this tragic drama. She married the conventional Mr Tanqueray, but when the past caught up with her and shattered her dream of respectable married bliss, she couldn't face life and committed suicide. Mrs Pat's magnificent portrayal of Paula won her recognition as an actress of outstanding quality. George Alexander gave a polished performance as Tanqueray but the play belonged to Mrs Campbell.

Mrs Patrick Campbell had been 'discovered' by Alexander, but this maddening woman rewarded him by laughing at his acting. He wrote her a polite note: 'Mr George Alexander presents his compliments to Mrs Campbell and would be obliged if she will not laugh at him on the stage in future.' She replied: 'Mrs Campbell presents her compliments to Mr Alexander and informs him she does not laugh at him on the stage, but waits till she gets home.' George Alexander believed in absolute politeness when dealing with his patrons at the St James's Theatre. Enormous hats for women were the fashion then, and Alexander tried to persuade them to remove their bonnets by inserting a notice in his programmes:

Mr George Alexander would respectfully request those ladies who frequent the St James's Theatre intent on viewing the performance to recollect the similar purpose in those who sit behind them. If therefore every large hat were left in the Cloak Room . . . the lady so doing would confer a great benefit on her immediate neighbours.

Pinero's next major play, *The Notorious Mrs Ebbsmith*, was produced at the Garrick Theatre in March 1895. Mrs Campbell again played the title role and fascinated audiences by the power of her emotional acting. This drama was considered Pinero's masterpiece by many of the critics. Mrs Ebbsmith, a strong-minded woman who had been pursued by scandal, formed a relationship with a married man in Venice. The latter was a weak character and his family did all they could to break up the romance; eventually they succeeded, thanks to a clergyman who arrived at the villa with his Bible. The unhappy ending was less tragic than *Mrs Tanqueray*. Mrs Patrick

Campbell was superb, and Forbes Robertson triumphed as the weak hero in the hardest part. John Hare was perfect as the Duke, the hero's cynical uncle.

Beerbohm Tree produced *Trilby*, by George du Maurier, at the Haymarket in October 1895. He was praised to the skies for his playing of Svengali, the rascally musician who hypnotized Trilby into a great singer. His make-up was astonishingly clever and audiences gazed in awe at this weird, uncanny, unkempt white-faced scoundrel. There was no more interesting villain on the stage than Svengali, said Clement Scott. Though it was Tree's greatest success, he himself called the piece 'hogwash'.

Wilson Barrett produced *The Sign of the Cross*, a melodrama with a religious theme, at the Lyric in January 1896. He was the author and also starred in it as Marcus Superbus, a noble young Roman in Nero's time who rescued a lovely Christian girl, fell in love with her, and was converted to Christianity. Nero condemned the girl to death unless she gave up her religion. She refused, and the play ended with Marcus and the girl going hand in hand into the arena. This very well constructed piece made a fine spectacle; Wilson Barrett gave a marvellous performance and the public adored every moment of it.

George Alexander presented *The Prisoner of Zenda* at the St James's in January 1896, adapted from Anthony Hope's novel by Edward Rose. George Alexander had a field day, playing three different parts in this cloak and sword melodrama. He was a courtier in the prologue, then doubled as Rudolf Rassendyll, the hero, and the drunken king Rudolf. Alexander directed this piece at a rattling pace and made the cardboard characters come to life, aided by a fine cast. The public loved the spectacle and always cheered when Alexander took on the entire Ruritanian army and made mincemeat of them.

Charles Wyndham, the actor-manager, was an incomparable light comedian and the comedies of Henry Arthur Jones fitted him like a glove. *The Liars*, produced at the Criterion in October 1897, was a comedy with an element of tragedy. Most of the characters were the liars of society who had taken a wrong turning until Sir Christopher Dearing (Charles Wyndham) came along, talked them out of their follies and put them on the right road. Wyndham as a gay, worldly bachelor dominated the piece and was always interesting. Mary Moore was outstanding as a foolish society woman playing with fire. The satire rang true and was biting and there were many witty lines.

J. M. Barrie's brilliant adaptation of *The Little Minister* was produced at the Haymarket in November 1897. His sentimental piece was beautifully interpreted by its two stars. Winifred Emery made an ideal 'Lady Babbie', and Cyril Maude carried off the role of the Rev. Gavin Dishart most admirably. His love scene with Lady Babbie drew vast enthusiasm from the audiences.

In 1897 Sir Augustus Harris presented *The Babes in the Wood* as the Drury Lane pantomime. Dan Leno and Herbert Campbell appeared as the two babes; Herbert Campbell was an extremely fat girl and Dan Leno made a lean boy. Leno was a funny man to his finger-tips and could express more with a grimace then many comedians could manage with very hard labour.

By 1898 Pinero's plays were being treated as a national event. *Trelawney of the Wells*, his sentimental comedy, delighted a first night audience at the Court in January 1898. It took place in the 1860s and Tom Wrench, his main character, was based on Tom Robertson, the playwright. The Philistinian respectability of the hero's home was contrasted with the gay, Bohemian atmosphere of a small theatre company. Paul Arthur made the success of the evening as Tom Wrench and Irene Vanbrugh scored as Rose Trelawney, the heroine.

The Belle of New York, an American musical play with an all-American cast, came to the Shaftesbury in April 1898 and conquered London in a night. Its melodramatic plot about a man about town who was reformed by a Salvation Army girl hardly mattered. The piece had gorgeous costumes, Dan Daly played the hero with dry humour and spirited dancing and, above all, there was Edna May as the Salvation Army lass who became a high kicker at the Casino. *The Belle of New York* was directed at a fast pace which was a revelation to the British public. George Edwardes was so impressed by the 'pep' of the chorus girls that he sent the Gaiety girls along to see it, and had the tempo of their dance routines speeded up.

Martin Harvey presented *The Only Way*, adapted from *A Tale of Two Cities*, at the Lyceum in February 1899. He played the heroic part of Sidney Carton, who went to the guillotine to redeem his past life and uttered the famous words: 'It is a far, far better thing that I do than I have ever done.' Martin Harvey's well judged performance and the sentiment of the piece delighted the public and he played this part as his standby for the rest of his career.

Charles Wyndham triumphed again when he produced *The Tyranny of Tears* by Haddon Chambers at the Criterion in April 1899. This comedy was about a weeping wife whose ability to turn on the tap almost wrecked her marriage. Wyndham made an excellent long-suffering husband, and Mary Moore was spendid as the weeping wife who had to play 'against the audience'.

In the same month *The Gay Lord Quex*, a fine Pinero play, was produced at the Globe. This comedy of intrigue had well drawn characters and witty lines, and such an ingenious plot that the audience were in suspense to the last moment as to how it would end. The most interesting character was Sophy, a Bond Street manicurist with managing ways who tried to find out if her foster sister was doing the right thing in marrying the notorious Lord Quex. In the big scene Sophy and Lord Quex had a trial of wits in another woman's boudoir. Irene Vanbrugh gave a marvellous performance as Sophy and John Hare played Lord Quex with his customary aplomb.

At the end of the century George Edwardes encountered hot competition from *Floradora*, produced at the Lyric in November 1899 with a particularly good score by Leslie Stuart. The slight story centred round a perfume called Floradora, manufactured on a Philippine island, and a wicked magnate who tried to steal the rights from an orphan girl. Evie Greene sang beautifully as the heroine and Ada Reeve sang and danced with gusto as a very unlikely duchess. The honours of the evening went to Willy Edouin, the principal comedian. The British public succumbed to the charm of its delightful sextet, 'Tell me Pretty Maiden', and the other numbers by Leslie Stuart, with the result that *Floradora* became a smash hit. Stuart made a fortune, his royalties averaging £300 a week. He had come from a poor Lancashire family, and it was the first time he had made big money. Success went to his head; he built himself an enormous house in London and spent money like a drunken sailor. None of his later shows did as well as *Floradora* and he died a poor man.

The last night of *The Toreador* took place on 4 July 1903; the Guv'nor arranged that it would also be celebrated as the last night of the old Gaiety. The public queued for hours to obtain seats for the performance and, although the doors had been opened early in the morning, there was such a heavy demand for seats that many people had to stand.

The auditorium of the Gaiety looked like a flower garden with great baskets of flowers hanging everywhere. Sitting among the audience was John Hollingshead, a frail-looking old man of seventy-five: he had been an invalid for some years and had recently gone bankrupt. Nellie Farren was well enough to attend the last night and so was Edward Royce, another of the old Merry Family Quartette.

After playing the second Act of *The Toreador*, the company presented *The Linkman* or *Gaiety Memories*, a nostalgic piece of entertainment about the old Gaiety which George Grossmith Jr, had devised. The linkman was the uniformed attendant who stood outside the theatre and called carriages and cabs for the playgoers, a descendant of the man who used to light people to their homes in an earlier age.

The Linkman opened with a sketch at the Gaiety stage door, in which any resemblance between Robert Nainby as the keeper and Jimmy Jupp was purely coincidental, then Connie Ediss appeared as an eccentric wardrobe mistress and performed an abandoned dance. Next came a scene in the Green Room, which made an excuse to introduce Gaiety stars past and present. Then there were excerpts from *The Shop Girl* with Connie Ediss and Arthur Williams, and from the burlesque, *Cinder Ellen up-too-late*. Seymour Hicks trod the Gaiety boards again and sang 'Her Golden Hair was hanging down her Back', and Hayden Coffin rendered 'Queen of my Heart' once again.

Teddy Payne, George Grossmith, Harry Grattan and Fred Wright joined forces with Evie Greene, Edna May, Ethel Irving and Hilda Moody to do a version of the 'Pas de Quatre', which had not been danced in the theatre since Hollingshead's day. All the artists wore the original costumes and it went so well that the highly sentimental audience insisted on an encore.

Finally, Teddy Payne and George Grossmith sang a topical duet entitled 'The Two Obadiahs', with Teddy Payne as the old Obadiah and Gee Gee as the young one.

Said the old Obadiah to the young Obadiah,
'The Gaiety will shortly be no more!'
Said the young Obadiah to the old Obadiah,
'They are putting up a better place next door.
When they pull the dear old playhouse down
They will not leave a stick,
They'll take off all the knockers
And wreck 'em double-quick.
And as a little souvenir I'd like to have a brick.'
Said the old Obadiah, 'So would I!'

An avalanche of property bricks descended on the two comedians on this cue. Then the audience called for Nellie Farren to appear on her stage again, but her rheumatism made this impossible. Edward Royce, however, was still quite hale and hearty and climbed up on the stage amid great cheers from the gallery. 'Ladies and Gentlemen,' he said, 'it is just thirty-one years since I first trod these boards. You cheered my fleeting footsteps then and you receive me in the same way tonight.'*

Just after midnight, when the full company had assembled on the stage, Sir Henry Irving walked on and delivered a valedictory in his beautiful voice:

I have just dropped in . . . as an old neighbour of thirty years standing who used to carry on a different kind of shop over the way (the Lyceum) and is still in that serious line of business: hell and that sort of thing . . .

In a few minutes Mr Edwardes will close the doors of the Gaiety for ever . . . and in a few weeks he will open the doors of the new Gaiety to a flood of popularity and prosperity which, I am sure, will keep him and the company and the public in the highest good humour for many years to come.

Some sad reflections were probably passing through Irving's mind as he stood there. When he had appeared at the Gaiety in *Uncle Dick's Darling* in its early days he stood on the threshold of his great career. Now his world was collapsing, for he was on the point of losing the Lyceum, which he regarded as the temple of his art. But George Edwardes was on the crest of the

* Pope, *Gaiety*.

wave with his musical comedies, which Irving hated because he thought they lowered the tone of the theatre. Besides this Irving knew in his heart that he had lost his position as leader of the British theatre to Beerbohm Tree.

However, Sir Henry continued to play his part on the last night of the old Gaiety. He singled out John Hollingshead in the audience and called him affectionately, 'my friend, the ever-green John Hollingshead, who established the Gaiety fame'. He invited Hollingshead to come up on to the stage, and when the old man arrived Irving shook him warmly by the hand.

Then the Guv'nor joined them on the stage and thanked John Hollingshead for his loyal and generous support when they went into partnership at the Gaiety. He also thanked Sir Henry Irving for honouring the theatre with his presence, and he reminded the audience that Irving had once appeared at the Gaiety with notable success in *Uncle Dick's Darling*.

'And now all I have to say is Farewell to the Old Gaiety,' concluded Edwardes. This was the signal for Hayden Coffin and Florence St John to lead the audience in 'Auld Lang Syne'. The artists on the stage then linked hands with the audience and sang it again. When the singing was over it was very difficult to persuade the audience that the time had come to leave the theatre they had loved so well: the Gaiety electricians had to lower the house lights almost to vanishing-point before the last people departed and the theatre was empty at last.

The Guv'nor gave a supper party on the stage to all the artists and his staff. There was champagne all round and every kind of summer delicacy had been provided for his guests.

Sir Henry Irving gave his last performance at the Lyceum a fortnight later, on 19 July. It was a charity matinee of *The Merchant of Venice* in which he played Shylock to the Portia of Ellen Terry. The public had no idea that this was the last time they would ever appear together on the stage. At the end Irving led her forward by the hand to acknowledge the applause of the audience. He was in tears, knowing that this marked the end of their wonderful partnership. Ellen Terry was also very moved.

'I shall never be in this theatre again,' she said to him after their last curtain call. 'I feel it—I know it!'*

* Irving.

IV

THE GREAT
IMPRESARIO (1903–1911)

12 New Gaiety

> *I am elderly enough to have seen two or three of the old Gaiety burlesques . . . What though 'the Sacred Lamp' has been snuffed out and the arc lamp of musical comedy installed? . . . The spell has not been broken. The spirit, the 'note', is as it always was. The temple stands true to its name, and true to that special and peculiar sort of gaiety with which we have always associated it.*
>
> SIR MAX BEERBOHM, *Around Theatres*

The new Gaiety was situated only a few yards away from the corner of the Strand and Aldwych. The building had been designed by Ernest Runtz and George Ford under the influence of the Florentine school of the Renaissance and was executed in Portland stone with bands of green marble round it. The most striking feature was a large green dome forty feet in diameter, ninety feet above pavement level: surmounting it was a green dome or cupola, on top of which stood the golden figure of a girl blowing a trumpet.

The decor of the interior had been carried out in the art-nouveau style. In the crush-room there were six panels with full length portraits of favourite Gaiety artists: Nellie Farren as the Street Arab; Katie Vaughan in *The Forty Thieves*; Letty Lind as a dancing girl; Sylvia Grey in *Monte Cristo, Junior*; Connie Gilchrist in *The Forty Thieves*; and Ellaline Terriss, the first leading lady of Gaiety musical comedies, in *The Runaway Girl*.

Although it rained all day on 26 October, it made no difference
to the box office: the public waited cheerfully in the rain to
try and get seats for the pit or gallery—the more expensive
seats had been sold already. It had been announced that King
Edward VII and Queen Alexandra would be present on the
first night, which was an added attraction. The Guv'nor could
not have wished for a greater compliment than to have Their
Majesties attend the première of *The Orchid*. He summoned the
company and read out King Edward's note to him 'I've loved
the Gaiety, I love you and I love the Girls. Am bringing Queen
Alexandra to the first night.'*

The decor of the new theatre was mainly dark brown with
yellow and a rich gold. The audience at the first night greatly
admired the appointments in the auditorium and thought
everything in excellent taste. The handsome new drop curtain
depicted a girl in diaphanous draperies with a girdle round her
waist and a real jewel glittering in her buckle. She held above
her head a lamp which actually shone because there was an
electric light behind it.

'It is no small honour to have the reigning sovereign among
the audience on the first night of a new theatre,' said *The Stage*.
But at eight o'clock, although there was no sign yet of the royal
party, Ivan Caryll took up his baton and conducted the
orchestra in the National Anthem. Then the curtain went up on
the first act, which took place in the colourful setting of a
horticultural college.

'Just as the opening chorus was over the familiar figure of the
King, accompanied by Queen Alexandra, was seen at the back
of the Royal Box. A roar of welcome rang out as their Majesties
came forward and took their seats, and so enthusiastic and
prolonged was the cheering that both King and Queen, beaming
with delight at the hearty spontaneity of their reception, half
rose in their places, and bowed and smiled repeatedly to their
loyal subjects.†

The Orchid had a lively score by Ivan Caryll, Lionel Monckton
and Paul Rubens. The highly involved plot began with an
explorer who had lost a valuable South American orchid and
then bought its duplicate for £5 from a simple gardener at the
ladies' horticultural college. Teddy Payne played the gardener

---

* Conversations with Miss Ruby Millar, a Gaiety Star.
† Mander and Mitchenson, *Lost Theatres of London*.

The royal opening of the New Gaiety—Connie Ediss, Edmund Payne, George Grossmith, Jnr, and Gertie Millar in *The Orchid*, 26 October 1903

who 'did all the dirty work', and he also arranged secret marriages for two couples who fell in love but had no money. But the Registrar muddled up the names with the result that the wrong couples set off to Nice on their honeymoons—and somehow or other the other characters in the show also landed up in Nice. Gertie Millar had her first starring part as Lady Violet, who was in love with a penniless doctor. Amongst the other characters was a pushing Cabinet Minister who always wore an orchid in his buttonhole—an obvious dig at the Right Honourable Joe Chamberlain, a controversial politician. Gabrielle Ray, playing the Minister's special secretary, became a star overnight.

A demure little figure in a grey Quaker dress, Gabrielle Ray wore a huge picture hat over her glorious golden hair; she danced exquisitely and was extremely pretty, with sparkling blue eyes. Walter Macqueen Pope, who was at the first night, said her dancing was a poem. 'It was a piece of silvery thistle-down floating on a sunbeam.' She never seemed to touch the stage when she was dancing: she just seemed to be blown here and there by the breeze. And when she kicked, up went her leg and her little golden shoe went far above her head quite effortlessly.*

Gabrielle Ray created a furore by coming on in the second act in pink silk pyjamas, which were a great novelty for women in 1903. She sang an absurd little number in her tiny voice and the Gaiety patrons lapped it up.

Connie Ediss, the outsize Cockney comedienne, had a number about the joys of fancy dress in which she mixed up things like Mrs Malaprop. And George Grossmith sang 'Bedelia', which he had brought over from America, and it scored the smash hit of the show. The Guv'nor was banking on having a big success to launch the new Gaiety, and the notices were most encouraging. The *Daily Telegraph* said:

Bright music, dainty dancers and picturesque costumes, coupled with a plentiful supply of clever artists and fascinating damsels, were the elements relied on for success in the past and in *The Orchid* they are to be rediscovered. . . . The stage pictures will vie in point of brilliance and taste with any yet presented by Mr George Edwardes. . . . Of the

* Pope, *Carriages at Eleven.*

young members of the cast Miss Gertie Millar distinguished herself most by her exquisite and charming manner, alike as an actress, singer and dancer. Her performance last night brings her into the very front rank of her profession.

The critic of the *Morning Leader* obviously enjoyed his evening:

It was a good thing to be alive at the new Gaiety last night. It was a splendid, uproarious night—everybody . . . waiting only to applaud the old favourites and help in the launch of a beautiful theatre on a career as famous and successful as that of the old. . . . *The Orchid*, with its gaiety, high spirits, pretty faces, superb staging and popular tunes, will start on a career of success to which it would be foolhardy to prophesy any term.

Finally, *The Times:*

It is no use . . . trying to judge the Gaiety by rational standards: only go prepared to surrender to her frivolity, and in a few minutes it is ten to one that your eye will be glued to her kaleidoscope, to be moved very rarely.

The Guv'nor discovered that a girl of fourteen had bluffed her way into the chorus of *The Orchid*. The 'delinquent' was Ruby Miller, a stunningly pretty redhead whom he had engaged on sight because her colouring contrasted so well with that of the other chorus girls. When it came out that Ruby was only fourteen, George Edwardes packed her off back to her family, who promptly sent her back to school. Ruby Miller had set her heart on becoming an actress and told Edwardes she would get in touch with him again when she grew up.

The Guv'nor interviewed every girl who applied for the chorus himself. He asked one of them, 'Do you run straight, my dear?' 'Oh yes, Mr Edwardes,' she replied, 'but not very fast and not very far.'

The Orchid came up to the Guv'nor's best expectations and ran for 559 performances; Gabs Ray soon became the most popular of all the picture postcard beauties. The late Herbert Farjeon, an outstanding revue-writer, was an ardent collector of the picture postcard girls in his youth. He recalled seeing rows

and rows of glossy musical comedy beauties in the alluring
windows of the stationers. Some of them were smiling to
display their dazzling white teeth, some peering coyly over
parasols, some swinging on swings, some perching on crescent
moons, some revelling in snow, some with their doggies, some
punting, some canoeing, some in pyjamas, some in furs.
Farjeon appreciated the charms of Marie Studholme, Gabs Ray,
Lily Elsie and the Dare sisters, but came out strongly in favour
of Gladys Cooper. He thought nobody was more beautiful than
Gladys Cooper, 'who did not need to smile, who always
maintained a certain but by no means forbidding dignity'.*
The price of the shiny sepia cards was 2d., while the coloured
ones sold for 3d. But the coloured postcards were hand tinted
and wildly inaccurate: a chinchilla muff would be striped with
gold paint and actresses wore dresses of pea green and raspberry
pink, and other impossible colour combinations. The picture
postcard boom was a godsend to the box office when leading
musical comedy actresses went on tour. Whenever Zena Dare
toured in Seymour Hicks's shows shoals of admirers of her
picture postcards came to the theatre to see her.†

The Coronation of King Edward VII, which had been
greeted with tremendous enthusiasm all over the country,
was a boon for the London theatres. Beerbohm Tree had
celebrated it with a revival of *The Merry Wives of Windsor* in
which he played Falstaff, with the addition of layers of padding.
He chose the two most eminent actresses of the day, Ellen
Terry and Madge Kendal, to play Mistress Page and Mistress
Ford. Though Ellen Terry was fifty-five and Madge Kendal
fifty-three, they romped through the comic scenes to the great
delight of the audiences.

In the autumn of 1903 Beerbohm Tree produced *Richard II*,
of which a leading critic wrote: 'Mr Tree is among the very
princes of producers of plays. . . . No one but an artist by
temperament could have such an elaborate framework for a
series of historical pictures. . . . As a spectacle Mr Tree's
production of *Richard II* surpasses anything we have seen.'
Tree gave a fine performance as the tragic king, but he dreamed
up several scenes that were not in Shakespeare's play. He

* Herbert Farjeon, *Morning Leader*, 1945.
   † Conversation between the author and Miss Zena Dare, who also
starred in the Guv'nor's musical plays.

brought real horses on to the stage for the lists at Coventry, and they gave so much trouble backstage that they almost wrecked the first night.

One of Beerbohm Tree's minor productions was *The Eternal City* by Hall Caine, a melodramatic novelist whose books used to sell like hot cakes. Success had made Hall Caine regard himself as an oracle and Tree allowed him to be present at rehearsals. Constance Collier, who had started at the Gaiety with George Edwardes, was Tree's leading lady. In one scene she and Tree quarrelled and he threw her on the ground in a rage. As they rehearsed Hall Caine suddenly cried: 'Stop!' and declaimed, 'I see in my mind an actor seizing a woman fiercely, and with tense muscles and bated breath hurling her right over his head.'

Beerbohm Tree appeared to go into a trance, then said, 'I remember seeing a famous actor seize a famous actress, lift her up by her feet, and dash her head upon the ground, not once, not twice, but three times.'

'In what play was that?' demanded Hall Caine.

'I understand it was called *Punch and Judy,*' said Tree mildly.*

Beerbohm Tree adored women; in fact he was such an enthusiastic sexual athlete that he could never stay faithful to his wife for long. This was wretched for Maud Tree, who loved him despite his affairs and got most upset whenever she discovered he had been out on the tiles. Maud Tree was a beautiful woman; she refused to take a lover, although she had plenty of offers. One of her most persistent admirers was Lewis Waller, the greatest matinee idol of his time; he was so popular that his female fans started the K.O.W. Club in his honour, K.O.W. being short for Keen on Waller.

The most embarrasing thing about Tree's amorous adventures was that several of them resulted in illegitimate children. Fortunately, Maud Tree was a woman of wit. 'Poor, dear Herbert!' she said. 'All his affairs start with a compliment and end with a confinement!'*

Beerbohm Tree occasionally visited prostitutes in the West End. It was reported that when a certain whore saw him standing naked in front of her she pointed at his member and said, 'Oh, what a beauty!' 'I come to bury Caesar, not to praise him!' retorted Tree.

* Pearson.

One of the most endearing things about Tree was that he treated everybody alike, from dukes to dustmen. He was very tolerant about people's faults, and never minded if an actor 'got into an advanced state of alcoholic decomposition' on a Saturday night. He never grew self important and used to say, 'The process of acquiring a swollen head is a pleasant one, it is only the subsequent shrinking that hurts.'*

While Beerbohm Tree's productions at His Majesty's continued to draw the town, Sir Henry Irving tried to make a come-back: he appeared at Drury Lane in a play about Dante by Victorien Sardou, the French playwright, who wrote well-carpentered pieces like *Diplomacy* and *Madame Sans-Gêne*. Sardou was incapable of portraying a great poet; his play was over-long, involved and hardly had a line of poetry in it. But Irving rashly went ahead and produced it at Drury Lane on 30 April. It was a spectacular failure: he lost £12,000 and swallowed up nearly all his savings.

He immediately arranged to take his company on a tour of the United States, where he still remained a great attraction. Billed as Irving's Farewell American Tour, it aroused great enthusiasm over there, but only made a small profit. Irving then set out on a strenuous farewell tour of the provinces, where he could rely on playing to packed houses. He managed to keep faith with his public and fulfil every engagement, but he was fighting a losing battle with his rapidly declining health. Unfortunately every play in his repertoire was designed as a vehicle for a great star: himself. Touring his plays put an enormous strain on him, yet he refused to take the advice of Bram Stoker and Harry Loveday, who wanted him to end the tour after six months. One night in February 1905 he collapsed when playing at Hanley, Staffordshire, and had to abandon the rest of the tour.

The doctors found that Irving had been suffering from emphysema of both lungs for a long time; he also had an acute attack of bronchitis and his heart condition was worse. Any ordinary man would have chosen this moment to announce his retirement, but Sir Henry Irving had an indomitable spirit. As soon as he had made a partial recovery he told Bram Stoker to book a provincial tour for him in the autumn.

But his second farewell tour only lasted a month. At Bradford

* Pearson.

he played Mathias in *The Bells*: it was the most exhausting part he ever performed, and at the end of the play he had to pause for ten minutes on the stage in order to recover his breath. Stoker and Loveday, most alarmed, persuaded him never to play this role again. On Friday, 13 October he presented Tennyson's play *Becket* at Bradford; Stoker and Loveday and the rest of the company sensed that he had to call on every ounce of his reserves in order to get through the exacting name part.

It was a bitterly cold night when Sir Henry Irving said good night to the company. He and Walter Collinson, his valet, drove off in a cab to the Midland Hotel where he was staying. He walked into the lounge and immediately collapsed into an armchair. The porter sent for a doctor. When Dr Vaughan Bateson arrived he found Irving lying on a sofa in his frock coat, with his smudged make-up still on his face; the great actor was already dead.

'We were all stunned with grief,' the doctor said. 'Women in leg-o-mutton sleeves and men in high white collars groped for handkerchiefs when I told them he was dead.' Bram Stoker, who had been summoned to the hotel, saw twenty men grouped round Irving, who lay at full length on the floor. His eyes were still open and Stoker couldn't believe he was really dead. So he knelt down by him and felt his heart to satisfy himself it was indeed death. Walter Collinson was sitting on the floor beside Irving, crying.*

The news of Sir Henry Irving's death reached London and the country mourned him. The British public, which had stayed away from his last seasons at the Lyceum, appreciated that he had been a great man and thousands of people turned out to watch his funeral procession on its way to Westminster Abbey. Irving had been such a towering figure that the theatrical profession turned out in force to pay their last respects to him. Amongst the mourners was George Edwardes, his 'old neighbour of twenty years'.

The Guv'nor was most heartened to find that all his patrons came back to the new Gaiety, where they found the same warm, human atmosphere as at the old theatre in the Strand. *The Orchid* bloomed until 1905, and was followed by *The Spring Chicken*, an adaptation from the French by George

* Bram Stoker, *Personal Reminiscences of Henry Irving* (Heinemann, 1907).

Grossmith, who appeared in it as a flighty French advocate who couldn't stop flirting in the spring. He was so carried away by the charms of the Baroness whose case he was handling that he neglected his wife. Teddy Payne and Connie Ediss were in fine form as an English husband and wife at large in Paris with their two awful children. Payne really went there to chase the pretty girls and made a dead set at Rosalie, a Breton girl (Gertie Millar). Connie Ediss followed him to Paris to try and catch him red-handed.

Teddy Payne had a number in which he was surrounded by the prettiest Gaiety girls, all disguised as Parisiennes; he admitted he was 'slightly past the age of forty-one'. Connie Ediss picked up his trail in Paris and then sang:

I don't say that husbands are all of them bad,
But I don't put very much trust in 'em,
I've pretty good eyes, as I always have had,
And never let people throw dust in 'em.
My husband comes over to Paris, says he,
On business alone, just for the day,
He never tells me what his business may be,
Nor why it is done on a Sunday.

The Spring Chicken was produced at the time of the Entente Cordiale, which was largely due to the efforts of King Edward. The Guv'nor brought in a topical touch when Gertie Millar appeared in the second act as the French Republic in a dress of red, white and blue, wearing the cap of Liberty.

Gertie Millar was not a beauty like Marie Studholme or Gabs Ray, but had greater appeal than either of them. She had a slim, graceful figure and a most arresting face, marvellous eyes and a bewitching little voice. She had come from a humble Yorkshire home; she had worked in a mill and worn clogs. She always laughed a lot in her shows, and many people thought it the most wonderful laugh in London.

The Spring Chicken came off after running for over 400 performances, and the Guv'nor presented *The New Aladdin*, a musical extravaganza based on the old pantomime story. The leading lady was Lily Elsie, whom the Guv'nor had brought in from the provinces. But the earthy patrons of the Gaiety found Lily Elsie too quiet and ethereal for their taste. The Guv'nor took the hint and brought out a second edition with Gertie

Millar replacing her. George Grossmith played the Genie of
the Lamp and Teddy Payne was Tiffin, a pageboy. The Guv'nor
had brought over from Paris a ravishing actress named Gaby
Deslys, who made a terrific impact in the show and kept every
red-blooded male on the edge of his seat.

Gaby Deslys appeared as The Charm of Paris in an episode
which had been specially devised by the Guv'nor to exploit her
sex appeal. Her two songs, 'The English Language' and 'Sur La
Plage', always brought the house down; although she had only
a wisp of a voice it had a delightful quality and she used it with
grace and suppleness. Her manner was piquant and extremely
arch, and when she sang 'Sur La Plage' she wore a décolleté
bathing costume which all the women thought *le dernier cri*
whilst the men couldn't take their opera glasses off her as she
sang:

When I take my bain-de-mer
At what do the men all stare?

Gaby Deslys was also a spirited dancer, and her act included a
special feature with Yuko-Tani, a Ju-Jitsu expert, in which she
wore a fetching gym tunic which was considered exceedingly
daring. Yuko-Tani just touched her hand and over she would go,
spinning like a top. Then the process was reversed and Gaby
Deslys gave him a spin in the air.

The Guv'nor came to watch them at rehearsals just when Gaby
was finding it very hard to get the correct grip on Yuko-Tani to
throw him. Edwardes, who then weighed 17 stone, innocently
asked Yuko-Tani how he managed to throw people about so
easily. The Ju-Jitsu expert thought he wanted a demonstration
and said, 'Come, I will show you.' He took Edwardes gently by
the hand and then—whir! up in the air, one spin round, and the
Guv'nor landed safely on his feet again. 'How did you do that?'
he gasped in bewilderment.

'Like this,' said Yuko-Tani, gripping the Guv'nor and
spinning him round in the air again. But unluckily Edwardes
landed on his back instead of on his feet. He got up and said
quite sharply, 'Don't do it—I don't like it. I'm too old for that
sort of thing.'*

Before Gaby Deslys appeared at the Gaiety, she had been
* Jupp.

one of the reigning stars of Paris and acquired a fabulous collection of jewellery from her many admirers. She brought all her gems over with her to London and used to arrive at the theatre in full regalia, with jewels on her fingers and neck, and in her ears and on her hair. When she left her room to go on to the stage she would deposit trinkets worth a king's ransom on her dressing-table.

Though *The New Aladdin* only had a brief stay at the Gaiety there was enough time for Gaby Deslys to become a legend. Men fell for her like ninepins, and offered her a small fortune to spend a night with them. One ardent Frenchman, who had chased Gaby Deslys all over the Continent to no avail, turned up to see her at the Gaiety one night half-mad with desire. He jumped up in the stalls and threw handfuls of gold and silver at her on the stage, then he whipped out his gold watch and chain and his pocket book and threw them at Gaby's feet, swearing that he adored her.

The next Gaiety show, *The Girls of Gottenberg*, was based on the extraordinary incident of the cobbler of Kopenik, who had put on a uniform and posed as an Army Captain and emissary of the Kaiser and managed to spoof the entire German hierachy. Produced on 15 May 1907, it had a cast headed by Gertie Millar, and George Grossmith. Teddy Payne was Max, valet to Prince Otto (George Grossmith), a feather-bed German soldier. Max dressed up in the Prince's gorgeous uniform and posed as a Captain and the special envoy of the Emperor, and thus managed to arrest a Colonel of Hussars and then a pompous Burgomaster. Gertie Millar played Mitzi, the devastating waitress at the 'Red Hen' Inn on the Rhine, and sang a slightly saucy number entitled 'The Titsy Bitsy Girl.' Teddy Payne gave an outstanding performance as the little valet who enjoyed every minute of his day as an important person.

He and Gertie Millar sang a charming duet together about the love affair of two little sausages. Payne also sang:

I'm the extra special envoy of the Kaiser,
Show me all the deference you can,
My credentials you may scan them
When you've played the German anthem
For the Kaiser's right-hand man.

Gladys Cooper made her debut in the chorus of *The Girls of*

Gottenberg. She was eighteen and breath-takingly beautiful; the Guv'nor had given her a three-year contract and promised to groom her for stardom. She worked very hard at the Gaiety and thought it was rather like being back at school, except that there was such a jolly atmosphere. Edwardes behaved like a second father to her and the other chorus girls, but all of them had to conform to the rules of the theatre. If they were not performing on the stage, Jupp made sure they stayed in their dressing rooms, and at the end of the show nearly all the girls wended their way home to their mothers. The girls in the 'Big Eight' led a totally different existence; in the normal way they went out to supper every night with their admirers.

Sometimes the chorus girls received letters from unknown young men in the audience which gave them a good giggle. One youth wrote to Gladys Cooper: 'Do come out to supper with me—I am sitting in the second row of the stalls and wearing a white carnation.'* The chorus girls often stayed late at the theatre to rehearse dance routines with Gertie Millar. Whenever they did, Gertie always sent up a bottle of champagne to the girls dressing-room. She had become rather a martinet in the theatre, but most stars in her position were the same. The company were all very fond of her and she never allowed her swift rise to fame to spoil her.

If Gertie Millar was appearing at the Gaiety, crowds waited outside the stage door to welcome her. As she came through the stage door the fans would fall back, leaving a gangway for her to pass down, and as she passed all eyes would follow her to her brougham. The public used to treat Gertie Millar like a queen, and she rewarded them with her lovely smile and a wave.

* Gladys Cooper, *Gladys Cooper* (Hutchinson, 1931).

13 The Merry Widow, English style

The applause went across the footlights like a prairie fire, accompanied by roars of cheers, warm and flowing with pleasure and affection.

W. MACQUEEN POPE and D. L. MURRAY,
Fortune's Favourite

Nearly all the Guv'nor's shows at the Gaiety paid off handsomely, but it was a very different story at Daly's after *The Country Girl* finished its run in 1904. *The Cingalee*, his next production, had an outstanding score by Lionel Monckton and Paul Rubens, was set in the colourful island of Ceylon, and had been put on the stage with no expense spared in typical George Edwardes style. One of the highlights was the Fire Dance, devised by Willie Warde and based on the traditional Cingalese ceremony held on the island during the Feast of the Fire. Huntley Wright and Rutland Barrington supplied the comedy, Hayden Coffin played the dashing hero, and there were two accomplished leading ladies. The first night went very well, the notices were excellent—yet *The Cingalee* never drew the public and was a very expensive failure.

The Guv'nor's next piece, *The Little Michus*, was a French operetta by André Messager with a Gilbertian plot about two girls, brought up as sisters, who got mixed up when they were babies. One of them was the daughter of an ordinary grocer, but the other was a wealthy General's daughter. There were amusing complications when Marie Blanche and Blanche Marie grew up and each had a young man anxious to marry her. Adrienne Augarde and Mabel Green played the 'sisters', and Robert Evett appeared as an Army officer in love with one of them. Huntley Wright as the General's orderly had to work overtime to extract some comedy from his part.

George Edwardes had engaged Adeline Genée, the famous ballerina, who was under contract to him at the Empire, to add lustre to the dancing. During rehearsals Miss Genée got into difficulties deciding on the steps she should dance before a character's first entrance. Edwardes suddenly rushed on to the stage from the stalls in his frock coat and top hat.

'I'll show you, my dear,' he said. Lifting up his tails to give the semblance of a skirt, the big man proceeded to show the ballerina how he thought the steps should go. All the staff held their breath in case he had offended her, but Adeline Genée just smiled and tried out the Guv'nor's routine. 'That's just what I mean, my dear,' he panted. 'I knew I had only to show you.'*

Unfortunately the mistaken-identity theme of *The Little Michus* failed to divert the public for long. The Guv'nor soon withdrew the piece and called it a 'nitter', which was his private word for a flop. However, *The Little Michus* threw another star into his lap: George Graves, a witty Irish comedian, who took over the part of General des Ifs from Willy Edouin. Though George Graves was still quite young, he was a most talented character actor: he had a very red nose, wore a peculiar wig and spoke in a high-pitched music-hall voice which was compared to the sound of the popping of champagne corks. He had a cosy stage presence and a charming way of taking the audience into his confidence: he would invent fantastic pets and beasties and then introduce them to the public. During the run of *The Little Michus* he had people rolling in their seats as he described the Gazeeka, a small beast of prehistoric ancestry:

Nature has become so neglectful as to forget to clothe him in any way, except for a little patch of fur on his chest . . . such a sweet-natured little fellow is he that to prevent the little patch of fur being in any way ruffled before it reaches

* Pope, *Carriages at Eleven.*

us, he sleeps on his back. But . . . when the moon's rays shine on him (he being of a light milky skin) the other animals mistake him for a turnip and nibble him.

Shame! . . . the young Gazeekas are pounced upon by the various slugs of the district, who attack the ankles of the Gazeeka, and he, being of a self-absorbed nature, doesn't notice until too late that the slugs have chewed through his equilibrium. Consequently, the next thing he knows is that he has lost his balance and is on his face in the suffocating mud. He generally remarks before dying, 'I think that will do for today.'*

The Guv'nor chose another French operetta for his next production at Daly's. *Les Merveilleuses*, later re-titled *The Lady Dandies*, was presented on 27 October 1906. The strong cast was headed by Evie Greene, Denise Orme, Robert Evett and W. H. Berry, a new comedian who had been discovered playing in a concert party at Broadstairs. Bill Berry, a big, cheerful man, had a pleasant singing voice and was an excellent dancer.

The Lady Dandies were an influential group of Parisian women at the time of the Directoire (1795). They set the fashions and were noted for the daring and eccentricity of their clothes, generally wearing scanty classical costumes in Roman style. Evie Greene played the leader of the 'Merveilleuses', Berry and two other comedians played rival police agents, and the production was extremely expensive. The libretto was by Victorien Sardou, whose plays were great money-spinners, but the piece was another 'nitter' and came off after 180 performances. The Guv'nor's flair for knowing what the public wanted seemed to have deserted him at Daly's; he had lost so much on his last three shows that there was very little left in the kitty for the next one.

Edwardes decided to try a Continental piece once more, and paid £1,000 for the English rights of *The Merry Widow*, a Viennese operetta which was the rage of Germany and Austria. He signed up Mitzi Günther, the original Merry Widow, before he had seen her in the flesh, and had a terrible shock when a prima donna weighing around fourteen stone walked into his office at Daly's. 'She has the voice of an angel, but no waist,' he remarked gloomily to Pat Malone, who was going to

* *Gaieties and Gravities*, George Graves (Hutchinson, 1931).

produce the piece for him.* The Guv'nor sent Mitzi Günther back to Vienna by the next train, but had to pay her a large sum in compensation. He commissioned Edward Morton, the author of *San Toy*, to write an English version of *The Merry Widow*. Then he and William Boosey, the managing director of Chappells, the music publishers, went to Vienna to see a performance of the operetta. George Edwardes and William Boosey were good friends and about the same age: two portly, middle-aged men with fresh complexions and greying hair.

On the Continental train they met some mutual friends and were very easily persuaded to join them in a game of poker. But Edwardes was dead unlucky and had lost several hundred pounds by the time they got into Vienna. Boosey and the other men were so sorry about it that they bought him a magnificent set of etched glass decanters in Vienna to console him.

George Edwardes and Boosey both felt that the Viennese production of *The Merry Widow* was much too heavy-handed and Teutonic to suit the British public. The Widow and Prince Danilo were two strapping singers of forty in the shade; Danilo, a marvellous tenor, acted as if he was a hero in grand opera.

They travelled home from Vienna with the same friends from England and played poker again on the train. This time Edwardes had a wonderful run of luck and won back more than he had lost on the way out. Although Edwardes was an extremely generous man in the ordinary way, he was a different person when it came to gambling. He loved to get the better of his opponents, so on returning to London he never gave Boosey and the others a present out of sheer devilment. However, Boosey and the gamblers all received handsome gifts the following year.†

At Daly's Pat Malone had bad news for the Guv'nor: the adaptation of *The Merry Widow*, by Edward Morton, was useless! It was partly Edwardes's own fault; being in a hurry when he explained the story of the operetta to Morton, he had left out things and muddled up the plot because his German was not fluent. He was now in a devil of a mess, with the piece scheduled to open at Daly's in three months' time! He sent for

* Hibbert, *Fifty Years of a Londoner's Life* (Grant Richards, 1916).

† Conversations with Julius Edwardes.

F

Captain Basil Hood, who was considered the best librettist in England since W. S. Gilbert, and commissioned him to do a new English version.

By working day and night, Basil Hood completed a first-rate adaptation of *The Merry Widow* in a few weeks. At this point the Guv'nor should have gone to Edward Morton and told him his libretto had been thrown out of the window and Basil Hood had written a new one. But Edwardes was too soft-hearted to do it; all he did was to make sure that Morton never came to any of the rehearsals, while he kept on postponing the unpleasant meeting with the author.

The Guv'nor picked Lily Elsie to play Sonia, the widow. It was an original choice because Lily Elsie was very young for the part at 21 and had never appeared in a big London success. But she was talented and extremely beautiful and he *knew* she was exactly right for the part. He took her to Vienna to see *The Merry Widow*, but she came back with a sinking feeling that her voice could not compare with Mitzi Günther's and she would fail dismally in the role.

He gave the part of Prince Danilo to Joe Coyne, a young American light comedian. It was a daring thing to do because Joe Coyne could hardly sing a note, although he was an attractive and graceful artist and a superb ballroom dancer.

During the first rehearsals both Lily Elsie and Joe Coyne felt they were wrong for the parts. Lily Elsie thought her voice too light for Franz Lehár's lovely score and Coyne worried because he had no voice at all. Joe Coyne, a comedian who always thought he was going to give a bad performance, was plunged into the depths of despair. He met a fellow actor at the old Cavour Bar in Leicester Square and told him, 'This is dreadful—it's ruin! I'm going back to New York!'

Coyne went and saw the Guv'nor and offered to give up the part of Danilo. Edwardes did his utmost to reassure him. 'You're going to be an enormous success, Joe, you wait and see.'*

The two principal comedians were George Graves and W. H. Berry. Graves played Baron Popoff, an absurd Ruritanian ambassador in Paris, and Berry was Misch, the simple-minded messenger at the Embassy. Elizabeth Frith played Natalie, Popoff's promiscuous wife, and Robert Evett was Vicomte

* Pope and Murray, *Fortune's Favourite*.

Camille de Jolidon. George Graves complained that there was hardly a funny line in his part of Popoff, so he invented Hetty the Hen, a pet whom he worked up into a star turn. Hetty had been inspired by one of the hens he kept at home in the country, which hardly ever laid an egg. Graves developed Hetty the Hen with great skill. 'Her self-satisfied cluckings (when actually laying an egg) so infuriated a neighbour that he mixed brass filings in her food . . . with the result that she laid a door-knob.' At one point in his recital George Graves used to say to the audience, 'Have you ever seen a peacock sitting at the end of a bed blowing a brass trumpet?'*

As the spring advanced the Guv'nor found himself at his wit's end for money. He had to ask Joseph Harker, the well known stage designer, if he would mind doing the *Merry Widow* sets for him 'on tick'. Later, when the Guv'nor was having a session with Fred Farren, his choreographer, Farren mentioned there was a 'a little account outstanding'. George Edwardes summoned his secretary, Charles Cannon, and demanded to know why Farren's account had not been paid. 'See that it is paid at once.' he said. 'I never heard of such a thing. I hate things outstanding.'† It was bluff: George had no funds available to settle the account. Fred Farren happened to meet Joseph Harker at Daly's and they had a drink together and compared notes. They discovered that George Edwardes had been owing money to both of them for the last three months, but Fred Farren said loyally, 'I don't mind if I work for nothing for the Guv'nor!'

'Neither do I,' said Joseph Harker.

Lily Elsie was making herself miserable trying to sing Franz Lehár's music as well as she could—she felt her voice would never be equal to his lovely song 'Vilia'. After one rehearsal she begged the Guv'nor to release her from her contract, but he wouldn't hear of it. George Graves happened to be at a rehearsal when Joe Coyne was attempting to sing a delightful Lehár number entitled 'The Prince's Children'. He was horrified to hear Joe Coyne 'murdering' the song in his feeble voice. Next time they rehearsed together, George Graves spoke out. 'Joe, if you try to sing that "prince's children"

* Graves.
† Pope and Murray, *Fortune's Favourite.*

bit I'll kick you in the stomach!'* Joe Coyne, feeling despondent, said, 'What do you expect me to do with it? Recite it?' 'Do anything!' cried George Graves. 'Have it framed as a text and hung over your bed. . . . Give it to the cat—anything! But don't—er—sing it, Joe!' Joe Coyne then proceeded to *recite* 'The Prince's Children'; he spoke the lyric to synchronize with the music in the background and enchanted the whole company with the effect he produced. The Guv'nor was so carried away that he instructed Joe Coyne to recite every one of his numbers in the piece.

In June Franz Lehár arrived at Daly's to conduct the final rehearsals of *The Merry Widow*. George Edwardes was dreading this visit; he knew he would have to exert every ounce of tact on the composer to avoid a catastrophe. In the first place he only had twenty-eight musicians in the orchestra at Daly's and the contract had stipulated thirty-four. Secondly, he knew Franz Lehár would consider Lily Elsie far too young to play the Widow. Worst of all, how was he going to justify to Franz Lehár Joe Coyne's method of 'singing' his numbers?

Lehár turned up punctually at the theatre: he was a dapper individual with a military manner acquired from the days when he was an army bandmaster in Vienna. He fumed at finding the orchestra six men short, but Edwardes persuaded him to run through his score with the present orchestra. Lehár said afterwards that they played admirably together—perhaps twenty-eight men might be enough after all.

Then George Edwardes introduced Franz Lehár and the German authors, Leon and Stein, to Lily Elsie, the English Merry Widow. The Germans were flabbergasted at the idea of a girl of twenty-one playing the part of Sonia. 'She looks more like ze Merry Widow's daughter zan ze merry widow,' said one of the authors.†

Edwardes knew that Lehár was likely to blow his top the moment he heard Joe Coyne 'reciting' his numbers, so it was vital to make sure the composer did not hear Coyne recite till the last moment. At every rehearsal Edwardes kept making excuses for Joe Coyne, saying he had a sore throat and was resting it for the great day. 'Save your voice, Joe!' he called out whenever Danilo was supposed to sing a number.

* Graves.
† Pope and Murray, *Fortune's Favourite* (Hutchinson, 1953).

He waited until the dress rehearsal before he sprang his surprise: then Joe Coyne recited all his songs (just as Rex Harrison was to do fifty years later in *My Fair Lady*). Franz Lehár was outraged that anyone should dare to recite his music! At his hotel he blew up and swore at George Edwardes for deceiving him about Joe Coyne's voice.

'But Joe Coyne is a very funny man,' protested Edwardes.

'I have not written funny music,' snapped Lehár.

Edwardes did his best to try and calm down the composer. He declared, 'Herr Lehár, that man will put a fortune in your pocket even if he does not *sing* your beautiful music!'*

Bill Berry, the comedian, had been carried away at the dress rehearsal by the quality of *The Merry Widow* score and the gay atmosphere of the piece. At the end he went over to George Edwardes and said, 'You've got a winner, Guv'nor!'

'Shush! Shush!' cried Edwardes, putting up a warning finger. 'Don't say that, Bill. Don't ever say it again! Say it's a nitter, Bill—a nitter!' he whispered.'†

On the morning of 17 June 1907 the Guv'nor was half demented with worry about the fate of *The Merry Widow*. The theatre libraries, generally so enthusiastic about his shows, had refused to buy any tickets until they had seen the first-night notices. They had no faith in Franz Lehár, an unknown composer from Vienna, and thought nothing at all of Lily Elsie and Joe Coyne as a box-office attraction.

Realizing what a state the Guv'nor was in, Pat Malone took him off to Richmond for lunch at the Star and Garter, and never left him alone till the evening. Edwardes had saved as much as he possibly could on the production. Mrs Fields, the wardrobe mistress at Daly's, had worked wonders, making up the artists' costumes from cheap materials so cleverly that on the stage they gave the illusion of being fashionable dresses. The sets had also been done on the cheap by Joseph Harker: one of them had been revamped from a set in *The Cingalee*. When the curtain went up that evening George Edwardes was so uncertain about *The Merry Widow* that he expected it to run for only six weeks.

The operetta centred round Sonia and Prince Danilo. They had once been in love, but after his father had forbidden the

* Pope and Murray, *Fortune's Favourite*.
† W. H. Berry, *40 Years in the Limelight* (Hutchinson, 1939).

marriage he had jilted her and she had married a millionaire on the rebound. Sonia was left a widow with a fortune at her command and lived in Paris, where Danilo worked as secretary at a Ruritanian embassy. They met again, but Danilo was too proud to admit he was still in love with Sonia: and though Sonia still loved him, she was determined to make him declare his love for her first.

When Joe Coyne made his first entrance as Danilo, the audience were amazed to see an ordinary-looking fellow instead of a tall, handsome hero like Hayden Coffin. But as soon as Coyne started to 'sing' about Maxim's restaurant in Paris, he held them enthralled, 'speaking the words . . . so clearly, with such quiet meaning, and in such perfect time, that the melody behind them, and the lilt of Maxim's and the ladies in its dancing notes, were brilliantly enhanced by it'.*

I go off to Maxim's
Where fun and frolic beams,
With all the girls I chatter,
I laugh and kiss and flatter,
Lo-lo, Do-do, Jou-Jou,
Clou-Clou, Margot, Frou-Frou!
For surnames do not matter,
I take the first to hand,
And then the corks go pop,
We dance and never stop,
The ladies smile so sweetly,
I catch and kiss them neatly!
Lo-lo, Do-do, Jou-Jou,
Clou-Clou, Margot, Frou-Frou!
Till I forget completely
My dear old Fatherland.

When Lily Elsie faced the footlights as Sonia for the first time she felt terribly nervous, but she suddenly sensed that the audience had been enjoying every moment of the show, and it gave her just the confidence she needed. At the end of the first act the gallery was screaming, 'Who loves Lily Elsie? We do!', and then the pit took it up. When the moment came for her to sing her lovely number, 'Vilia', she rose to the occasion

* Pope and Murray, *Fortune's Favourite.*

and sang it effortlessly and with exactly the right feeling:

> Vilia, O Vilia! the witch of the wood,
> Would I not die for you, dear, if I could!
> Vilia, O Vilia, my love and my bride!
> Softly and sadly he sighed . . .

In the second act there was a sextet entitled 'Women', sung by six men including Joe Coyne and Bill Berry:

> Women, women, women,
> Women, women, women,
> You may study their ways if you can,
> But a woman's too much for a man,
> It is deeper than diving for pearls
> Courting girls, girls, girls, girls, girls!
> With her fair flaxen hair, eyes of blue,
> She's a long way too knowing for you,
> She is dark, she is fair, you may smile, you may frown,
> Never mind, you will get done brown!

Bill Berry remembered how the audience at the first night responded to 'Women'. 'It has a marvellously attractive and lilting tune and, as we danced around the stage, we could hear and *feel* the audience keeping in time with us . . . tapping their fingers on the arm of their chairs, and kicking anybody's else's hat under the seat in front.'*

Lily Elsie and Joe Coyne danced the Merry Widow Waltz together in this act. To the intoxicating strains of Lehár's music this perfectly matched couple danced almost as if in a dream, waltzing in reverse in the Viennese style. At first Coyne held her round the waist, and the second time he held her round her neck. The British public had never seen such dancing before, and in the space of two minutes Lily Elsie and Joe Coyne had the house at their feet. Everyone began to sway in unison with the wonderful melody and the waltzing couple. And when they finished dancing the applause broke out: the men in evening dress cheered and beat their hands until they were sore, the women cheered shrilly, and the pit and gallery went quite mad. Sonia and Danilo had to dance the Merry Widow Waltz again and again.†

* Berry   † Pope and Murray, *Fortune's Favourite.*

When the final curtain fell on Sonia and Danilo embracing happily at Maxim's, pandemonium broke out in the theatre. 'The applause went across the footlights like a prairie fire.' The audience yelled for Lily Elsie and Joe Coyne, for George Graves and Bill Berry, then for Elizabeth Frith and Robert Evett, the two other principals. Finally, they shouted for the Guv'nor, and Edwardes appeared on the stage.

Knowing that he had found a colossal winner for Daly's at last, he immediately ordered a brand new production of *The Merry Widow* with no expense spared. Everybody in the theatre was cock-a-hoop about their success; the only unhappy person connected with the show was Edward Morton, the librettist, who had come to the first night in all innocence and found there was not one of his lines left in *The Merry Widow*. Though his name was on the programme as the author, everybody knew the libretto was by Basil Hood. Morton was so angry about it that he sued George Edwardes. A settlement was agreed out of court under which Edwardes had to pay royalties both to Basil Hood and to Edward Morton.

The *Era* gave *The Merry Widow* an excellent notice:

> There are airs in *The Merry Widow* with a lilt in them which ring in one's ears after they have been heard once. . . . The part of the Merry Widow is played most delightfully by Miss Lily Elsie, who has caught exactly the spirit of light-hearted gaiety, touched occasionally with deep feeling, necessary to the part. She is merry and grave, tender and cool, in turn . . . her whole performance reached a high standard of excellence, placing her at once in the front rank of the bright particular stars of light opera. . . .
>
> Mr Joseph Coyne played the character [*Prince Danilo*] throughout in the vein of pure comedy, and although the romance with which the [*German*] authors have evidently invested the part was absent, Mr Coyne made a manly figure of the Prince and evidently got great fun out of the role.

Even *The Times* found very little to carp at in the piece.

> . . . The applause seemed to increase its volume as the evening went on: we have hardly ever attended so up-roarious a first night: and the waltz-tune was caught up at

once and whistled incessantly between the second and third acts. The charm of that waltz lies . . . not so much in its air as in its harmonization, and still more in the strange and almost entirely beautiful dance executed to it by Miss Lily Elsie with the help of Mr Coyne. . . .

The Merry Widow . . . is a genuine light opera: it is not overlaid with buffoonery . . . it has a good story to tell and tells it pleasantly: and the music . . . is not blatant, nor sugary, nor cheap: its content is not exhausted at a first hearing.

Miss Elsie . . . is gentle, appealing, very charming, a little strange and remote, she is in everything delightful—except 'merry'. . . . The quintessence of her came out in that dreamy swaying waltz . . . whatever the [*German*] authors may have intended . . . this is the most strongly individual work that has appeared on our lyric stage for some time . . . it is clear that the original part [*Prince Danilo*] was written for a singer: and it is all to Mr Coyne's credit that, being no singer, and being obliged to trust to his pleasant gift of quiet drollery, he gave his part the prominence intended for it. If he cannot sing he can dance. . . .

George Graves was singled out for his brilliant characterization He made such a hit with his invention, Hettie the Hen, that he had to come forward on the stage every night of *The Merry Widow* and give the audience the latest bulletin on Hetty.

Daly's box office was besieged next day. The theatre libraries, which had scorned the piece only the day before, were now begging the Guv'nor to sell them tickets. *The Merry Widow* was an ideal show for the Edwardians: men and women of all classes succumbed to its music and romance, and people went to see it time and again just for the pleasure of watching Lily Elsie and Joe Coyne dancing the Waltz together. King Edward VII saw it four times: some of his subjects went ten, twenty and even fifty times. Although George Edwardes had to pay royalties to two authors—Basil Hood and Edward Morton—it made very little difference to him because *The Merry Widow* was making a fortune.

After Franz Lehár heard Joe Coyne recite his songs on the first night, he decided that the effect was most artistic and afterwards, whenever *The Merry Widow* was performed, he insisted that Prince Danilo *must* recite his songs. But nothing could stop Joe Coyne worrying: in spite of the glowing notices, in spite of the terrific applause he received at every performance, in spite of the long run, he was convinced that he had given a rotten performance.

One can only describe *The Merry Widow* as a phenomenon. It toured all over the British Isles and broke records, and it repeated its success in the United States and in every English-speaking country. It ran for a year at the New Amsterdam Theatre, New York, and took a million dollars.

In America they cashed in on its success and opened Merry Widow beer cellars, and sold Merry Widow chocolates, cigars and beefsteaks. And, as was only to be expected, some smart aleck put a Merry Widow corset on the market.

The Merry Widow smashed every record at Daly's during its run of over two years, and made Lily Elsie and Joe Coyne stars of the first magnitude. It grossed over a million pounds in London and was seen by over a million people; 200,000 copies of the Merry Widow Waltz were sold in London alone. Women were wearing the huge Merry Widow hats from Mayfair to Mile End. And George Edwardes was in clover again; his financial worries were over for the next two years.

14 The Trouble with Three Theatres

> *George Edwardes needed the resources of a bank*
> *to produce all the plays that appealed to him. . . .*
> *He depended on his theatrical coups to pay for*
> *his betting losses.*
>
> D. FORBES WINSLOW, *Daly's*

Audiences were still queueing up for *The Merry Widow* and Lily Elsie was the toast of the town when the Guv'nor presented *Havana*, with a score by Leslie Stuart, at the Gaiety. Its leading lady was Evie Greene and the principal comedian was Alfred Lester, a clever and original artist whose gloomy expression became his trademark. *Havana* got off to a poor start: it would probably have had a better chance at Daly's. The Guv'nor took W. H. Berry out of *The Merry Widow* and put him into *Havana* in order to strengthen the comedy side. Bill Berry made a great personal success; his cheerful manner was infectious and his two numbers, 'Filibuster Brown' and 'How Did the Bird Know That?' became very popular.

Berry had been given some sound advice by the Guv'nor when he first came to London under his management. 'Berry! Make sure of a good entrance, me lad, and a good exit,' said Edwardes. 'What comes in between doesn't matter so much. But get 'em from the word go and the rest is easy.'*

Bill Berry was *too* successful in *Havana* from Alfred Lester's

* Berry.

point of view. He was getting more laughs in the show than Lester and, since he had a much better voice, he had taken over the number 'Filibuster Brown' from him. The comedian brooded over his grievances and decided to go and see the Guv'nor one night after the show. Edwardes was playing bridge in his office with Walter Pallant, the Gaiety chairman, and Leslie Stuart and other cronies. On hearing that Alfred Lester was coming to see him to complain about Berry, Edwardes said to them, 'Now for the love of Mike don't mention the name of Bill Berry to him! It might slip out, but if it does it'll be a red rag to a bull.' Alfred Lester came into the office looking the picture of misery. George Edwardes got up from his chair, beamed at him and said, 'Hello, *Berry*, how are you?'* There was a dreadful silence, then it took all the Guv'nor's tact to calm down the infuriated comedian.

Gladys Cooper appeared in *Havana* as one of the Touring Newspaper Beauties and had one line of dialogue: 'It looks like the top of a hatpin—is it real?' This inane remark ought to have been pretty easy to remember, but Gladys Cooper was a perfectionist and rehearsed it in the dressing-room for hours. She yearned to become a real actress and play proper parts and felt that George Edwardes was not giving her a fair chance. This raging beauty had her work cut out to keep the stage-door johnnies at bay; she was engaged to Herbert Buckmaster by this time and took a serious view of her status.

Buckmaster was a pleasant young man of good family who did nothing in particular, which caused her conventional father to refuse to consent to them getting married, But Gladys Cooper defied the ban and eloped with Herbert Buckmaster after the last night of *Havana*. Buckmaster himself achieved a minor celebrity by founding Buck's Club, which is still flourishing in 1974.

Two of the other Touring Newspaper Beauties with Gladys Cooper were Trixie and Hope Hillier. Hope Hillier can still remember her first sight of Gladys Cooper—'She came into the dressing-room looking so beautiful that I had to gasp for breath.' The Hillier sisters were living far out at Woodford in Essex, so if they went out to supper with a masher he drove them to Liverpool Street afterwards and they caught the last train to Woodford. But sometimes Hope Hillier, better known today as Mrs Mirabel Topham of Aintree, missed the last train to

* Jupp.

Woodford and had to get out at a junction five miles away and walk home across Epping Forest. 'I was not in the least frightened,' said Mrs Topham. 'At that hour in the morning there were only a few tramps sleeping rough in the forest, and they used to call out good night to me. We girls certainly had some energy in those days.'*

The next Gaiety show, *Our Miss Gibbs*, had an excellent cast headed by Gertie Millar, Teddy Payne and George Grossmith. While George Edwardes was rehearsing it, Julia had a letter from Lucy Carr Shaw, Bernard Shaw's sister, who had appeared in *Dorothy*. Lucy Carr Shaw mentioned that Shaw's comedy *Arms and the Man* had been made into an operetta called *The Chocolate Soldier*, with a score by Oscar Straus. It was a tremendous success in Germany, said Lucy Carr Shaw, and added, 'Why doesn't your George produce my George's operetta in England. Please ask your George if he would like to do it.'†

Julia passed on her suggestion to George that he might like to buy the English rights of *The Chocolate Soldier*, but he turned it down. He disliked Shaw, possibly because Shaw always knocked the Gaiety shows when he was drama critic of the *Saturday Review*. Apart from that, he knew Bernard Shaw was a most efficient businessman who handled all his own contracts, and was afraid he would demand enormous royalties. It was one of the biggest mistakes of his career: the English version of *The Chocolate Soldier* had a world-wide success almost comparable with *The Merry Widow*.

Our Miss Gibbs, produced at the Gaiety on 23 January, 1908, was a cast iron winner for the Guv'nor. Gertie Millar played Miss Gibbs, a lass from Yorkshire who worked at Garrods department store where 'they sell every conceivable thing from enamel chains to aeroplanes and from pianolas to petticoats'. Everyone knew that Garrods was really Harrods, and the stage set was more or less a replica of the famous luxury store in Knightsbridge. Teddy Payne was Tim, Miss Gibbs's breezy Yorkshire cousin who calls in to see her on his way to a brass band competition, and Grossmith was the Honourable Hughie, a young man about town with a strange ambition to become an amateur cracksman like Raffles. The score was by the old team

* Conversation with Misses Trixie and Hope Hillier.
† Hibbert.

MR GEORGE GROSSMITH Jnr.
as
"The Hon Hughie"

MR EDMUND PAYNE as "TIM"

of Monckton and Caryll, and the book by James Tanner and 'Cryptos', which was a nom-de-plume for the Guv'nor. Miss Gibbs had a big romance with an earl who worked at Garrods incognito. Then the plot revolved round the theft of the Ascot Gold Cup—a subject dear to the heart of George Edwardes on account of his horse Santoi.

Our Miss Gibbs received wonderful notices. The *Daily Chronicle* critic said:

> Altogether the best and brightest Gaiety show we have had for five or six years . . . there is a new spirit pervading *Our Miss Gibbs*. There is true, fresh, observant humour peeping out here, there and everywhere . . . . There is . . . a spirited championship of the typical middle-class shop girl as respresented by 'Our Miss Gibbs' herself. With it all the piece is light and jolly and sparkling . . . it is a dream of splendour and beauty. . . .
>
> Those who know and love Mr Edmund Payne can imagine him, with . . . a brilliantly suggested Yorkshire accent, in a stumpy little white top hat, a suit of ill-fitting pepper and salt, and a handbag in one hand and a vast brass trumpet in the other. While Mr Payne was on the stage . . . with his open-hearted comradeship with his cousin (Gertie Millar) there was not a dull moment. . . . With the admirable story are interspersed songs and dances and little mimic scenes between Mr Payne and Miss Gertie Millar, many of which are the prettiest that have been heard at the Gaiety. . . .

Lionel Monckton had written all Gertie Millar's numbers and had given her a Yorkshire one since she really was a Yorkshire lass. He also wrote her a number entitled 'Moonstruck', one of the highlights of the show. The lights were lowered and Gertie Millar tripped on to the stage in a dark blue pierrot costume with a bow under her chin, wearing a pair of large white gloves. The chorus, dressed as light blue pierrots, danced in the background as she sang:

> I'm such a silly when the moon comes out,
> I hardly seem to know what I'm about,
> Skipping, hopping,
> Never never stopping,

I can't keep still although I try;
I'm all a-quiver when the moonbeams glance,
That is the moment when I long to dance:
I can never close a sleepy eye
When the moon comes creeping up the sky.

Her contemporaries said that Gertie Millar danced like a moonbeam herself, and she was supposed to have the tiniest feet on the stage. People who saw her dance 'Moonstruck' seemed to remember it for the rest of their lives.

George Grossmith made a big hit with his inconsequential song 'Yip-i-addy-i-ay', yet when the Guv'nor first heard it he couldn't stand it at any price, and said, 'I won't have that beastly thing in my theatre.' However, Edwardes thought so highly of Gee-Gee that he had made him one of his lieutenants, and he agreed to let him try out his number on the first night. It became the most popular number in the show within a week and is still played today:

Yip-i-addy-i-ay, i-ay,
Yip-i-addy-i-ay,
I don't care what becomes of me,
When she plays me that sweet melody.
Yip-i-addy-i-ay, i-ay!
I just want to shout out Hooray!
Sing of Joy!
Sing of Bliss!
Home was never like this,
Yip-i-addy-i-ay.

Ruby Miller, the precocious schoolgirl who had wangled her way into *The Orchid*, had grown up and become an actress. She wrote to the Guv'nor to ask if he would take her back at the Gaiety, and he engaged her as a showgirl and as Gladys Cooper's understudy in *Our Miss Gibbs*. With her good looks and spectacular red hair Ruby became a favourite of the mashers— 'resplendent young men in their tails, their opera hat and cloak lined with satin, carrying tall ebony canes with gold knobs and gardenias in their buttonholes'.*

A titled admirer sent Ruby Miller a bunch of orchids with

* Ruby Miller, *Champagne in my Slipper* (Herbert Jenkins, 1962).

£5 notes wrapped round each stem. Jupp, at the stage door,
returned all the fivers to him with this message: 'I'm sorry,
m'Lord, but Mr Edwardes does not allow his young ladies to
receive gifts of money.' However, his Lordship made up
amply for his *faux pas* by sending her a magnificent Fabergé
emerald and diamond bracelet the following night.

A Russian Grand Duke gave a party for Ruby Miller at
Romano's, and during the evening he asked her to lend him her
slipper. She took it off and he filled it with champagne and,
bowing to her, drained the contents from the back of the shoe.
'That was a charming gesture, sir, but it has left my slipper
somewhat damp,' said Ruby. A few days later she received half
a dozen pairs of slippers of all colours from H. and M. Rayne,
the theatrical shoemakers. There was a note inside:

DEAR MISS RUBY MILLER,
    That was the best champagne I ever drank. Thank you for
the loan of your slipper.

x.*

After *Our Miss Gibbs* Gertie Millar left the Gaiety for good.
The Guv'nor took this important decision because he had just
bought a third theatre for his musical plays—the Adelphi—
and had arranged to present her in *The Quaker Girl* there
instead of at the Gaiety. He had bought it on the optimistic
theory that if he had three theatres instead of two under his
management, it would help to spread the enormous risks
involved in the production of musical shows. Before *The
Quaker Girl* opened, he spent £20,000 on modernizing and
re-decorating the Adelphi Theatre.

But Gertie Millar was irreplacable at the Gaiety; it meant the
break-up of the marvellous team of Gertie Millar, Teddy
Payne, George Grossmith and Connie Ediss, and regular patrons
complained that the theatre was never the same after she left
it. Max Beerbohm had written when he saw her in *Our Miss
Gibbs* that 'Miss Gertie Millar . . . has achieved an exquisite
style in comedy, of a kind precisely fitted to the tasks laid on it,
and this, with her charm, is all-sufficient. One cannot imagine
her at any other theatre than the Gaiety, nor imagine the
Gaiety without her.'

* Miller.

After *The Merry Widow* came off in 1909 the Guv'nor presented *The Dollar Princess* at Daly's with Lily Elsie and Joe Coyne as the co-stars. The Guv'nor was only paying Lily Elsie £10 a week when she first played the Merry Widow; he then raised her salary to £20, but even that was a stingy reward for her ability to bring the customers to Daly's in their thousands. Lily Elsie, who had started life as Elsie Cotton in Yorkshire and been a child actress, was very shy and nervous and no match for George Edwardes when she had to interview him about her salary.

It took her a long time to screw up her courage to ask him for another rise, and when she did see him in the office Edwardes talked so much about other matters that she never got a word in edgeways. Then he told her how busy he was and bundled her out of the office, assuring her that the only way to keep healthy was to eat a pound of green apples every day. Lily Elsie should have asked Marie Tempest to give her six lessons in how to deal with the Guv'nor.

The Dollar Princess was by Leo Falls, a German composer, and its plot had echoes of *The Admirable Crichton* about it. Joe Coyne played an eccentric American oil king who insisted on having impoverished European aristocrats as his servants. He fell in love with the housekeeper, who turned out to be a bogus Russian countess. His sister Alice—played enchantingly by Lily Elsie—fell in love with her well bred English secretary (Robert Michaelis). Alice proposed to him, but he was too proud to marry her for her money. He left on the spot, though he loved her dearly, and went to California and struck oil. Alice followed him there and they swiftly got married.

The Guv'nor had great hopes of *The Dollar Princess* and was disappointed that it only ran for a year. After a first night he always held a full rehearsal for the company. He would sit at a table on the stage with his back to the footlights and begin by saying: 'Now, boys and girls, you were all very good last night, very good indeed . . . but the show's too long—we must cut out at least half an hour of the dialogue . . . now we'll run through the show and see what we can cut.'

On one occasion Willie Warde, who played small parts as well as doing dance arrangements, spoke up: 'You don't want to cut any of mine, do you, Guv'nor? I've only got one line: "Four pounds six and ninepence." That's all I've got to say.'

'There you are,' said Edwardes solemnly. 'Make it eightpence-halfpenny—we'll *never* get the curtain down!'*

The Guv'nor reopened the Adelphi with Gertie Millar in *The Quaker Girl* on 5 November 1910. Joe Coyne joined her as co-star and Lionel Monckton wrote one of his best scores for it. *The Quaker Girl* was a winner after the Guv'nor's heart and ran for 550 performances. The late Sir Noël Coward saw it when he was a schoolboy and adored it so much that he used to save up his pocket money every week so that he could afford a seat in the gallery. He would gaze down from the 'gods' on Gertie Millar, whom he worshipped from afar.

'Her quality was unique and unmistakable, and will always live in the hearts of those who saw her,' he said. 'She was the essence of enchantment in the theatre. . . . And *The Quaker Girl* was the epitome of what a musical comedy ought to be.'†

Gertie Millar was superb as Prudence, the Quaker Girl, who found life desperately dull until Tony—played by Joe Coyne—descended on her. This young American diplomat from Paris flirted with her and sang:

When a bad, bad boy like me
Meets a good, good girl like you

After Tony had taught Prudence to dance in an irresistible number entitled 'The Dancing Lesson', a French dressmaker turned up and went into ecstasies about her Quaker clothes. Prudence was easily persuaded to leave her dull, religious home and come to Paris to model new fashions with Tony as her escort. There were troubles in Paris, where she found Tony philandering with an actress, but it was all smoothed out by the finale. Other popular numbers in *The Quaker Girl* were 'Thee loves me and I loves thee', sung by Gertie Millar and Joe Coyne as a duet, and 'Come to the Ball'.

The *Daily Chronicle* gave it a marvellous notice, like the rest of the Press:

A beautiful theatre, a beautiful production, with taste in every frill of the costumier and every fancy of the scenic

* Forbes Winslow.

† Sir Noël Coward, Introduction to Raymond Mander & Joe Mitchenson, *Musical Comedy* (Peter Davies, 1969).

painter . . . and a play which is in one respect . . . among the
very best produced by Mr George Edwardes. . . . As 'a farce
for music' this is the most ingenious piece of sheer construc-
tion on Mr Tanner's part. . . . Most important of all, there is
Miss Gertie Millar as The Quaker Girl herself. It is, of course,
the daintiness, neatness and perpetual intelligence of this
artist that is at the heart of the whole escapade. . . .

The Quaker Girl was an ideal musical comedy to open the
Adelphi with, but the Guv'nor's later shows at this theatre were
not nearly as entertaining. He soon found that running three
theatres meant harder work for him in his middle age and
brought him more worries than before. George Edwardes in his
fifties was going grey and had begun to look an old man.
Racing was his main diversion: he followed the fortunes of his
big string of racehorses as keenly as ever and spent most of his
weekends at Ogbourne Maisey, without Julia.

Sometimes he went over to Ireland for a short weekend and
visited his stud at Ballykisteen, where Santoi had been installed
and had already sired some good winners. Santoi had an
abominable temper which had caused him in his racing days to
bite one of his jockeys and anyone rash enough to come too
near him in his stall. Before he went to stud the vet had
suggested it might change his ugly nature if they could find a
donkey to keep him company. Major John Edwards, George's
trainer, who was also his brother, bought a donkey for half a
crown which settled down in perfect bliss with Santoi and
always slept with him in his stall. Henceforth he became a
reformed character and was never known to bite anyone
again.

Santoi went on to sire winners of a thousand races and was
still alive in the twenties, siring his last winner at the venerable
age of twenty-eight.

George Edwardes was a compulsive gambler. He had been
backing horses for years and nothing could stop him continuing
to do so. 'Jommy Edwardes', his young nephew, came over on a
visit from St Petersburg and was taken to the races by George
Edwardes. The boy's eyes nearly popped out when Uncle
George handed him two crisp white £100 notes and said, 'Put
it all on such-and-such a horse to win—it's a good thing!'*

* Conversation with Julius Edwardes.

The horse started favourite and won, and Edwardes promptly collected the money.

George Edwardes's eldest daughter, Dorothy, who was always known as 'Pops', had married Cuthbert Sherbrooke, a member of a well known banking family. Edwardes gave them his house at 6 Park Square as a wedding present, and he and Julia moved into number 11—a bigger house—with the three younger children, D'Arcy, Nancy and Norah. He had a lift installed in the new house because he was starting to get short of breath. Edwardes recognized that 'Pops' had good taste and a feeling for the theatre, and sometimes discussed his theatrical problems with her.

He still indulged in transient affairs and Julia continued to ignore them. She and George kept up appearances in front of the children; she glossed over his absences from Winkfield Lodge at some weekends by inventing trips to the Continent for him. D'Arcy Edwardes was at Eton and was going to follow the family tradition and go into the Army. Nancy and Norah were not the brightest of scholars; perhaps it was their father's fault that they found *Ruff's Guide to the Turf* more fascinating reading than the works of Charles Dickens.

Pops sometimes went racing with her father. He always dressed very correctly in a tight-fitting morning coat on these occasions, whereas he generally wore a lounge suit in the theatre. Pops noticed that, as soon as the horses came into the straight, her father's heart started beating so fast that she could almost see his muscles rippling away under his morning coat. She didn't enjoy going racing with him as much as she might have because she kept worrying about the reckless way he backed horses.*

In the summer of 1910 George Edwardes had his first intimation of heart trouble. The doctors found he was suffering from high blood pressure and warned him to take things more easily for his health's sake. He weighed about seventeen stone and was told to take off at least one stone. But he was so preoccupied with his three theatres and his racing interests that he could never stick to any weight-reducing programme and never got down to a proper diet.

On 17 August he travelled to Germany to take the cure at

* Conversation with Julius Edwardes.

Bad Nauheim near Frankfurt, but it failed to work on him. Back in London he started courses of intense massaging in an effort to get his weight down. His friend Chance Newton found him 'enduring the most drastic rubbing and pommelling at all hours of the day'.

The Gaiety chorus was becoming a matrimonial agency for girls with ambitions to marry into the peerage. It began in the nineties when Connie Gilchrist, a star of the Old Gaiety, had married the Earl of Orkney. Then Rosie Boote, who had charmed London when she sang 'Maisie was a Daisy' in *The Messenger Boy*, went off and married the Marquess of Headfort at the turn of the century. After Connie Gilchrist and Rosie Boote had started the fashion, a score of the Guv'nor's budding stars left him to marry peers or men of title, while other Gaiety Girls settled for a banker or a stockbroker. The Guv'nor, finding this was playing ducks and drakes with his theatrical plans, had a 'nuptial clause' inserted in every contract.

When George Edwardes heard that a certain Gaiety Girl had been led to the altar he burst out: 'It's ingratitude, sheer ingratitude! I've done everything for her—taught her to pick up her aitches, clean her fingernails, had her teeth looked to, her appendix removed, her hair dyed, dressed her from her underclothes to her boots, and now, when she looks like making good, she *marries*!'*

Debutantes were competing with the other girls to get into the Gaiety chorus, while upper-class youths were joining the ranks of the chorus boys. Soon after the accession of George V two immaculate chorus boys were chatting together on the stage before the curtain went up.

'I wonder is dear old George in front tonight?' said one of them.† G. M. Salter, the stage manager, overheard them. Shocked by their impertinence, he said pompously, 'I must ask you to remember that when you have occasion to refer to Mr George Edwardes in this theatre, you must refer to him as *Mister* George Edwardes and in no other manner!' 'Oh, I was talking about the King, old boy,' drawled the chorister.‡

The Guv'nor heard bad reports of one of his touring shows at Sheffield. He went up to the theatre incognito with Frank Tours, his musical director, and another of his lieutenants, and they sat down among the audience in the dress circle. George

* Booth, *London Town*.　　　† Glover.　　　‡ *Ibid.*

Edwardes thought the conductor of the orchestra so appalling
that he asked Frank Tours who he was. Tours knew nothing
about him and George shouted, 'Even if you can't tell me
where he comes from, I can tell you where he's going to!'*
People sitting near them started to shush George Edwardes.
The leading man began his solo and made a hash of it. The
Guv'nor interrupted—just as if he was conducting a rehearsal
at the Gaiety—and shouted, 'Go back—go back—it's all
wrong!'

Edwardes had created such a disturbance that his two
lieutenants firmly conducted him out of the theatre. It was
the last time he ever interfered with one of his provincial
tours.

Chance Newton and George Edwardes were lifelong friends
and George sometimes nattered to him about his theatre
troubles when they lunched together. Chance Newton told him
he was wasting a lot of money on artists' salaries.

'Why are you paying so-and-so £80 a week if you don't use
him?' asked Newton.

George replied in a superior voice, 'My boy! you can't see
an inch before your nose. I must do this sort of thing to keep
other managers from getting these people!'†

However, the Gaiety Girls passed their days quite heedless of
the Guv'nor's problems and most of them had a whale of a time.
They led the fashion parade at Ascot, wearing huge picture hats
or small toques made entirely from flowers which matched their
frocks. On Ascot Sunday crowds used to wait at Boulter's Lock,
Maidenhead, to catch a glimpse of the Gaiety girls in their
summer hats and dresses being poled up the river by their young
swains.

At some time or another almost every girl at the Gaiety was
driven down to the Star and Garter at Richmond for the
evening. J. B. Booth of the 'Pink 'un' recalled a happy summer
evening there by the riverside. Dinner was served in the big
dining-room with large bow windows, with an orchestra playing
waltz tunes in the background. The Star and Garter was
illuminated by Chinese lanterns which produced an enchanting
effect as the moon rose over the river. The restaurant drew its
clientele from all types. There were young bloods dining
tête-à-tête with pretty girls; City men having a family night

* Jupp.   † Newton.

out with their wives and children; and bachelor parties of rowing men who had come straight in from the river. Booth spotted a charming little Gaiety girl, whose doctor's certificate had only recently been handed in to the stage manager, 'recuperating' with the aid of her dashing young Guardee escort.* But he was far too good a sport to report her to the Guv'nor.

* Booth, *London Town*.

15 Twenty-Five Years a Manager

> *Has he not given happiness to thousands nightly?—and to give happiness to the greatest number has been defined as the highest form of morality.*
>
> SIR HEBERT TREE, speaking about George Edwardes at his Jubilee dinner at the Savoy—
> 5 November 1911

The Guv'nor could not find a leading lady for the Gaiety who came within a mile of Gertie Millar. The actress he chose to replace her, Phyllis Dare, was very young and pretty and an English Rose type. A delightful dancer and a good singer, she had a wistful charm and a touch of sentiment in her personality; but she was not at home at the Gaiety where the patrons liked their stars pert and rather impudent.

Phyllis Dare made her debut in *Peggy* on 4 March 1911, as a manicurist at a London hotel who was wooed and won by a charming young man from the upper crust. Teddy Payne played Albert Umbles, a hairdresser who worked with Peggy and was once engaged to her. George Grossmith had some amusing moments as a man about town reduced to working as a street hawker at the French seaside, but this didn't stop his romance with Olive May.

The score by Leslie Stuart was written in a slow tempo, and his numbers were not nearly as lively as those of Lionel

Monckton and Ivan Caryll. *Peggy* failed to bring in the Gaiety patrons and came off after 270 performances, which was a 'nitter' by the Guv'nor's standards.

During the show one of Gabs Ray's admirers sent her the biggest present that had ever been delivered at the Gaiety: a complete grapevine trained to grow in the shape of a half-hoop. It was brought to the stage door in a cart and needed four men to carry it inside. The vine stood ten feet high and had twenty bunches of perfect grapes: it had been cultivated for eight years as an experiment. When it stood inside the hall of the stage door it looked like the handle of a gigantic fruit basket.

Although *Peggy* had been a disappointment, the Guv'nor still hoped to build up Phyllis Dare into a big star. He gave her a second chance in *The Sunshine Girl*, which took place at Port Sunshine, another name for Port Sunlight, Lever's huge model soap factory outside Liverpool. Phyllis Dare played Delia Dale of the Perfume Department, who was in love with Vernon (Basil Foster) but had no idea he had just inherited the factory. Wishing to keep this a dark secret—so that she would love him for himself—he persuaded his friend, Lord Bicester (George Grossmith) to take over the soap factory instead. But things went wrong when Floot (Teddy Payne) arrived on the scene: this petty crook on the run blackmailed Lord Bicester into making him general manager, and then proceeded to turn everything upside down.

Connie Ediss played Mrs Floot and made a hit with her number, 'I've been to the Durbar', and there was a popular quartet entitled 'What did the butler see?' Paul Rubens, who was starting to rival Lionel Monckton, wrote the score and also collaborated on the lyrics and the book. He was deeply in love with Phyllis Dare and they were engaged; but he had consumption and felt it would be wrong to marry her until he was sure of a reasonable chance of being cured. Rubens had started writing songs when he was a Cambridge undergraduate. Charming, witty and kind, he thoroughly enjoyed the social side of life: he worked hard and played hard and managed to get along with very little sleep.

For a time Robert Courtneidge was in joint management with George Edwardes at various theatres; later he became a leading producer of musical plays in competition with the Guv'nor. Sometimes Courtneidge used to call on Paul Rubens

at midnight to discuss a new number, the composer would
hurry in from a party and start talking about his new song with
great enthusiasm, as if he had just started the day. A chance
suggestion from Courtneidge would be quite enough to set his
agile brain working; Rubens would sit down at the piano and
gradually shape out the words and music. Courtneidge used
to leave him polishing his number as he smoked a cigarette,
looking as if he hadn't the slightest intention of ever going to
bed.*

The Guv'nor tried out *The Sunshine Girl* at Brighton before
bringing it in to the Gaiety. Paul Rubens was suffering from a
bout of consumption at the time, but he called in at the theatre
stage door and left a new number he had just written for
Phyllis Dare. It was a very sentimental song with a lovely
melody and became immensly popular:

> I love the moon, I love the sun,
> I love the wild birds, the dawn and the dew,
> I love the forest, the flowers and the fun,
> But best of all I love you, I love you!

Produced in October, 1911, *The Sunshine Girl* ran for 336
performances; this was an improvement on *Peggy*, but it was
not an out-and-out winner for the Guv'nor. Connie Ediss sang
a song in praise of Brighton—which happened to be her home
town—and followed it with one of her wild, abandoned dances:

> Take me on the boat to Brighton,
> Put me on the pier at Brighton,
> That's the place for me,
> London by the sea,
> Leave me there and I shall be as happy as can be.
> Oh, when I leave my own back garden
> I don't look for Baden-Baden,
> I've travelled once or twice
> To Monte or to NICE
> But Brighton's Nice enough for me!

Gladys Cooper had left George Edwardes after the run of
Our Miss Gibbs and started a new career on the legitimate

* Robert Courtneidge, *I Was an Actor Once* (Hutchinson, 1930).

stage. This event prompted *Theatre* to write the following piece:

> Bow down your heads, O lovers of Musical Comedy, for beautiful, charming, fair-haired Miss Cooper has forsaken you. No more will she trip divinely down the stage and say with her adorable smile as she did in *Havana*: 'Hello, people—people, hello.'

Gladys Cooper left because she felt she was getting nowhere under the Guv'nor's management. He paid her only £5 a week and kept promising her wonderful parts that never materialized. He was always willing to see her, but whenever she went to his office to ask him for a rise the conversation went roughly like this:

GLADYS COOPER Good morning, Mr Edwardes, I have come to ask you if—

GEORGE EDWARDES Sit down, my dear . . . I'm glad you have come because I want to tell you about a wonderful play I saw in Vienna last week. I shall do it in London soon, and there's a lovely part for you . . . I'm keeping my eye on you, you see, my dear.

GLADYS COOPER Thank you, Mr Edwardes, I love being with you, but don't you think you could——?

GEORGE EDWARDES Of course I can't afford to put on a new production till things improve—but as soon as I can I'll get to work. . . .

GLADYS COOPER But you see I was wondering if you could possibly see your way——

GEORGE EDWARDES I know you ought to have more to do, my dear. . . . So you shall. But there's a part in that play I saw that'll suit you down to the ground. . . . I'm very busy just now, my dear, so if you'll just run along . . .*

Gladys Cooper's account of her interviews with the Guv'nor has the ring of truth, and he richly deserved to lose her to the legitimate theatre. One can understand why George Graves used to call him 'the old sprucer'.

Although *The Dollar Princess* had been a disappointment to

* Cooper.

the Guv'nor at Daly's, he had high hopes of his next production, *The Count of Luxembourg*. In the first place Lily Elsie starred in it, and secondly the score was by Franz Lehár; he believed that this combination made it a cast-iron certainty. *The Count of Luxembourg* opened in a blaze of glory on 20 May 1911 with King George V and Queen Mary present in the Royal Box and Franz Lehár conducting the orchestra.

Playing opposite Lily Elsie as the Count was Bertram Wallis, a very handsome actor with a fine voice who was a worthy successor to Hayden Coffin. Huntley Wright was a Grand Duke infatuated with Angela, played by Lily Elsie. He had been so kind to her that she agreed to marry him, but first it was essential for her to have a title. She therefore agreed to go through a marriage ceremony with the spendthrift Count of Luxembourg (Bertram Wallis), in which the bride and groom never saw each other and agreed to have a divorce three months afterwards. However, Angela and the Count came face to face and fell in love at sight and vowed that their marriage should be a genuine one after all. It all ended happily by the end of the second act.

Franz Lehár's score was superb from a musical point of view, but lacking in popular appeal. Lily Elsie and Bertram Wallis had a duet entitled 'Are You going to Dance?' which led into the Staircase Waltz in which they danced up and down an elaborate staircase. The Guv'nor was banking on it being as popular as the Merry Widow Waltz. Incidentally, he had just raised Lily Elsie's salary to £100 a week, so he must have been confident it was a winner. The advance booking was excellent and so were the first-night notices. But the critic of the *Daily Chronicle* put his finger on the flaw in this operetta.

Far and away the most splendid production that has been seen at Daly's—from beginning to end a voluptuous dream of luscious music and dazzling light . . . of riotous carnivals and sighing love songs. . . . Just as the production is more gorgeous (than *The Merry Widow*) so Franz Lehár's music is more elaborate, more decorative, full of ingenious orchestrations. . . . It is better music . . . but without the same definite and simple imspiration. The great waltz of the evening is the one in which Mr Bertram Wallis and Miss Lily Elsie waltz up a flight of stairs. . . . But the waltz is not of the kind that everyone can hum the moment after they have heard it played for the first time—as with *The Merry Widow* and *The Chocolate Soldier.* . . . This is so with the whole evening. It is delicious while it lasts. . . . But one comes away with few definite musical remembrances.

Miss Lily Elsie is still without rival in her own marvellous art. Looking really beautiful . . . she still gives the strange impression of a being from another world, where stage romances are life-and-death affairs, and a touch of the finger-tips, a glance, a whisper, are matters of almost religious ecstasy. . . .

In spite of Miss Elsie's 'marvellous art', the public had little time or inclination for *The Count of Luxembourg*, so the Guv'nor cut his losses and took it off. During the run Lily Elsie told him she was going to marry the Hon. Ian Bullogh and that she had made up her mind to retire from the stage on her marriage. This was even a worse blow to Edwardes than the failure of *The Count*: Lily Elsie was one of the greatest stars he had ever handled, and leading ladies of her calibre did not grow on trees.

It has already been said that George Edwardes's passion for racing was almost on a par with his love of the theatre. The year 1911 turned out to be one of the most successful he ever had on the Turf; his horses won a total of £5,345 in races on the Flat, but this was a drop in the ocean to Edwardes, who was such a reckless punter that he could lose £5,000 in a week.

Edwardes continued to live in hopes of repeating the big gambling coup he had pulled off with Fairyfield in 1898. Fairyfield was a two-year-old entered for a selling race at Kempton Park, and he believed it was a certainty. If the horse had been ridden by its regular jockey, Allsopp, it would probably have started favourite but, on the advice of Teddy Hobson, who did all Edwardes's betting commissions, they put up an apprentice named Aylin. Fairyfield ran at Kempton at odds of 100–8 and won—and Edwardes netted £18,000.

George Edwardes was deeply in the red and he ought to have made stringent economies. He could easily have halved his expenses by selling all his racehorses or his estate at Ogbourne or the breeding establishment at Ballykisteen. But, after thinking the matter over, he decided there was no need to make any change in the pattern of his life for the time being and pinned his hopes on his three theatres—the Gaiety, Daly's and the Adelphi. He reasoned that if he could only produce a smash hit at each of them in 1912 he would be solvent again and be able to carry on racing in the style to which he had grown accustomed.

The first years of the new century marked a turning-point in the British theatre: the playwrights of the New Drama, with Bernard Shaw at their head, came into their own and eclipsed the old guard, led by Pinero and Henry Arthur Jones. *Mrs Dane's Defence*, one of Jones's greatest successes, was produced in October 1900 at Wyndham's. Mrs Dane had changed her name after being involved in the scandal of her lover's death. She got engaged to a Judge's son, which was a great mistake, as the Judge grilled her into confessing the truth about her past. Thus the Judge broke up his son's romance, but the rather odious character was so skilfully played by Charles Wyndham that he retained the audience's sympathy. The play was a superb piece of theatre at the time, and Lena Ashwell gave a highly intelligent, memorable performance as Mrs Dane.

Marie Tempest established herself as a leading comedy actress in *The Marriage of Kitty*, a slight comedy produced at the Duke of York's in August 1902. It was written by her husband, Cosmo Gordon Lennox, and produced by Dion Boucicault. Marie Tempest acknowledged that, after she had left George Edwardes and Daly's Theatre, Boucicault had taught her everything about acting.

Lewis Waller appeared in *Monsieur Beaucaire*, a romantic cloak-and-sword drama, at the Comedy in October 1902. Waller was perfect in his role of a French nobleman masquerading as a barber at Bath in order to win the love of a proud English beauty. Booth Tarkington's piece bristled with intrigues; the audience lapped it up and greatly appreciated Waller's splendid display of swordsmanship.

His performance as D'Artagnan in *The Three Musketeers* had established Waller as the finest actor of his time in costume drama. He wore doublet and hose as to the manner born, and his verve and panache made the most far-fetched situations credible to audiences. Women flocked to see this prince of matinee idols and watched him, enthralled, as he made love to his leading ladies. Lewis Waller was a short man off the stage, and when he appeared in contemporary parts he never made the same overwhelming impact.

After Seymour Hicks and Ellaline Terris had left George Edwardes, they appeared under the management of Charles Frohman, mostly in musical comedies. Seymour Hicks presented *Bluebell in Fairyland* as a children's entertainment at the Vaudeville on 18 December, 1901. Bluebell was a London flower girl who lived in a garret with her two little sisters. After reading them the story of the Sleepy King one Christmas night, she was visited by fairies who transported her to fairyland where she set out on a mission to find the Sleepy King who had been asleep for 300 years. After adventures all over fairyland she and her schoolboy friends, Blib and Blob, located the King in the bowels of the earth and restored him to his throne. On returning to her garret, Bluebell had a call from a dear old philanthropist who insisted on adopting her and her sisters.

Ellaline Terriss as Bluebell captivated audiences with her unaffected charm and sang 'The Honeysuckle and the Bee', a delightful number by Walter Slaughter. Seymour Hicks, who had also written the show, doubled the parts of the Sleepy King and Dick, a crossing-sweeper friend of Bluebell's. The piece had a very long run and was revived on several occasions.

The Catch of the Season, another of Hicks's biggest successes, was a simple Cinderella story in a Mayfair setting presented at the Vaudeville on 9 September 1904. Angela, the down-trodden daughter of an improverished baronet, was condemned to stay at home while her papa went off to the ball of the year with Lady Crystal and her two ghastly daughters. The ball was given by the young Duke of St Jermyn's, who had already met Angela incognito. Angela's aunt proved herself a fairy godmother and sent her off in style to the Duke's Ball where she created a sensation and won her 'Prince Charming' with the greatest of ease.

This musical comedy was effectively staged, had lively, pointed dialogue and tuneful numbers by five different composers. Zena Dare as Angela had an overnight triumph in her first starring role. She was very young and charming, sang well and acted intelligently. Seymour Hicks played the Duke in his usual dashing style.

Sometimes Seymour Hicks and Ellaline Terriss appeared in straight plays, the most notable being J. M. Barrie's delightful

G

sentimental comedy *Quality Street,* produced at the Vaudeville in September 1903. Phoebe and Susan Throssel were two unmarried sisters who lived in Quality Street during the Napoleonic wars, fully expecting Captain Valentine Brown to come back and marry Phoebe. But when he returned after nine years he found 'Phoebe of the ringlets' had become a tired and faded schoolmistress, and lost interest in her. Phoebe, who was only thirty, decided to dress up as her young 'niece'; she went to the Officers' Ball and flirted outrageously with Valentine Brown and other officers. Brown came to his senses next morning: he called at Quality Street and declared himself in love after all with the 'noble' Miss Phoebe who had only grown old because she had worked so hard running a girls' school with her sister Susan.

Ellaline Terriss made a perfect heroine, alternating between Phoebe and her non-existent niece, Miss Livvy. Seymour Hicks carried off the role of Captain Valentine Brown, and Marion Terry played Susan with distinction.

One of the theatrical occasions of 1902 had been the production of *The Admirable Crichton* at the Duke of York's. The public warmed to Barrie's delicate satirical fantasy about a helpless peer's family who were shipwrecked on an island and all brought under the dominion of Crichton, their perfect butler. But once they had been rescued, all of them reverted to their old roles of servant and master. In this superb play H. B. Irving gave a splendid performance as Crichton and Irene Vanbrugh was excellent as Lady Mary, his 'slave' on the island. Produced by Dion Boucicault, *The Admirable Crichton* had a long run and was revived several times.

Arthur Bouchier produced *The Walls of Jericho* by Alfred Sutro at the Garrick in October 1904. He played a man who made his pile in Australia and returned to London to find Society rotten to the core, and in the process of corrupting his wife. He blew down his part of 'the walls of Jericho' and persuaded his wife to return to Australia with him to a better life. This satirical drama presented a realistic picture of the Edwardian 'smart set' and was played to perfection by Arthur Bouchier and Violet Vanbrugh as the man from Australia and his wife.

1904 was a historic year for the British theatre. Harley Granville-Barker leased the little Court Theatre for a season of *avant-garde* plays which was so successful that it continued till 1907. The principal author performed was Bernard Shaw and for the first time British playgoers began to appreciate this Irish genius. In *John Bull's Other Island*, produced in 1904, he broke all the rules of the well made play and had scarcely any plot; but he held the audience's attention with his witty, pungent dialogue and his interesting Anglo-Irish characters. Such long speeches had not been heard for years in an English theatre. Granville-Barker as Mr Keegan stood out among the actors.

In late December 1904 *Peter Pan*, the most popular of all Barrie's plays, opened at the Duke of York's. Peter Pan's story, with its flight to the Never-Never Land, appealed to both children and grown-ups, even if it failed to please every critic. Nina Boucicault as Peter Pan shared the acting honours with Gerald du Maurier, who doubled the roles of Mr Darling and Captain Hook.

In February 1905 Fred Terry and Julia Neilson appeared in *The Scarlet Pimpernel*, adapted from Baroness Orczy's book, at the Haymarket. This melodramatic piece of hokum made their fortunes. Fred Terry was an ideal Sir Percy, the aristocrat who rescued victims of the French Revolution, and Julia Neilson was equally satisfactory as Lady Blakeney, who was blackmailed into exposing her husband as the Pimpernel by that diabolical villain Chauvelin.

Man and Superman, one of Shaw's best plays, was produced at the Court in May 1905. John Tanner, its hero, was a revolutionary Socialist clearly modelled on Shaw himself. The other main character was Anne Whitfield, a forceful young woman determined to bring Tanner to the altar. It was a battle of the sexes with the odds on Anne and the life force. Every character rang true, and Shaw had the gift of making his audiences laugh at the same time as he expounded his philosophy. Granville-Barker gave a magnificent performance as Tanner and Lilah McCarthy made a perfect Ann Whitfield.

Pinero's last outstanding play, *His House in Order*, was produced at the St James's in February 1906. Nina, once the family governess, became the second wife of a cold-blooded M.P. who regarded his late wife as a paragon. After Nina had been humiliated by everybody for her failings, she suddenly discovered love letters which proved that the first wife was an adulteress who had her son by another man. Hilary, Nina's sympathetic brother-in-law, dissuaded her from exposing the truth to her husband; but in the end he learnt the truth and started to appreciate Nina. The play was an overwhelming triumph for Irene Vanbrugh as Nina, with George Alexander a tower of strength as Hilary.

Somerset Maugham scored his first success in the theatre with his realistic comedy *Lady Frederick*, produced at the Court in October 1907. Lady Frederick, a fascinating Irish widow who was heavily in debt, had a charming young lord dangling by a string. But she decided it would be better for them not to get married and, to cure his illusions about her, she insisted on him staying in her boudoir while she proceeded to make up her face and bring various artificial aids to help her look young and beautiful. Ethel Irving gave a magnificent performance in this highly entertaining play.

Jack Straw, Maugham's next play, was a very light comedy starring Charles Hawtrey, which was produced at the Vaudeville in March 1908. The following month his *Mrs Dot* was presented at the Comedy and provided a wonderful vehicle for Marie Tempest. In 1909 Lewis Waller produced Maugham's comedy *The Explorer* at the Lyric, while *Lady Frederick*, *Mrs Dot* and *Jack Straw* were still running, giving Somerset Maugham the unique distinction of having four plays running in London at the same time.

The Arcadians, a 'fantastic' musical play, was produced by Robert Courtneidge at the Shaftesbury on 18 April 1909. It had an original opening in Arcady in 'a setting as beautiful as anything the domains of musical comedy have shown us'. The nymphs and shepherds of Arcady were still living the simple life when a middle-aged businessman named Smith landed there in his airplane. Smith was changed into Simplicitas and sent to England with two delectable Arcadian damsels to convert the natives to the simple life. They arrived at Ascot, where Simplicitas Smith rode a rogue horse to victory. Then he and the Arcadian girls opened a restaurant to try to popularize the ideal pure life. The mission failed and Smith reverted to his old gross self, but the end was reasonably happy.

One factor in the enormous success of *The Arcadians* was the music by Lionel Monckton and Howard Talbot. There were also two outstanding comedians: Dan Rolyat as Simplicitas

Smith and Alfred Lester as a miserable jockey who never won a race in his life and sang, 'I've gotter motter, always merry and bright.' Florence Smithson made a great hit as the leading Arcadian damsel and Phyllis Dare pleased the public in the role of the heroine. Robert Courtneidge had proved that George Edwardes had no monopoly of the best muscial plays in town.

The Chocolate Soldier, described as 'an authorized parody of Bernard Shaw's play *Arms and the Man*', opened at the Lyric on 10 September 1910. The score by Oscar Straus put it in the comic opera class; it had already had a big success in Germany, and the Guv'nor had missed the chance of presenting it in London. In Shaw's play the Bulgarian heroine saved the chocolate soldier from being shot by the soldiers by hiding him in her bedroom, but despised him for being a coward. The German operetta sweetened the situation and changed names and characters; it had the heroine, Nadina, her mother and her girl cousin all helping to shelter the Swiss chocolate soldier and all falling for this 'lady-killer'. After the war the chocolate soldier returned the Colonel's coat with love letters from all three ladies inside it. Nadina rejected her bogus hero, Alexis, and enthusiastically accepted a proposal from the chocolate soldier, who had just inherited six Swiss hotels.

The Chocolate Soldier was an assured success from the first act, when Constance Driver as Nadina captured the audience with her clever acting and her sweet rendering of 'I love you only', a Straus waltz that became a world hit. C. H. Workman sang splendidly as the chocolate soldier and did wonders with the part.

The Great Adventure by Arnold Bennett was presented at the Kingsway Theatre on 25 March 1913. Like Barrie, Maugham and Galsworthy, Arnold Bennett had made his name as a novelist before he established himself as a dramatist. His whimsical piece was about a famous painter, Ilam Carve, who was so tired of the public's adulation that he let his dead valet be buried in his own place at Westminster Abbey. Carve then had the time of his life, living absolutely free of disturbance with his homely Cockney wife who never talked about art. But unfortunately Ilam Carve couldn't stop painting; a Bond Street expert recognized his work and tracked him down. Then his valet's wife turned up and accused him of bigamy.

However, Carve managed to keep his secret intact from the world, and only a small circle of people knew the truth.

The play, constructed in a number of short scenes, had the good fortune to be produced by Harley Granville-Barker and had a very long run. Henry Ainley, a handsome matinee idol, played Ilam Carve with wonderful delicacy and finesse. But Wish Wynne as his homely wife 'stole' the play, making her a real woman and not a caricature.

John Galsworthy's first play, *The Silver Box*, had been one of the outstanding pieces in Granville-Barker's season at the Court. Barker produced *Justice*, a tragedy by Galsworthy, at the Duke of York's in February 1910. Galsworthy wrote with passionate indignation about a lawyer's clerk who forged a cheque to help the unfortunate woman he was in love with. He was arrested, tried, and sent to prison in solitary confinement, which broke his spirit. He committed a petty crime on his release and, rather than return to prison he took his own life. Granville-Barker produced the court scene, the prison scene and the rest of the play with a realism that the British public had never seen before. Churchill, then Home Secretary, was so moved by *Justice* that he took steps to have the law changed so that such an ordeal as solitary confinement could not happen to future prisoners. By 1910 Shaw, Galsworthy, Barrie and Maugham took over as the leading dramatists and the plays of Pinero and Henry Arthur Jones, had become old-fashioned.

The Guv'nor celebrated his twenty-fifth year as a theatre manager on 26 November 1911; the London theatre managers organized a banquet in his honour at the Savoy Hotel. Sir Herbert Tree, who had succeeded Sir Henry Irving at the head of the profession, took the chair with Sir George Alexander as his deputy. Every theatre manager in London turned up to honour Edwardes, and his Jubliee dinner was also attended by playwrights, actors, singers, musicians, first nighters, newspaper men and 'a sprinkling of lords, none of whom had married a Gaiety Girl'.*

Beerbohm Tree had been knighted in 1909 when he was appearing as Sir John Falstaff in his revival of *The Merry Wives of Windsor*. There was a scene in which Falstaff was lying on the ground, surrounded by village children who were all pinching

* *Sporting Times*, November 1911.

him. Ellen Terry and Constance Collier as the two 'Wives' had to come to his rescue and say, 'Arise, Sir John.' But the evening after he had received the accolade, they changed the words of Shakespeare and said, 'Arise, Sir Herbert,'* This was the first time Tree had been called by his title and the audience at His Majesty's burst into loud cheers.

Sir Herbert Tree made an extremely eloquent speech at the Guv'nor's Jubilee dinner. After congratulating him on completing twenty-five years as a manager, Tree spoke about his prosperity.

> But prosperity alone could not bring together the assembly of men who are sitting round these tables tonight. It is the man no less than the manager: it is rather the man than the manager that we regard.
>
> George Edwardes was predestined by fate to be successful and by character he was predestined to shed the rays of his success on others and to make them happy. He is a man, I believe, who would have won success in any walk of life or on any turf of life . . .. Had he not been a manager of many theatres he might have been a barrister. I can imagine how he would have cajoled a jury with his dulcet accents. . . .
>
> Again, had he been a doctor, my lords and gentlemen, what a bedside manner. . . . As a General—well he who can run three theatres and manage three choruses and a corps de ballet, to him the command of an army corps would be but a pleasant hobby. I know what it is to manage one theatre: what must it be to manage three? . . . Apart from this, he is interested in countless tours. How large, then, is his control, and how many there are to be grateful to him for their daily bread.
>
> . . . Has he not given happiness nightly to thousands?— and to give happiness to the greatest number has been defined as the highest form of morality. George Edwardes has given to gaiety all the adjuncts of beauty on which he could lay his hands—beauty of scenery, beauty of dancing and music, as well as beauty of limb. . . .

Sir Herbert Tree then led up to the presentation of a loving cup to George Edwardes:

* Collier.

What greater compliment could any man ask than that which is so spontaneously given to our friend tonight? True, he has won on the Turf . . . the Ascot Gold Cup. Tonight, he wins in the human race yet another gold cup. Here it is.

My dear Edwardes, in asking you to accept this cup we wish you many sunshine days, and many years to shed your genial rays on those among whom your life is passed. And in those years to come . . . you will, I am sure, prize none of your possessions higher than this, for no man can have a more precious possession than that which we have bestowed on you tonight—this loving cup of friendship.

It was a great moment for George Edwardes when Sir Herbert Tree presented him with a massive gold loving cup; he always treasured this night that his friends in the theatrical profession had given him. When he rose to speak he was so overwhelmed with emotion that at first he seemed lost for words. Then he gathered himself together.

I am, believe me, deeply sensible to . . . the honour you offer me this evening. I confess myself fortunate, very much beyond my deserts, to have the esteem, the sympathy, the goodwill of such a gathering. I feel a proud man . . . in the presence of such a distinguished company, among whom I am flattered to see so many representatives of the calling with which I have been associated all these long years.

. . . If I have sometimes felt more than a little elated when I have found myself praised immoderately in the newspapers . . . praised for certain changes—and I hope, improvements— which I have tried to introduce into the play with music, my vanity . . . is rudely chastened now and then when a sterner critic tells me bluntly that I have all the time been doing my best . . . to destroy the British theatre. . . . If I have cultivated my own little patch in the world of the theatre to some use and advantage, then I am satisfied. . . . I hope I may say for this Cinderella of the drama that it is a little better cared for, better housed, more considerately treated, better dressed, than it used to be in the old days.

I know that . . . there are serious-minded people who will have it that the only function of the theatre is to improve our minds. That is not my philosophy. If I may quote

Shakespeare for my own ends, 'My true intent is all for your delight.' No one has a greater admiration than I for the work accomplished by our leading theatrical managers . . . by Sir Herbert Tree, who has for years been doing single-handed the work of a national theatre, by Sir George Alexander . . . who has done so much for English comedy and the English authors . . . by Sir Charles Wyndham, the incomparable, and by other gentlemen too numerous to mention, whom I see here tonight.

George Edwardes's remark that Tree was doing the work of a national theatre was entirely justified. For the past six years Tree had been presenting a Shakespearian Festival at His Majesty's which opened on 23 April, Shakespeare's birthday. The plays were all produced up to his usual high standards and performed by an all-star cast. Sir Herbert Tree ran his festivals at a loss, but thought them well worth it. As for Sir George Alexander, he had given Oscar Wilde every encouragement to write *Lady Windermere's Fan*, his first success, and had also produced *The Importance of being Earnest*, besides outstanding plays by Pinero and Henry Arthur Jones; while Sir Charles Wyndham excelled as an actor and produced the plays of Jones and other leading dramatists at his theatres, the Criterion, the New and Wyndham's.

It is sometimes asked what the musical play has done for the art of the theatre [*continued Edwardes*]. I think I may fairly say that it has done something, for I am surprised when I look around and see how many actors and actresses who have graduated under my management have since taken honours in the 'higher schools of drama'. . . .

Graduates of the 'George Edwardes Academy' included Marie Tempest, Constance Collier, Gladys Cooper, Ellaline Terriss, Marie Löhr, Ethel Irving, Billie Burke, Fanny Ward, Evelyn Laye, Seymour Hicks, Dennis Eadie and George Arliss.

To you, Sir Herbert Tree, I am indeed grateful for the signal compliment you have paid me in presiding at this dinner . . . and to you, gentlemen, one and all, who have paid me the honour to come here I feel myself greatly indebted for an evening which you have made memorable for me. It has been worth waiting twenty-five years for!

They had all given him a wonderful evening for his jubilee at a time when the theatre world still regarded George Edwardes as a great impresario. If only he had retired then and handed over his theatrical interests to his lieutenants—men like Pat Malone, George Grossmith and Sydney Ellison—his story might have had a different ending.

The public's taste in entertainment was undergoing a radical change, and George Edwardes's musical plays had lost their former appeal. Musical shows can lose thousands if they fail, and the Guv'nor might have considered cutting down his other commitments while he was having a bad patch in the theatre. Although he would never have given up racing altogether, he might have sold his estate at Ogbourne or his breeding establishment at Ballykisteen. But he was so deeply involved in the sport of kings that he never seriously contemplated it. He carried on racing in his customary style in the firm belief that he would produce a string of winners at the Gaiety, Daly's and the Adelphi to enable him to pay for his ventures on the Turf.

Unfortunately his shows only played to average business, while one or two of them were outright nitters. But the Guv'nor was rather like Mr Micawber, and always hoping that another *Merry Widow* would turn up and come to his rescue.

V

END OF THE ROAD
(1912–1915)

16 A Different Public

Will there never come a season
Free from incoherent rot,
Free from rhyme that has no reason
And 'books' that have no plot,
When a girl in man's apparel
Will not make the pittites roar,
When the Ivans cease to Caryll,
And the Rubens Paul no more?

Vanity Fair,
lampoon on Gaiety musical comedies—1909

The Guv'nor continued to plan his future productions at the Gaiety and Daly's just as if the British public was as keen as ever on seeing the same type of musical plays he had been giving them for nearly twenty years. But since the death of King Edward a new public was demanding different kinds of entertainment. The Gaiety type of musical comedy, which had attracted huge audiences ever since *A Gaiety Girl* and *The Shop Girl*, had become old fashioned, whilst the craze for waltz time, which was the secret of *The Merry Widow*'s appeal, was on its way out.

A new type of music known as ragtime, and later as jazz, had originated in the United States and been popularized by Scott Joplin, a Negro musician, with numbers like the Maple Street Rag. The infectious jazz rhythm had already conquered the dance halls of America; Tin Pan Alley had vulgarized it and made it the nation's most popular music. Irving Berlin had already written 'Alexander's Ragtime Band', a wonderful number which became the world's number one hit. Jazz was about to invade Britain, whilst Edwardes also had to face strong competition from revues, which had gathered a wide following both in London and the provinces; there will be more about them later in the chapter.

But the biggest threat to him was a new entertainment at first called the Bioscope, then known in America as the motion picture and in Britain as the cinematograph. There had been a demonstration of 'the new Biograph' from America at the end of a variety programme at the Alhambra Theatre in 1897. The reporter of a weekly paper went to see it and wrote this entertaining piece:

> Wonderful! But my eyes! and the whizzing and whistling, and twittering of nerves, and blinking and winkings that it causes to not a few of the spectators. . . .
>
> It is a nightmare! There's rattling and shattering and there are sparks, and there are showers of quivering snow-flakes always falling, and amid these appear children fighting in bed, a house on fire, with inmates saved by the arrival of fire-engines . . . followed by warships, pitching away at sea, sailors running up riggings and disappearing into space, trains at full speed coming directly at you, and never getting there . . . and then, the trains having vanished, all the country round takes it into its head to follow as hard as ever it can: rocks, mountains, trees, towns, gateways, castles, rivers, landscapes, bridges, telegraph poles, all whirling . . . and racing against each other . . . and then suddenly all disappear into space! Phew! We breathe again! But O heads! O brandies and sodas! O whiskies and waters! Restoratives quick!

By the end of the century nearly every music hall in the country put on cinematograph shows. When Edward VII died in 1910, R. W. Paul had produced a newsreel film of the funeral in which the clarity of the pictures amazed the public, and it had a tremendous success. Soon after Mack Sennett's two-reel comedies came over from the States, introducing the Keystone Cops and 'Fatty' Arbuckle to the British public. Pearl White and her cliff-hanging serials followed close behind. Less than five years after Paul's newsreel of King Edward's funeral along came Charlie Chaplin, a funny little fellow in a bowler hat and baggy trousers, to become the greatest star in the world. Films henceforth were the favourite entertainment of the masses.

The Guv'nor had been king-pin of British musical plays for so long that he was reluctant to admit that the public had lost their enthusiasm for his type of shows. By 1912 he realized at last that films were the coming entertainment. He tried to buy an interest in two of the leading cinema circuits, but was unable to obtain satisfactory terms from their owners. It was too late after that; Edwardes had run short of money and needed every penny he could lay his hands on to keep his theatres running.

As 1912 drew to a close he was working late every night at Daly's, trying to sort out the up-to-date position of the box-office returns of his musical plays in London and on tour. Julia kept urging him to take a break, and he promised her that he would try to take a week off at Christmas. Edwardes had found he was deeply in the red; he had already been forced to borrow money to keep a show on at the Adelphi, and was desperately casting around for a solution to his financial troubles.

A week before Christmas the stage manager found him slumped in his chair in the office, unconscious. He had suffered a stroke as a result of high blood pressure, brought on by financial worries over failures at his three London theatres. They moved him to his house at Park Square, where he soon recovered consciousness.

It was assumed by the theatre world that the Guv'nor's débâcle was entirely his own fault, and no doubt his extravagant way of living and his theatrical failures were the main cause of it. However, the family papers prove beyond a shadow of doubt that Julia deserved part of the blame. She was hard up at this critical moment in his affairs, and there was no earthly reason why she should have been. She had an income of £3,000 a year, George had also put money aside for her in his good years, but Julia spent money like water and for years she had been a drain on his resources. Ever since he had bought Winkfield Lodge and put it in her name, she had insisted on playing Lady Bountiful to her friends and relations, who all regarded George Edwardes as a millionaire. She had also caught the betting fever from him and lost hundreds of pounds backing slow horses.

Unfortunately, George and Julia were not on good terms in 1912. She spent nearly all her time at Winkfield Lodge, while George was generally at 11 Park Square or at Ogbourne, where his horses were being trained. In one letter, Julia even stated that he had banned her coming to Park Square at all. Although he strongly denied this, one can sense from their correspondence that he was more or less leading the life of a bachelor. His letters to Julia, written in the autumn of 1912, reveal a great deal about their unsatisfactory relationship.

11 Park Square, N.W.

MY DEAR JULIA   *20 Sept 1912*

To come to Winkfield on Sunday is more than I could stand . . . [he complains about the lack of respect shown to him by his daughter Nancy].

Re Money

. . . Winkfield has cost a lot, has it not, and now Oylers Bill comes in over £300 . . . I don't blame you about Winkfield but I asked you not to spend too much money out. How can you in reason expect me to save and provide for you when I am dead or don't make it? . . .

Why do you worry yourself about Mlle? [the children's ex-governess] . . . Tell her to get out. You cannot help being unfair and unjust (re 15 years) but perhaps you don't mean it and only say it to hurt.

                    Your affectionate husband,

                                                    GEO. EDWARDES

On 1 October he wrote her a much more serious letter in which he castigated her for her crazy extravagance. Since it is of crucial importance, I quote the letter almost in full.

Daly's Theatre Offices,
  31, Lisle Street,
    Leicester Square   *1 October 1912*
MY DEAR JULIA

. . . I am sorry but I have no money to invest—on the contrary I have had to borrow myself lately. . . . Your object in life seems to be to help others. Like Addie Gunn

[Michael Gunn's daughter], Sybil Gray, Mlle and others so as to put me to as much inconvenience as possible.

. . . On the last occasion when I paid £100 to pay some debts you promised me you would never pawn anything again, and these tickets you must be aware are enough to drive me out of my mind. Will nothing stop you pawning? Apart from the damage it does to my credit and so worries and upsets me that it seriously interferes with my work— I have no mind for anything—I don't know where I am and I never know what is going to happen.

The Winkfield bills are still to come in . . . and further you want £100. Your object is either to break me or your mind does not realize what you are doing—it is terrible to have to write like this but nothing seems to make any impression on you. You don't care what pain and worry it causes me but if anyone wants anything you give it to them!

What it is coming to is this: I must sell Ogbourne and anything else but 11 Park Square. Winkfield is yours if you would like it . . . I have struggled long enough—I cannot go on—it is no good. I am nearly 60 and I don't want to be knocked out and bankrupt now. It's terrible but I must face it— it is better to know now than when it is too late.

Your affectionate husband,

GEO. EDWARDES

P.S. If you would only be sensible and reasonable how happy you would make me and I hope yourself.

For several years Julia had been pawning her jewellery to settle her pressing debts and she couldn't get out of the habit. Although George Edwardes had tried to bring her down to earth he failed to make any impression on her. He wrote her another letter from Biarritz, when he was taking a cure to try to get his liver working properly.

Palace Hotel,
  Biarritz   *14 December 1912*

MY DEAR JULIA

. . . If you cannot live on £1,500 a year why not engage somebody to show you how to do it?—as a matter of fact at the present moment you are getting nearly £30 a week for the box at the Adelphi . . . and then there is your own money. So practically apart from taking the jewellery out of pawn by me . . . you are always in a helpless state . . . So you ought really to consult your sister [*Mrs Emma Cass*] and your daughter [*Mrs Dorothy Sherbrooke*] to know what is the best thing to be done—for it is serious—far more serious than you think. I will say this in conclusion. . . . Read this to Mrs Cass and Dorothy—hear their views—but I don't suppose you will do this or they might remove the present spectacles you are wearing.

Your husband,

GEO. EDWARDES

Edwardes made such a swift recovery from his stroke at the end of 1912 that he had no idea that he had reached the end of the road. His doctors ordered him to give up all work for the time being, and he went to Bournemouth to try to build up his strength.

While he was out of action, *The Girl on the Film* had gone into rehearsal at the Gaiety with Pat Malone producing it. This crude burlesque of the way they made the early silent films opened on 5 April 1913. George Grossmith played the actor/writer/producer of a pioneer British film company, with Connie Ediss as the Manageress. Grossmith shot *Napoleon and the Miller's Daughter* on location in Lincolnshire, and was too stupid to realize that his leading actress was really a girl and not an effeminate young man. Once he had established her sex, he fell in love with her only to find himself up against the formidable opposition of her father, the General. All the talents of George Grossmith and Connie Ediss couldn't stop the piece from failing.

When Edwardes returned to London he interested himself in *The Marriage Market*, which was in rehearsal at Daly's. He paid several visits to the theatre, but, realizing he was not fit enough to take up the reins again, he never stayed long. Dorothy Sherbrooke knew how worried her father was about Daly's, which belonged to him; he was only managing director of the Gaiety and was on the point of selling the Adelphi. He talked matters over with 'Pops' and decided to let her take charge at Daly's until he had completely recovered. Dorothy

Sherbrooke soon got the hang of theatre management; she was enthusiastic and energetic and had a flair for the theatre, and was helped by Edwardes's secretary Charles Cannon, Pat Malone and the rest of the staff.

The Marriage Market, produced on 19 May 1913, had a cast headed by Gertie Millar, Robert Michaelis, Sari Petrass, W. H. Berry and G. P. Huntley. The plot concerned a 'mock' marriage market for tourists in South California run by Bald-Faced Sandy. But on one occasion he had a real priest conducting the ceremonies, so every unsuspecting couple found themselves well and truly married. Jack married Mariposa, a rich Senator's daughter, who thought it was a trick and promptly walked out on him. However, Jack turned up as a deck hand on her father's yacht and proved his genuine affection for her, and it all came right in the end.

Robert Michaelis and Sari Petrass played the hero and heroine, and Gertie Millar had a second romance with G. P. Huntley, a new comedian. This run-of-the-mill piece got its deserts and only had a short run. Gertie Millar was losing her box office appeal: she had never managed to adjust her lively style of acting to the slower tempo and more sentimental atmosphere of the pieces at Daly's.

While George Edwardes's musical plays flopped, the new revues came into fashion. Revues sprang from the music halls; they discarded all semblance of a plot and consisted of brief sketches and solo turns loosely linked together round a central theme. It was due to the enterprise of Albert de Courville, an ex-reporter of the *Evening News*, that the first jazz revue came to London. De Courville persuaded Edward Moss, head of the powerful Moss Empires, to send him over to the States to study the way the Americans produced their shows, and also to book American turns for a new spectacular revue he intended to produce at the Hippodrome Theatre, London.

De Courville returned from the States full of enthusiasm for the new musical rhythm; he had signed up a number of artists and bought new numbers. In collaboration with Max Pemberton he wrote a Hippodrome revue called *Hello, Ragtime* which he put into rehearsal in the summer of 1912. De Courville insisted on the Hippodrome orchestra adapting its style to the proper sense of the rhythm and syncopation of jazz; he had brought over from the States a trap drummer, a cornet player and a trombonist to assist them. Julian Jones, the Hippodrome conductor, loathed the syncopated music at first and told de Courville: 'This is not music—it's against all the principles of music!'* It was only when they had almost reached the dress rehearsal that Julian Jones admitted that the new music was quite effective.

Albert de Courville had signed up two American stars, Ethel Levey, whom he had discovered in Paris singing 'Alexander's Ragtime Band', and Shirley Kellogg. He also engaged Ned Wayburn, an American dance instructor, to train the chorus girls in the new steps. Wayburn, a rough diamond, drilled the girls like a sergeant major to enable them to carry out his precision routines. His dance routines created a stir in the West End because they were a complete contrast to the artistic and delicately staged routines in George Edwardes's musical comedies.

De Courville decided that *Hello, Ragtime* would be a non-stop revue and have no curtain waits. The Hippodrome staff rose magnificently to the occasion; De Courville had engaged the best stage carpenter in town and had recruited expert flymen who operated behind the scenes with split-second timing, 'arranging for the lowering and raising of cloths, backings, borders and curtains'.†

Lord Northcliffe, de Courville's former boss, sat in the Royal Box at the first night and watched him win his spurs as a theatre producer. The audience were bowled over by the syncopated music, and the pep of Ethel Levey and Shirley Kellog and their technique of putting over their numbers. The perfectly drilled chorus girls were another factor in the success of *Hello, Ragtime*. This revue played to packed houses for a year; the public had to book their seats a month in advance.

Hello, Ragtime was still running in May 1913 when the Guv'nor went to take the 'cure' at Bad Nauheim, near Frankfurt. The doctors forbade him to write any letters and tried to stop him receiving any; but he managed to drop a line to Julia:

I have got to avoid all excitement whatever . . . to see no one and to talk to no one for at least another 3 weeks.

* Albert de Courville, *I Tell You* (Chapman & Hall, 1928).
† De Courville.

My heart is certainly quieter and the baths are really wonderful. . . . All I want to hear is that you are well and nothing about theatres or racing.

He wrote to her again the following month:

Park Hotel,
  Bad Nauheim.   *10 June 1913*

MY DARLING JULIA

Here I am quietly settled down. The Doctors won't tell me anything at present but keep very quiet—write no letters, receive no letters.

If you and Norah were to try that electric treatment you have no idea what good it would do you. No bread, no potatoes, and not drinking at meals and you would take off 4 stone before you could say knife.

Goodbye, my darling wife. Love to the children.

Your affectionate husband,

                                                    GEO. EDWARDES

However, George was not the only man who had written to Julia that year. She had received a most touching letter in March from an old admirer who had fallen in love with her in the days when she sang in Gilbert and Sullivan. He was Arthur Diósy, the expert who had been responsible for 'japanning' the production of *The Geisha* at Daly's, who had written to her from Penzance where he was staying on a lecture tour.

The Queen's Hotel,
  Penzance   *17 March 1913*

MY DEAR EMPRESS JULIA

As usual in the winter I am on the 'lecturing tramp' . . . Fate has brought me, for the first time, to this picturesque spot, and I am in *Penzance*: in other words: 'Alone in the Pirates' Lair!' The dear *Pirates*! You may imagine how memory got to work when I found, staring me in the face from every hoarding in the town, a poster . . . announcing that the Redruth Amateur Operatic Society had been performing *The Pirates of Penzance* in this very place that gave them their name! What delightful memories it recalled!

Memories of the sunny days of youth, of the happy times when I used to wait, with panting heart, at the dirty little stage-door in Hollywell Street . . . for the glorious moment when you appeared and allowed me the blissful privilege of sitting by your side, perched up on the driver's bench of the rattling old bus. all the way to the corner of Boscobel Gardens. I see you before me now, as I saw you so many times from the stalls, with your bewitching smile, your merry eyes, your dimple—I see your ruby velvet hat with the turned-up, scalloped brim, I hear your fresh young voice singing 'Go, Brave Man, Go!' to Barrington [*playing the Sergeant of Police*] and his Bobbies.

Oh! Julia dear, how I loved you then, and—as we are both grandparents now—I may say, how I love you still! It was all so young, and good, and pure between us and my love for you kept me straight as an arrow at a time when young men mostly sow plentiful wild oats. Dear me, how long ago it was! But I feel not a week older—my heart is as young as in those days! . . .

The years roll by—they find me still and always, your
devoted old friend,

ARTHUR DIÓSY

George Edwardes returned to London in the autumn, although the cure at Bad Nauheim had failed to work for him. He called in sometimes at Daly's, but never stayed for long; it was extremely depressing to find business so poor at all his theatres. He wrote to Julia on her birthday.

Daly's Theatre Offices,
  31, Lisle Street,
    Leicester Square   *11 November 1913*

Here you are Darling. I hope the cheque will please you and my only regret is that it is not £1,000. But if you could only realize how bad things are. I can assure you we are approaching a crisis in the country, and we shall want every farthing we can beg, borrow or steal.

May you be happy and never know care is the wish of your husband on this your Birthday.

GEO. EDWARDES

His reference to 'approaching a crisis in the country' probably meant that the tours of his musical plays—on which he was relying to make his profits—had fallen off badly at the box office. He had found in the big provincial towns that his musical comedies and operettas were being ousted by the new revues.

Since the Jubilee dinner, Sir Herbert Tree had been as busy as usual with his elaborate productions at His Majesty's. During a hiatus in his work there, Tree and his wife arranged to appear on the bill of the Palace Theatre in a short play by Rudyard Kipling. On arriving at the Palace for their first rehearsal, they found the stage occupied by a team of half-dressed acrobats, all of whom were sweating like pigs. Although Tree took most things in his stride, he couldn't help feeling rather embarrassed as he and Maud passed them on the stage. An acrobat in an old sweater slapped Sir Herbert Tree heartily on the back and said, "'Allo, 'Erbert, 'ow are yer? Glad to see yer on the 'alls.' Tree paused to get his breath, then smiled and said politely, 'I'm very well, thank you—you don't know my wife Maud? Maud—the Two Whacks! The Two Whacks—Maud!'*

In 1914 Tree arranged to produce Bernard Shaw's *Pygmalion*, which had already been performed with great success in several European countries. Shaw had written the play specially for Mrs Patrick Campbell to play Eliza Doolittle, although Mrs Pat was over forty-five and Eliza was supposed to be a flower-girl of eighteen. Tree agreed to play Professor Higgins but Shaw, convinced that he knew exactly how his play ought to be performed, insisted on producing it himself.

Thus three of the greatest egotists in the history of the theatre started working together. The West End was soon buzzing with the news that the word 'bloody' was going to be spoken in a modern play for the first time in living memory. Shaw tried to keep the rehearsals of *Pygmalion* to a regular time-table, as Granville-Barker had always done at the Court Theatre; but it was impossible because Sir Herbert Tree had a maddening way of walking off in the middle of a scene to talk to his horde of visitors. Journalists, backers, fellow actors

* Pearson.

and just friends of his from the Garrick Club kept turning up at His Majesty's to watch his rehearsals.

As soon as Tree left the stage Mrs Patrick Campbell refused to rehearse without him and retired to her dressing-room. Bernard Shaw would be left holding the prompt book, muttering curses because everything at His Majesty's seemed to be in a state of chaos. Sir Herbert Tree once stayed away two hours talking to the correspondent of *The Times*, and Shaw let fly on his return. 'Ah, here's our absentee landlord. Good of you to come, Sir Herbert. Are you *sure* you can spare the time?'*

Tree always liked to 'improve' the plays he produced at his beautiful theatre by putting in extra scenes and business; but Shaw was the producer this time, and he fought tooth and nail to stop him changing a single line. Tree never learnt his part properly, and was never word-perfect at rehearsals. On top of this, Mrs Pat generally threw a tantrum once a week. Sometimes Bernard Shaw refused to stay in the 'madhouse' for another minute and walked out. But he always came back the next day, to be greeted most cordially by Sir Herbert Tree, just as if he was making a social call. 'Hello, Shaw, how good to see you again!' Tree would say. 'How are you? Anything I can do for you?'†

Tree, who had made his great reputation as an actor by his skill in playing a fantastic range of parts from Svengali to Colonel Newcombe, began to fret because Higgins was really a straight part which called for no elaborate make-up or special business. One morning he came to rehearsal leaning on a stick and explained to Bernard Shaw that Higgins had to use a stick because he was a bachelor, and all bachelors drank too much port and suffered from gout and so they limped. 'Why stop at a limp and a stick?' roared Shaw. 'Why don't you put a patch on your eye, have one leg and a parrot on your shoulder, then we can do *Treasure Island!*'

The final rehearsals took place during the week of 6 April, but on the Monday morning Sir Herbert Tree received a bombshell: Mrs Patrick Campbell had not turned up at the theatre and nobody knew where she had gone. It transpired that she had eloped with George Cornwallis-West and married him that

* Richard Huggett, *The Truth about Pygmalion* (Heinemann, 1969).
† Huggett.

morning after he had obtained his decree absolute from Jennie, the former Lady Randolph Churchill. Nobody had the foggiest idea when Mrs Pat was coming back!

'Oh, my God!' wailed Tree.

Mrs Patrick Campbell turned up at His Majesty's on Friday morning—the day of the dress rehearsal. She never apologized to Sir Herbert for her outrageous behaviour. All she said was, 'George is a golden man,' referring to her new husband, George Cornwallis-West, then she addded, 'Now let's rehearse!'*

Basil Dean, who was Tree's assistant producer, retained a vivid memory of Mrs Pat. 'I can see her now, standing erect and formidable in front of the inner doors of the stage entrance. She was dressed in a fashionable sable toque and tippet, wore a large bunch of Parma violets in her buttonhole, and carried a little dog in her arms.'†

The dress rehearsal went very badly indeed: afterwards Bernard Shaw sent Tree and Mrs Pat pages of notes on how they should each play their roles. But Sir Herbert Tree arrived at his theatre on Saturday 11 April in a defeatist mood, sure that *Pygmalion* was going to be a fiasco. He ignored Shaw's notes on Professor Higgins, whereas Mrs Pat memorized every point the author had made on Eliza Doolittle.

The popular newspapers had featured the fact that she was going to speak That Word tonight at His Majesty's. Tree suddenly got in a panic about the word—although Shaw's play had already been passed by the Censor. He went to Mrs Pat's dressing-room before the curtain went up and begged her to say anything but 'Not bloody likely'. But Stella Patrick Campbell told him Bernard Shaw was a great play-wright and she wouldn't dream of changing a word he had written.

The public had read so much about *Pygmalion* in the Press that half London wanted to get seats for the first night. That evening the West End had its biggest traffic block since George V's Coronation, with all vehicles converging on His Majesty's from Haymarket, Piccadilly, Pall Mall and Lower Regent Street. Sir Herbert Tree was so uncertain of his lines that he devised a special system to get him through his first night

* Pearson.

† Basil Dean, *Seven Ages* (Hutchinson, 1970).

ordeal. He had 'difficult' speeches pinned to the backs of the columns of the stage, and to chairs and tables; in one scene he had them pinned on to a desk and on the mantlepiece; in another on the piano. Besides his pieces of paper he had a squad of prompters at hand in case of an emergency: they were distributed all round the back of the stage, behind doors and windows, behind a fireplace, behind a sofa, underneath Higgins's desk and under Mrs Higgins's big table.

The first night of *Pygmalion* attracted a capacity audience, who were rewarded by a golden evening in the theatre. Mrs Pat as Eliza Doolittle overcame the difficulty of being twenty-five years older than the part and, from her first entrance as the flower-girl, she gave a superb performance. Tree played Higgins with just the right obstinacy and aggression and yet conveyed the childishness of the Professor. The audience, who had been enthralled from the start, were all waiting for Act III when Higgins presents Eliza Doolittle to his mother and her smart friends. At length Eliza duly said, 'Not bloody likely!' The audience held their breath for a moment, stunned: they could hardly believe that Mrs Pat had actually spoken That Word. And then they began to laugh, and the laughter went all round His Majesty's Theatre. It went on and on in fresh waves and seemed as if it was never going to stop.

Bernard Shaw was furious. Feeling that the audience's laughter had ruined his play, he walked out of the theatre. However, the notices of *Pygmalion* were marvellous. The *Daily Telegraph* said:

Here is Mr Shaw in his most benign mood. . . . When Sir Herbert Tree made a little speech at the end he explained there had been so much laughter that Mr Shaw had left the theatre in despair.

. . . Save for a lack of speed the performance was brilliant. Mrs Patrick Campbell's Cockney accent was exactly right and supremely funny. The whole attitude of the girl was excellently managed. With very delicate art we had the gradual progress of Eliza suggested. Her comedy was rich and rare. . . . Sir Herbert Tree, as Higgins, has a part in which his wit and his power of inventing byplay have full scope, and he used them to delightful advantage. There were a thousand and one little touches of oddity, all perfectly right and vividly expressive. . . .

Pygmalion was the hit of the 1914 season. When it was still playing to capacity in July, Sir Herbert Tree took it off because long runs bored him. It was something George Edwardes would never have done in a month of Sundays.

17 A Hopeless Case

*That curious mixture of human weakness and
great ability, of strength of purpose and tenderness
of heart, whose faults were endearing and whose
qualities inspired.*

W. MACQUEEN POPE on George Edwardes
(*Shirtfronts and Sables*)

There were to be no more golden evenings in the theatre for
George Edwardes, who never recovered from his stroke in 1912.
It was as much as he could do now to summon up the energy
to pay a visit to Daly's to see how Dorothy was managing to
cope with everything in his place.

In the spring of 1914 Pat Malone produced *Adele* at the
Gaiety. This feeble musical comedy had a great number of
Americans in the cast: on the first night the two leading
comedians were almost inaudible and the audience gave it
'the bird'. Pat Malone rashly walked on to the stage and a voice
from the gallery shouted, 'We'll report you to the Guv'nor!'*

Adele only lasted a few weeks, making the third successive
flop at the Gaiety. In the summer the theatre went dark—
the first time it had been closed since the première of *The
Orchid*. Behind the scenes discussions were taking place about
a reconstruction of the Gaiety Company; the time had come
to find another managing director to replace the Guv'nor.

Meanwhile, George Edwardes had returned to Bad Nauheim
for a check-up. Soon after his arrival he wrote to Julia:

* Pope, *Gaiety*.

Grand Hotel,
  Bad Nauheim   *10 June 1914*

MY DARLING JULIA

I have not written to you before as I thought I had better
wait and see how I really get on. My heart of course is
marvellously better and the danger of 'angina pectoris' has
gone for the time being. The heart is now regular and does not
throb out of my chest as it did. I shall be here another 10
days, then I must get some mountain air as a pick-me-up—
they call this the 'Nach Cure'. . . .

. . . I hope to see you all soon nearly if not quite myself.
        Ever your loving husband,
                                              GEO. EDWARDES

George was writing to Julia in a much warmer strain: now
that there was no other woman in his life, some of his old
affection for her had returned. During the next few weeks he
began to make a little progress at Bad Nauheim. But before
he had made a real recovery Julia wrote to him asking
urgently for money, and upset him so much that he had a
relapse.

Grand Hotel,
  Bad Nauheim   *Monday morning*

O Julia dear, you little know how your letter has upset
me. I shall never be well, dear, believe me that is so. The
doctors say it has been principally caused by worrying and
excitement to get money. I have been doing well lately but
I am afraid it's no good now.

God knows I have given you all I can and you little
know (and didn't want to believe) the struggle I have had
to keep my head up. Dorothy knows as you won't believe
me. Time after time you have faithfully promised me to
'stop pawning' but you dishonourably broke your word. If
you put a match to Winkfield and burn it there would be
a chance for us all—but you will go on Spending!

Another blow like this morning and it will be all over
with me—you can take everything, but there will be nothing
to have and you won't listen. I have wired Dorothy to give
you the £1500 out of the ins [*insurance*]. Don't answer this

letter as I shall rest in bed for a time and it would upset me
again. My nerves are awful . . .

   Please God things may come right.

GEO. EDWARDES

Julia's S.O.S. for another large sum was the worst medicine
in the world for a man with a heart condition who had been
ordered to keep quiet and not upset himself about money.
George Edwardes began to go downhill again and the doctors
insisted on keeping him at Bad Nauheim. He was still there on
4 August, the day Britain declared war on Germany. He was
given twenty-four hours in which to leave the country but,
with his usual optimism, he refused to take the war seriously
and stayed on at Bad Nauheim, thinking it would all be over
by Christmas. It was a fatal mistake: the Germans interned
him and virtually kept him a prisoner at the Grand Hotel.
They allowed him to walk only a distance of one mile from the
hotel and made him go to bed at nine o'clock every night.

This compulsory detention was particularly hard on a
complete extrovert like George Edwardes; every time he went
for a walk the people of Bad Nauheim jeered at him and upset
him. The atmosphere at the Grand Hotel had changed in a
day: he had always been treated with great respect by the staff,
but now they did not conceal their contempt for him and the
waiters openly laughed at him. The town was so noisy in wartime that it got on his nerves. 'All the time, at all hours, they are
shouting and ringing bells to celebrate victories,' he complained.

His health deteriorated rapidly and he had a second stroke in
September. A Chicago newspaper reported that George
Edwardes, the famous impresario, was in danger of dying at
Bad Nauheim and that the doctors believed he could never
survive unless the Germans would allow him to return home to
England. America being still neutral, the American Consul in
Germany took up George Edwardes's case, and the Germans,
anxious to keep on the right side of the United States, agreed
to release him.

The doctors at Bad Nauheim advised that George Edwardes
should be sent back to England via Switzerland, which was the
shortest route, but the authorities decided to send him back
the long way via Rotterdam. 'A railway train is as good as
any place to die in,' said a cynical high official.

'I have had enough of Germany to last me for the rest of my life,' George Edwardes told a newspaper reporter on his return to England. His hair had gone white: he was very weak and stooped a lot: his hand shook and he found it impossible to concentrate for very long. They sent him down to Bournemouth, a town he was very fond of, in the hope that the tranquil atmosphere of this Mecca for invalids would help him to recuperate.

In 1915 the Gaiety re-opened with *Tonight's the Night*, a musical comedy presented by George Grossmith which put it right back on the map again. Gee-Gee had become an impresario and gone into partnership with Edward Laurrilard, a man of Dutch extraction whose English was very hard to understand. Laurrilard used to open a conversation disarmingly by saying, 'Well, there you are, you see.' The Guv'nor had lost all connection with the Gaiety, which was being run by a reconstructed company whose managing director was Alfred Butt, a powerful figure in the entertainment world, who already controlled the Empire, Palace, Victoria Palace, Adelphi, Globe and Queen's Theatres.

George Grossmith had given himself a typical role as the Hon. Dudley Mitten in *Tonight's the Night*; the leading comedians were James Blakely and Davy Burnaby, and Leslie Henson, a low comedian with a very funny face and a hoarse, croaking voice, played a small comedy part. Paul Rubens had written the score and Gee-Gee introduced two American songs by Jerome Kern.

The outstanding one, 'They Didn't Believe Me', was sung as a duet by Gee-Gee and lovely Haidee de Rance, playing June.

And when I tell them—
And I'm certainly going to tell them—
That I'm the man whose wife one day you'll be,
They'll never believe me—
They'll never believe me—
That from this great big world
You've chosen me.

When *Tonight's the Night* opened at the Gaiety on 14 April 1915, there was a total black-out in the West End. Britain and the Allies had made a disastrous start in the First World War and Britain was taking the German air attacks very seriously indeed. War had wrought a complete change in theatre habits: nobody at the Gaiety was in evening dress that night and nearly every woman in the house wore sombre clothes. The audience was mainly composed of war workers and soldiers home on leave who had come to the theatre yearning to be entertained. The show was fast, amusing, well mounted and highly entertaining. George Grossmith had gone out of his way to ensure the chorus girls were as glamorous as in the Guv'nor's day.

Leslie Henson made a tremendous hit in the small part of Henry; it was already clear that he could replace Teddy Payne (who had retired at the age of fifty and died suddenly in 1914). *Tonight's the Night* received splendid notices; the *Era* said:

> The Gaiety is a theatre with a tradition. It is expected to provide its patrons with the jolliest, funniest, liveliest type of musical comedy that can be seen anywhere. It has a name for the prettiest chorus girls, the catchiest music and the handsomest mounting, as well as the wittiest comedians. . . .
>
> *Tonight's the Night* is in every particular up to the required standard . . . the music of Paul Rubens is full of haunting melody. Two of the most successful numbers are by Mr Jerome Kern. Mr Grossmith . . . is as characteristically amusing as ever. He has a delightful mock serious duet— 'They Didn't Believe Me'. . . . Mr Leslie Henson strikes out a new line, very quaint and individual. . . .

After George Edwardes had been at Bournemouth a few months his blood pressure shot up alarmingly. The doctors decided to move him to Turnberry, Scotland, because they now felt he was in need of bracing air. He was installed at the luxurious Station Hotel, and put on a very strict regime; but even then there was no improvement in his heart condition.

Edwardes had a third stroke a few weeks later and was ordered to stay in bed, which was sheer misery to a man of his temperament. As he was too ill to write to Julia himself, he had to dictate this letter.

Station Hotel,
   Turnberry *June 1915*

MY DEAR JULIA

I have been very seedy or I would have written myself. . . .
I had a letter from Dar [*his son, D'Arcy*]. I tremble when I
think of him [*he was an officer at the Front*]. Please God he
will get through all right. If the worst is to happen it must.
I can't help it. . . .

Your affectionate husband,

GEO. EDWARDES

It was their thirtieth anniversary on 9 July. George sent
Julia a cheque and she wired him: 'Five hundred thanks my
dearest Georgie. All my good wishes to you. Fond love from
your thirty years wife. JULIA.'

Another letter, in July, was also largely written for him by
somebody else.

Station Hotel,
   Turnberry *20 July 1915*

MY DARLING JULIA

I am getting on slowly and very much better than I was
at Bournemouth. My liver was all out of order and those
wretched doctors in London would not believe it. . . .

I enclose a letter from D'Arcy—you might write to him
for me as I can't. I know only too well that poor little
Dorothy has got all the work to do and I wish to God I was
strong enough to take it from her shoulders, but I am not.
I am only getting to the stage that I can walk, but I will
go back to work directly I can. I hope all is well. The war I
am sure will soon be over. . . .

[*In his own handwriting*]: The doctor swears he will make
me right if I keep quiet for six weeks more and *not talk*.
Goodbye my darling wife.

Your affectionate husband,

GEO. EDWARDES.

By this time he had begun to despair of ever being cured,
but was desperately trying to convince himself that he still had
a chance; he also did his best to gloss over to Julia and the

H

family the gravity of his illness. He wrote to her again a month later when there was really no improvement in his condition.

Station Hotel,
   Turnberry   *10 August 1915*

MY DARLING JULIA

I am still not well enough to write myself. I'm still very weak . . . 5 weeks in bed makes you very weak. My liver and kidneys were very bad—that's what makes me so giddy sometimes. I can hardly stand but the doctors here say I shall be alright.

               Your loving husband,

                       GEO. EDWARDES

He added a postscript in his own handwriting:

I am feeling better—the doctors say I am getting better every day. Will *soon be able* to write myself.

However, by the end of the summer the doctors despaired of finding a cure for George Edwardes. They considered him a hopeless case, and sent him home to Park Square. Julia and Dorothy and the three younger children knew that he had come home to die.

George Edwardes was very fond of Bill Berry, the comedian, and used to say it was a tonic just to hear his cheerful voice. Berry received a message at Daly's that the Guv'nor would like him to drop in and see him. He promised to come, although he was dreading the meeting: everyone in the theatre world knew that George Edwardes was dying.

When Berry arrived at Park Square, Dorothy Sherbrooke warned him not to stay too long with her father. Berry remembered the last time he had seen the Guv'nor, before the war, when he had been 'his dear old bluff and handsome self, a fine figure of a man with a twinkle in his eyes'.* The comedian found Edwardes sitting at a table by the window, so altered that he hardly knew him. His body was thin and shrunken, his hair had gone snow white and his face was thin and pointed.

  * Berry.

His hands had become painfully thin and were quite helpless. But what distressed Berry more than anything was that the Guv'nor had lost his glorious resonant voice: now he only spoke in a weak and quavering whisper.

Edwardes wanted to offer Bill Berry a cigar, but couldn't manage to say the words. Berry did his best to sound merry and bright, but it was impossible to keep it up, knowing only too well that it was the last time he would ever see George Edwardes. 'Well, good-bye, Guv'nor,' he said, shaking his hand. 'Do buck up and come back to Daly's. We're all waiting for you.'*

Captain D'Arcy Edwardes was granted special leave by the War Office to come home from the Front to see his father. D'Arcy, a charming young man and a devoted son, spent all his leave at Park Square. One afternoon Dorothy came into her father to tell him that D'Arcy was due to return to his regiment and would be coming in to say good-bye to him in a few minutes.

George broke down and cried. 'Tell him not to say good-bye,' he begged her. 'Tell him to pretend he's coming back again next week—not good-bye!'† Perhaps he had a presentiment that D'Arcy was going to be killed in action.

George Edwardes died peacefully at home on 4 October and was buried at Kensal Green Cemetery. Many members of the theatre staff of the Gaiety and Daly's came to pay their last respects to the Guv'nor. Many of the authors and composers who had written his shows and the artists who had played in them were also at his funeral.

Although the Guv'nor had died right in the middle of the First World War, Franz Lehár and the other German composers who had worked for him sent him a magnificent wreath. There was very tight security in Germany at this period of the war, and nobody ever discovered how the composers had managed to smuggle it out of the country.

People were surprised to learn that George Edwardes had not died a wealthy man. The impresario who had employed two thousand people in his heyday, whose musical plays had made fortunes for composers, authors and stage stars, had left total debts of £80,000. The major assets in his estate of £49,780 were Daly's Theatre, and his royalties; but he still owned

* Berry.   † Bloom.

H*

11 Park Square, the estate at Ogbourne Maisey and the stud at Ballykisteen.

After his death Dorothy Sherbrooke managed Daly's in partnership with Robert Evett, the actor, who had been one of the principals in *The Merry Widow*. Evett's experience in the theatre and his tact in dealing with artists were most helpful. However, their first joint production, *The Happy Day*, was a 'nitter'. Its star was José Collins, an extremely attractive brunette with a superb singing voice, who was the daughter of Lottie Collins, who had once sang 'Ta-ra-ra boom-de-ay' for the Guv'nor at the Gaiety.

Robert Evett and Dorothy Sherbrooke signed up José Collins for another show. Evett bought an unproduced play by Frederick Lonsdale, which he felt would make a splendid vehicle for José Collins, and changed its title to *The Maid of the Mountains*. It was a sink-or-swim venture becaue their money was running out: Evett and Dorothy cut all expenses to the bone and agreed not to take any salary until *The Maid of the Mountains* had had a chance to establish itself. José Collins made a handsome gesture and agreed to work for only £50 a week at first.

Evett engaged Oscar Asche to produce *The Maid of the Mountains* on the strength of his sensational success with the production of *Chu Chin Chow*, a musical play based on the story of Ali Baba and the Forty Thieves. Oscar Asche also starred in it at His Majesty's with his wife, Lily Brayton. Oscar Asche had written the book and the lyrics himself: but when he had finished *Chu Chin Chow* no manager would consider it until Asche arranged to have rough models of the sets done. Henry Dana accepted the piece for His Majesty's while Sir Herbert Tree was in America. Tree saw *Chu Chin Chow* on his return and was astonished to see so many semi-nude females on the stage. Asked his opinion of the piece, he replied, 'More navel than millinery.'*

The Maid of the Mountains opened at Daly's on 1 February 1917 and succeeded beyond Dorothy's wildest dreams. José Collins gave a wonderful performance in the main part, and it became one of the most popular shows of the wartime theatre and ran for 1,352 performances. The war had been over three years ago before it came off. How the Guv'nor would have

* Pearson.

loved to have been in his box at the last night! By then the George Edwardes estate had discharged all its debts and earned a profit of over £100,000.

George Edwardes was a gambler who saved very little while his theatres were booming, and consequently, when the public grew tired of his musical plays, he had no reserves to fall back on. But other impresarios of musical plays have duplicated Edwardes's story time and again because musicals cost so much to produce that it is easy to lose a fortune with an outright failure. Since the Guv'nor's day the two outstanding showmen of the English-speaking theatre were probably Flo Ziegfeld in America and Sir Charles B. Cochran in Britain; both of them suffered from Edwardes's complaint and went bankrupt several times.

George Edwardes should not only be remembered as the man who established musical comedy and made his fortune. He deserves full credit for the part he played in raising the standards of the actors and actresses in musical plays—particularly the chorus girls and small-part artists. His human touch is what made the Guv'nor the best loved theatre manager of his day.

The Guv'nor was admired as a great showman who never pretended to be anything else. During his speech at the Jubilee dinner he summed up his career admirably:

'. . . if I have cultivated my own little patch in the world of the theatre to some use and advantage I am satisfied. . . . I hope I may say for this Cinderella of the drama that it is a little better cared for, better housed, more considerately treated . . . than it used to be in the old days.'

Perhaps the last word about George Edwardes was said by Sir Herbert Tree when proposing his health at the Savoy.

'Has he not given happiness nightly to thousands?—and to give happiness to the greatest number has been defined as the highest form of morality.'

He would have been pleased with such an epitaph.

Acknowledgements

As well as individuals mentioned in the Foreword I am grateful to the following for permission to quote from copyright material: D. Forbes Winslow, *Daly's* (W. H. Allen); D. F. Cheshire, *Music Hall in Britain* (David and Charles); Raymond Mander and Joe Mitchenson, *Musical Comedy* (Peter Davies); Guy Deghy, *Paradise in the Strand* (Richards Press); W. Macqueen Pope, *Gaiety, Theatre of Enchantment*; *Ghosts and Greasepaint*; *Shirtfronts and Sables*; and *Nights of Gladness* (all Robert Hale); Sir Max Beerbohm, *Around Theatres*; *More Theatres*; and *Last Theatres* (Hart-Davis); Raymond Mander and Joe Mitchenson, *Lost Theatres of London* (Hart-Davis); Ada Reeve, *Take it for a Fact* (Heinemann); Richard Huggett, *The Truth about Pygmalion* (Heinemann); W. Macqueen Pope, *Carriages at Eleven* (Hutchinson) and (with D. L. Murray), *Fortune's Favourite* (Hutchinson); George Grossmith Jr, *G.G.* (Hutchinson); Robert Courtneidge, *I Was an Actor Once* (Hutchinson); Gladys Cooper, *Gladys Cooper* (Hutchinson); W. H. Berry, *Forty Years in the Limelight* (Hutchinson); George Graves, *Gaieties and Gravities* (Hutchinson); Ellaline Terriss, *Just a Little Bit of String* (Hutchinson); Ursula Bloom, *Curtain Call for the Guv'nor* (Hutchinson); Basil Dean, *Seven Ages* (Hutchinson).

I also wish to thank Bridget D'Oyly Carte, Ltd, for permission to quote W. S. Gilbert's lyrics, and am most grateful to Messrs Chappell and Co. and Ascherberg, Hopwood and Crew, Ltd, for their permission to quote lyrics from the following shows: *The Shop Girl, The Circus Girl, The Runaway Girl, The Toreador, The Spring Chicken, The Girls of Gottenberg, Our Miss Gibbs, The Sunshine Girl, The Merry Widow, The Geisha* and *San Toy*. I also thank Messrs Ascherberg, Hopwood and Crew, Ltd, for permission to quote the lyrics of 'Ta-ra-ra Boom-de-ay' and 'They wouldn't believe me', and Messrs Stainer and Bell for permission to quote the lyric of 'Man About Town'.

Bibliography

ARCHER, WILLIAM. *The Old Drama and the New*. Heinemann, 1923.

ASCHE, OSCAR. *Oscar Asche*. Hurst & Blackett, 1929.

BAILY, LESLIE. *The Gilbert and Sullivan Book*. Cassell, 1952.

BANCROFT, GEORGE. *Stage and Bar*. Faber, 1939.

BEERBOHM, SIR MAX. *Around Theatres*. Hart-Davis, 1953.

——*More Theatres*. Hart-Davis, 1969.

——*Last Theatres*. Hart-Davis, 1970.

——*Herbert Beerbohm Tree Memories*. Hutchinson, 1920.

BENSON, SIR FRANK. *My Memories*. Ernest Benn, 1930

BERRY, W. H. *Forty Years in the Limelight*. Hutchinson, 1939

BLOOM, URSULA. *Curtain Call for the Guv'nor*. Hutchinson, 1954.

BOLITHO, HECTOR. *Marie Tempest*. Cobden-Sanderson, 1936.

BOND, JESSIE. *The Life and Reminiscences of Jessie Bond*. London, 1930.

BOOTH, J. B. *London Town*. Werner Laurie, 1929.

——*Pink Parade*. Butterworth, 1933.

——*A Pink 'Un Remembers*. Werner Laurie, 1937.

——*Sporting Times*. Werner Laurie, 1938.

CHESHIRE, D. F. *Music Hall in Britain*. David & Charles, 1974.

COLLIER, CONSTANCE. *Harlequinade*. John Lane, 1929.

COURTNEIDGE, CICELY. *Cicely*. Hutchinson, 1953.

COURTNEIDGE, ROBERT. *I Was an Actor Once*. Hutchinson, 1930.

CRAIG, GORDON. *Henry Irving*. Dent, 1930.

DEAN, BASIL. *Seven Ages*. Hutchinson, 1970.

DE COURVILLE, ALBERT. *I Tell You*. Chapman & Hall, 1928.

DEGHY, GUY. *Paradise in the Strand*. Richards Press, 1958.

——and WATERHOUSE, KEITH. *Café Royal*. Hutchinson, 1955.

GLOVER, JAMES. *Jimmy Glover and his Friends*. Chatto, 1913.

GRAVES, GEORGE. *Gaieties and Gravities*. Hutchinson, 1931.

GROSSMITH, GEORGE, JR. *G.G.* Hutchinson, 1933.

HICKS, SIR SEYMOUR. *Twenty-Five Years of an Actor's Life*. Alston Rivers, 1910.

——*Between Ourselves*. Cassell, 1930.

——*Vintage Years*. Cassell, 1943.

HIBBERT, H. G. *Fifty Years of a Londoner's Life*. Grant Richards, 1916.

——*A Playgoer's Memories*. Grant Richards, 1920.

HOLLINGSHEAD, JOHN. *Gaiety Chronicle*. Constable, 1898.

——*Good Old Gaiety*. London, 1903.

HUGGETT, RICHARD. *The Truth about Pygmalion*. Heinemann, 1969.

IRVING, LAURENCE. *Henry Irving*. Faber, 1951.

JUPP, JAMES. *The Gaiety Stage Door*. Cape, 1923.

LESLIE, ANITA. *Edwardians in Love*. Hutchinson, 1972.

MANDER, RAYMOND and MITCHENSON, JOE. *The Theatres of London*. Hart-Davis, 1961.

——*Lost Theatres of London*. Hart-Davis, 1968.

——*Musical Comedy*. Peter Davis, 1969.

MANVELL, ROGER. *Ellen Terry*. Heinemann, 1968.

MILLER, RUBY. *Champagne from my Slipper*. Herbert Jenkins, 1962.

MILLWARD, JESSIE. *Myself and Others*. London, 1923.

NAYLOR, S. *Gaiety and George Grossmith*. London, 1913.

NICHOL, ALLARDYCE. *A History of English Drama, 1850–1900*. Cambridge University Press, 1959.

——*English Drama, 1900–1930*. Cambridge University Press, 1973.

PEARSON, HESKETH. *Gilbert and Sullivan*. Hamish Hamilton, 1935.

——*Bernard Shaw*. Collins, 1942.

——*The Last Actor-Managers*. Methuen, 1950.

——*Beerbohm Tree*. Methuen, 1956.

——*Gilbert, His Life and Strife*. Methuen, 1957.

POPE, W. MACQUEEN. *Haymarket, Theatre of Perfection*. W. H. Allen, 1948.

——*Gaiety, Theatre of Enchantment*. W. H. Allen, 1949.

——*Ghosts and Greasepaint*. Hale, 1951.

——*Shirtfronts and Sables*. Hale, 1953.

——*Carriages at Eleven*. Hutchinson, 1954.

——*Nights of Gladness*. Hutchinson, 1956.

——*St. James's, Theatre of Distinction*. W. H. Allen, 1958.

——and MURRAY, D. L. *Fortune's Favourite*. Hutchinson, 1953.

REEVE, ADA. *Take it for a Fact*. Heinemann, 1954.

ROBERTS, ARTHUR. *Fifty Years of Spoof*. John Lane, 1927.

ROBERTSON, GRAHAM. *Time Was*. Hamish Hamilton, 1931.

SALA, G. A. *London Up to Date*. A. C. Black, 1894.

SCOTT, MRS MARGARET. *Old Days in Bohemian London*. London, 1919.

SHORT, ERNEST. *Sixty Years of Theatre*. Eyre & Spottiswoode, 1951.

STEEN, MARGARET. *A Pride of Terrys*. Longman, 1962.

STOKER, BRAM. *Personal Recollections of Henry Irving*. Heinemann, 1906.

TERRISS, ELLALINE. *Ellaline Terriss*. Cassell, 1928.

——*Just a Little Bit of String*. Hutchinson, 1955.

VANBRUGH, IRENE. *To Tell my Story*. Hutchinson, 1948.

VINCENT, W. T. *Recollections of Fred Leslie*. Kegan Paul, 1894.

WILSON A. E. *Edwardian Theatre*. Arthur Barker, 1951.

WINSLOW, D. FORBES. *Daly's*. W. H. Allen, 1944.

Index

Theatres (*except* Daly's *and* The Gaiety (London), *which are indexed individually*) are grouped alphabetically under 'theatres'. *Abbreviations:* G. & S.—Gilbert and Sullivan, G. E.—George Edwardes, J. H.—John Hollingshead.